Wild GOURMET

NATURALLY HEALTHY
GAME, FISH AND FOWL
RECIPES FOR
EVERYDAY CHEFS

Fresh Caught Trout in Foil

Wild GOURMET

NATURALLY HEALTHY
GAME, FISH AND FOWL
RECIPES FOR
EVERYDAY CHEFS

Introduction by Marc Mondavi
With Suggested Wine Pairings

Recipes by Gourmet Chefs
Jon Bonnell | Daniel Boulud | Travis Brust
Michael Chiarello | Josh Drage | Chris Hughes
Bob Hurley | Emeril Lagasse | Scott Leysath
Jorge Morales | Daniel Nelson | Holly Peterson
Susan Prescott-Havers | Anthony Scanio | Hank Shaw

Wild Game Processing, Preparation and Cuts
Chef Daniel Nelson

BOONE AND CROCKETT CLUB
MISSOULA, MONTANA | 2014

WILD GOURMET

Naturally Healthy Game, Fish and Fowl Recipes for Everyday Chefs

Library of Congress Catalog Card Number: 2014948492
ISBN: 978-0-940864-93-1
e-ISBN: 978-1-940860-02-2
Published November 2014

Published in the United States of America by the
Boone and Crockett Club
250 Station Drive, Missoula, Montana 59801
Phone (406) 542-1888
Fax (406) 542-0784
Toll-Free (888) 840-4868 (book orders only)
www.boone-crockett.org

Printed in Manitoba, Canada

In a civilized and
cultivated country,
wild animals only
continue to exist at
all when preserved
by sportsmen.

Theodore Roosevelt

Contents

Introduction

The tradition of pursuing and harvesting game has been passed down for generations and shared by family and friends. I was a teenager when a close friend first introduced me to hunting. It was my friend and his father who taught me hunter safety, honorable pursuit of game, hunter ethics, as well as the respect and connection with the wilderness. I have learned through years of hunting and my experiences across the world that the sport extends beyond what many people believe it does. It is not only a means to legally regulate animal populations, it connects individuals to nature and the outdoors and contributes to wildlife management through the proceeds of license sales and excise taxes—not to mention the $90 billion it contributes to the U.S. economy.

The meals of game and fowl that I've harvested and shared with family, friends, and new acquaintances are filled with memories surrounding a healthy and organic lifestyle. It gives all of us a stronger connection to the animals we pursued and took. It also allows me to introduce non-hunters to the many benefits of hunting. I share my love for hunting with my four daughters and wife. Most meals in my household consist of the meat we shoot. That is one of the reasons this publishing project is so important to me.

An important feature of this book is the inclusion of wine suggestions for each recipe. Wine pairing can be as simple or complex as you wish to make it. Literally there are hundreds of thousands of brands from around the world and hundreds of varietals. In simple terms, the richer and heavier the food, the bigger and bolder the wine should be. The lighter and more delicate the food, the lighter the wine. Red wine with meat and white wine with fish is not the rule anymore. Often times, I pick wine based on the mood I am in. Do not be afraid to experiment—it's fun!

Our family has owned Charles Krug winery since 1943 when my grandfather Cesare purchased it. For decades, my brother Peter and I have worked closely with our father Peter, Sr., to run our family-owned winery. I studied viticulture and enology at the University of California, Davis, and marketing at California State University, Sacramento. After my studies, I returned to the winery and immersed myself in every aspect of winery operations. I worked alongside my father to further my knowledge of winemaking and applied the expertise I had acquired at Davis to our numerous vineyard holdings.

Today, I am on the road with a busy travel schedule overseeing winemaker dinners, sales meetings with the distributor network and chain meetings around the country. Through my work, I have the opportunity to meet and work with some of the finest chefs across the U.S., which ultimately spawned the idea for *Wild Gourmet*.

We worked closely with more than a dozen of the nation's top chefs to put together the great variety of recipes that appear in this book. We wanted to provide top-notch recipes that would offer different ideas on preparing wild game meals, while also making sure the recipes were something that everyday chefs could easily prepare. We're confident you will find new and exciting ways to cook and serve game and will no doubt impress the guests at your table when you serve them the fruits of your days in the field, at sea or by river's edge. All of these professionals need to be recognized for their contributions to the book and for their support of the Boone and Crockett Club.

While you're enjoying your wild game meal with a delicious glass of wine, be sure to remind everyone at the table about the far-reaching benefits of being a sportsman. Maybe, just maybe, they'll want to join you in the field next season.

Marc C. Mondavi
Vice President of Communications, Boone and Crockett Club
Co-Proprietor, Charles Krug Winery

Preface

Theodore Roosevelt, George Bird Grinnell and a handful of other sportsmen founded the Boone and Crockett Club well over a century ago. Their dedication and foresight resulted in our nation's first conservation organization that tallied a long list of accomplishments, which ultimately helped shape the course of conservation and protect our hunting heritage. Today B&C promotes wildlife conservation and related policy; guards hunting ethics; supports wildlife research and education; and maintains a scientific record of North American big game animals.

B&C entered the book publishing arena in 1893 with our first book, *American Big Game Hunting*, and we've continued our publishing tradition ever since. Our books are just one way to spread B&C's mission as well as our vision for the future of wildlife. We're excited to introduce a new genre with the release of *Wild Gourmet*, B&C's first-ever cookbook.

The recipes featured in *Wild Gourmet* include the preparation and cooking of all types of game, fish and fowl harvested across North America, ranging from rabbit to walleye. We've divided the book into three chapters: game (both small and big), fowl (including upland and waterfowl), and fish/seafood. Several of the recipes were field-tested by B&C staff members to ensure they were easy to make and delivered a delicious meal. You'll note that many recipes list a specific type of game in the ingredients list—don't hesitate to substitute what you have in the freezer. For instance, the braised venison with tomatillo and poblano peppers recipe on page 21 was prepared with a black bear roast instead of a venison neck roast as listed in the ingredients. The results were fantastic; black bear like I've never tasted before!

Along with the recipes, *Wild Gourmet* also includes additional information that both new and seasoned sportsmen (no pun intended) will find interesting, not to mention helpful. Chef Daniel Nelson of the Gourmet Gone Wild (GGW) program has provided an in-depth and fully illustrated chapter explaining different game-processing techniques, including his best cooking practices for various game, as well as recommended internal temperatures and food safety tips.

Gourmet Gone Wild was created in partnership with the Boone and Crockett Club, Michigan State University, Michigan United Conservation Clubs, and Michigan Department of Natural Resources. In a later chapter, B&C professional member Jordan Burroughs provides an overview of the program and how it's introducing young professionals to conservation, hunting, and fishing through the locavore movement. After attending initial GGW events—which focus on gourmet preparation of wild game

Opposite: Theodore Roosevelt and his hunting companions enjoy a meal together during his 1905 spring bear hunt in Colorado.

From *Outdoor Pastimes of an American Hunter*

and fish—these young professionals connect through hands-on events where outdoor instructors impart their knowledge to gain new support for fishing, hunting and conservation, while continuing to highlight the culinary and health benefits of eating wild fish and game.

Additionally, nutrition is important to all of us. However, nutritional information hasn't been readily available for many game and fowl species until recently. Moira Tidball, a human ecology nutrition resource educator, has provided a detailed table of the nutrition content of wild game and fish species that have known nutritional data in the USDA database. She also gives us the nutritional comparisons of farm-raised versus wild game meat.

Wild Gourmet is more than just another cookbook. For some, it may simply provide new ideas for preparing their game. But for others, it may be a stepping stone to take to the field this coming season and harvest their first rabbit, deer or quail. If you have the chance, now is the time to introduce someone new to hunting or fishing and demonstrate the many benefits the sporting life provides. It's one way sportsmen can ensure that our hunting heritage stays strong for future generations.

Julie Tripp

Director of Publications, Boone and Crockett Club

Game

ANTELOPE | BEAR | CARIBOU | ELK | RABBIT | SQUIRREL | VENISON | WILD BOAR

Wild Game Stock

DANIEL NELSON

Wild game stock and stocks in general are incredibly easy to make and take to freezing quite well, the key is to make saving the bones part of your routine when processing. Bone mass is one of the best and most wasted benefits to whole game butchering. You will need a small, portable, and easy to use hand saw designed for field butchery; I have a small sawzall that I reserve solely for processing and it is battery powered so I can take it afield if convenient. You will also need a large stainless steel pot. Always avoid the cheaper aluminum pots which cause bad tasting acid reactions. I would suggest buying one larger than you think necessary, as this recipe can easily be expanded. Roast bone marrow is packed with glutamates that give it a deep earthy flavor. The savory flavor is often categorized as umami, and this venison stock is chock-full of it, making it a perfect base to many game and non-game recipes alike.

COOK TIME: 3 to 4 hours

3 Pounds heavy marrow bones cut into 2-inch pieces, OR 2 fowl carcasses, OR 3 pounds fish carcasses. Leaving bits of meat attached to bone is preferred. Using more bone mass will give you a more viscous stock capable of thickening pan sauces.

½ Cup rendered duck fat

1 Large yellow onion roughly chopped in skin

½ Head of celery, roughly chopped including leaves

2 Cups carrots, roughly chopped and not peeled

6 Cloves of garlic

2 Tablespoons kosher salt

2 Tablespoons mixed peppercorns

2 Bay leaves

Any fresh herbs you enjoy, such as thyme, parsley, rosemary, and/or sage

8 Quarts water

2 Tablespoons tomato paste

2 Anchovy filets

1 Cup red wine, Bordeaux or cabernet

1. Mix **duck fat, bones, onion, celery, carrots, garlic, salt,** and **peppercorns** on a heavy tray. Roast in a 425°F oven for 10 to 15 minutes until browned.
2. Deglaze tray with **red wine** being sure to scrape any brown bits off the pan.
3. Scrape with rubber spatula everything on the roasting tray into a large stainless steel stock pot and add the **water, herbs, tomato paste,** and **anchovy filets.** Mix and simmer liquid for several hours until total liquids have been reduced by half.
4. Strain out all ingredients reserving the stock. Cool and store in an air-tight container or cooler for up to 7 days or freeze in heavy plastic bags for up to 9 months.
5. To save space for freezing you can slowly simmer the liquids further reducing by as much as you have time for. Take care not to boil your liquids as this will alter chains of fatty and amino acids and change the flavor profile of your stock.

Braised Squirrel Aurora

HANK SHAW

3 Squirrels, cut into serving pieces, or
   1 rabbit

5 Cloves garlic

¼ Cup almonds

25 Green olives

   Flour for dusting

3 Tablespoons olive oil

1 Large onion

1 Small hot chile, minced

1 Cup white wine

½ Cup chicken broth, rabbit or other
   light broth

1 Pound fingerling potatoes (optional)

   Parsley for garnish

If you have an old squirrel, which you can tell by the teeth, which are yellowy and separated, or by the ears, which are tattered, or by the feet, which look well-worn, braising is a must. Squirrels can live several years, unlike cottontail rabbits, which typically only last a year or so. This makes their meat a bit more complex and considerably denser. But an old squirrel can be tough if not braised.

I almost always cook squirrels with some sort of nut sauce. Call me macabre. This recipe is an adaptation of a Spanish rabbit dish I found in *Penelope Casas' Delicioso! The Regional Cooking of Spain*, which I highly recommend. It's a luxurious, thick stew that cries out for crusty bread. The combination of almonds and olives is also a hit.

Figure on one Eastern gray squirrel per person. Or you can use 2 fox squirrels or Western grays to feed 3 people, or 1 cottontail for two people. If you are not a hunter, 1 domestic rabbit will feed 2 to 3 people. And yes, you can use chicken thighs and legs, too.

PREP TIME: 15 minutes   **COOK TIME:** 2 hours

1. Toast the **almonds** in a dry pan if they are not already roasted. Pound them with the **garlic cloves** and a pinch of **salt** in a mortar; you could also buzz them in a food processor or chop them fine by hand. Pit and slice the **olives** in half or chop roughly.
2. Pour the **olive oil** in a Dutch oven or brazier—something ovenproof with a lid—and heat it over medium-high heat. Salt the **squirrel or rabbit** and roll it in the **flour**. Brown the meat on all sides over medium heat. Take your time and do this in batches so you do not crowd the pan. Remove the meat from the pot as it browns and set it aside.
3. While the squirrel is browning, slice the **onion** in half. Grate one half through a coarse grater, and roughly chop the other half. You could also slice it in half-moons.
4. When all the meat is browned, add the **white wine** and **broth** and scrape off any brown bits stuck to the bottom of the pot. Bring this to a rolling boil. Here is a tricky part: You want to cook it down to the point where when you put the meat back into the pot, the liquid comes up only about halfway. You do not want to submerge your meat. How long you'll need to boil depends on the size of your pot.
5. When the liquid is boiling, add the **almond-garlic mixture**, the **chile** and the grated **onion**. Mix well and let boil for a minute. Add the **squirrel** back to the pot. Make sure it is not totally submerged. Halfway is ideal. Cover the pot and simmer gently for 45 minutes.

CONTINUED...

6. After 45 minutes, take the pot out and add the sliced **onion**, the **olives** and the **potatoes**. Mix everything together. If the stew looks too dry, add a little more broth—but remember this is a "dry stew," not a soup. I eat this with a fork and a piece of bread, not a soup spoon. Add just enough broth to keep everything from drying out. Cover the pot again and return to the oven for at least another 45 minutes, maybe an hour. Check the meat and potatoes: The squirrel should be thinking about falling off the bone and the potatoes should be cooked through. When this is done, turn the heat off and let it cool—covered—for 10 minutes on the stovetop.

TO SERVE

Spoon out portions and garnish with **parsley**. Serve with crusty bread.

Smoked Elk Tenderloin

JORGE MORALES

I typically use an electric Char-Broil vertical smoker, which is a great product that maintains a consistent temperature. However, your favorite smoker will do the job well too! For the best results, soak the wood chips for 30 minutes while the rubbed loin is in the refrigerator prior to smoking.

PREP TIME: 40 minutes, including 30 minutes of inactive time.   **COOK TIME:** 90 minutes

3 Pounds elk tenderloin

1 Cup rub, recipe follows

SPICE BLEND FOR ELK RUB

½ **Cup paprika**

¼ **Cup kosher salt**

¼ **Cup sugar**

¼ **Cup brown sugar**

¼ **Cup cumin**

¼ **Cup chili powder**

¼ **Cup black pepper**

2 **Tablespoons cayenne**

ELK RUB

1. Combine **all ingredients** thoroughly.
2. Rub the **spice blend** into the **meat** with your hands, applying it generously all over the meat.
3. Refrigerate the rubbed tenderloin for 30 minutes to allow the spices to infuse the meat.
4. Pre-heat your smoker. Light the wood (pecan or mesquite are the preferred woods, although hickory or other nut woods will work) and heat the smoker chamber to 225°F. Once you reach this temperature, adjust the damper to maintain it.
5. Center the tenderloin in the smoker chamber and close the lid. Check the smoker temperature every 30 minutes to be sure it stays the same. Smoke for 1½ hours.
6. Insert a meat thermometer into the thickest part of the loin, continue smoking until the internal temperature of the meat reaches 120°F. Remove from the smoker, let rest 10 minutes, and serve.

SUGGESTED WINE VARIETALS

RED
Cabernet Sauvignon \ Malbec \
Merlot \ Petite Sirah \ Petit Verdot \
Rhone Blend \ Zinfandel

Leg of Venison on a String

MICHAEL CHIARELLO

I have a hook set beneath my fireplace mantel for the sole purpose of cooking meat this way. The meat is suspended by heavy string from the hook and the leg spins slowly while it cooks. Every time you pass, give it a gentle twirl so the venison spins in front of the heat while it roasts. Here's the cool thing about this method: the venison will spin until the string is unwound and then, due to the meat's weight, it will keep spinning in the opposite direction until it reaches full twist and begins unwinding again. People of every age get a kick of watching it to see how long it spins without a touch. This method works for any leg of venison from 6 to 12 pounds. Remove the pelvic bone but keep the leg intact and scrape down the bone midway if needed so you have a sturdy place on the bone that will hold the weight of the venison. If you don't have a mantel hook, buy the hook and install it before you make the recipe so the hook has time to set in place. I fill a spray bottle with a saltwater solution and spray the meat about every 10 minutes. Before you begin cooking, allow 2 to 3 hours for the venison to come to room temperature after it's come out of the fridge. Note the image at left is a lamb leg, not venison, but it gives you an idea how the recipe is prepared.

Prep Time: 15 minutes   **Cook Time:** 1 to 2½ hours

LEG OF VENISON
1 **Leg of venison, 6-12 pounds (see headnote)**

SALTWATER SOLUTION
3 **Cups water**

²/₃ **Cups kosher salt**

MINT PESTO
See recipe on page 26

1. When the **venison** has been out of the fridge for at least 2 hours, start a fire in your fireplace. Allow the fire to burn until the flames have died down and the glowing wood provides a steady, even heat.
2. For the saltwater solution: fill a medium saucepan with the **water**, add the **kosher salt** and bring to a boil over high heat.
3. Turn off the heat and allow the solution to cool. When it's cool, transfer it to a spray bottle and have the bottle handy on the hearth.
4. Trim any excess fat from the venison and discard.
5. Tie a 2-foot long piece of butcher's twine or kitchen string securely around the bone at the end of the venison leg. Test it to make sure it will hold the venison's weight.
6. Tie the other end of the twine to the fireplace hook so the venison is suspended; the bottom of the venison should be about 8 to 12 inches above the fire.
7. Place a pan at least 9 by 13 inches under the venison to catch all the drippings.
8. The leg will begin to spin; give the heel a twist in the direction in which it is turning. Every 10 minutes or so, check to see if the venison is turning on the string. If it's not, give it a gentle push so it spins.
9. After about 15 minutes, begin to baste with the saltwater solution every 5 to 10 minutes, spraying the venison all the way around.

CONTINUED...

SUGGESTED WINE VARIETALS

RED
Cabernet Sauvignon \ Malbec \
Merlot \ Petite Sirah \ Petit Verdot \
Syrah \ Zinfandel

10. Feed the fire from both sides (but not from the front), pushing the wood to the center as it burns. At this point don't add any more wood, but let the flames die down so the embers are cooking the venison.
11. After 90 minutes, begin basting the venison with the **mint pesto**. (Set aside about ½ cup of the pesto for basting; save the remaining pesto as a condiment to serve at the table.)
12. The venison will roast for between 1 and 2 hours for a 6-pound leg and 2 ½ hours for a 12-pound leg. Check for doneness by inserting an instant read thermometer in the thickest part of the leg, but don't let it touch the bone. For medium rare meat, the temperature should be 130°F.
13. Transfer the venison to a sheet pan, cover lightly with a sheet of aluminum foil, and let it rest for at least 15 minutes.
14. By the time the venison is done, everyone who has given it a push feels invested, so I like to carve the venison at the table where everyone can see. Use a napkin to hold the leg by the heel, at an angle, with the butt end resting on the platter. Slice away from yourself, at a sharp angle, with the knife blade almost parallel to the bone. Carve slices first from the thick, meaty section of the leg, then, turning the leg over, from the smaller muscle on the other side. Holding the knife at a slight angle with the edge pointing upward, remove small slices from the shank.

TO SERVE

Serve a slice of each cut onto every plate, tip the platter, and spoon carving juices over each serving. Add a generous spoonful of mint pesto to each plate.

Adapted from *Michael Chiarello's Live Fire: 125 Recipes for Cooking Outdoors*, Chronicle Books 2013.

Herb Crusted Venison Filets with Horse-Radish Sauce

CHRIS HUGHES

Tender cuts of venison are best prepared simply and cooked quickly. Keep the final doneness to rare or medium-rare to prevent drying out this very lean meat. This recipe is like a good pair of cowboy boots—easy everyday fare and, with a little polish, it's great for more elegant events.

COOK TIME: 25 minutes

1. Rub **filets** with **olive oil**. Sprinkle a generous amount of **salt** over filets.
2. Rub filets with **mustard**. Mix **pepper**, **rosemary** and **thyme** then season meat with the herb mixture.
3. Cover or wrap the meat with plastic and allow to sit at room temperature for 1 hour. (Alternatively, meat can be seasoned in advance and placed in the refrigerator, just be sure to pull meat from refrigerator 1 hour before cooking.)
4. For sauce, mix **sour cream**, **mayonnaise**, **horseradish**, and **mustard** to create the sauce. Chill until ready to serve.
5. Heat oven to 425°F or prepare a medium-hot grill. Roast/grill venison filets to rare or medium-rare. For rare, pull meat when internal temperature is 115° to 120°F, about 15 to 20 minutes total cooking time. For medium-rare, pull meat when internal temperature is 120° to 125°F, about 20 to 25 minutes total cooking time.

TO SERVE

Let filets rest for 5 to 10 minutes before slicing. Slice filets across the grain into ¼-inch medallions and serve with the horseradish sauce.

3 – 5 Pounds boneless venison or elk, or boneless pronghorn loin

2 Tablespoons extra-virgin olive oil

3 Tablespoons Dijon mustard

3 Tablespoons cracked black peppercorns

2 Tablespoons fresh rosemary, finely chopped

2 Tablespoons fresh thyme, finely chopped

Kosher salt, to taste

HORSERADISH SAUCE

¼ Cup sour cream

¼ Cup mayonnaise

¼ Cup prepared horseradish

1 Tablespoons Dijon mustard

SUGGESTED WINE VARIETALS

RED
Cabernet Sauvignon \ Malbec \
Merlot \ Petite Sirah \ Petit Verdot \
Rhone Blend \ Syrah \ Zinfandel

Chicken Fried Rabbit

JORGE MORALES

CHICKEN FRIED RABBIT

2 Cups buttermilk

2 Cups all-purpose flour

1 Teaspoon paprika

½ Teaspoon mustard powder

½ Teaspoon onion powder

½ Teaspoon garlic powder

4 Rabbit hindquarters, about 8 ounces each

Oil for frying

Lemon

1 Jar of pickled watermelon rind, available at most supermarkets

Enjoy this fresh take on a classic by serving your chicken fried rabbit with a semolina corn cake, candied bacon, and pickled watermelon rinds.

TOTAL TIME: 1 hour, 30 minutes

CHICKEN FRIED RABBIT

1. Pour the **buttermilk** into a bowl big enough to hold all four pieces of rabbit. Soak the **rabbit** in buttermilk for about 30 minutes.
2. In another large bowl, combine the **flour** with **paprika, mustard powder onion** and **garlic powders**. Season with **salt**.
3. Remove the rabbit from the buttermilk and give it a shake to remove any excess buttermilk. Toss the rabbit well in the **seasoned flour**, making sure to completely cover the meat.
4. Pour **oil** to the depth of 1 inch in a large sauté pan and heat to 350°F over medium-high heat. A thermometer is really helpful for monitoring the oil's temperature.
5. Using tongs, carefully drop the rabbit pieces into the oil. Fry until golden brown, about 3 minutes per side.
6. Using a slotted spoon or tongs, transfer the rabbit from the pan to a plate lined with paper towels. To finish, give the rabbit a nice squeeze of **lemon juice**.

SEMOLINA CORN CAKE

1. Bring the **water, milk** and **salt** to a boil. Slowly whisk in the **polenta**, turn heat to low and continue to whisk for about 5 minutes or until polenta is smooth and creamy. Spread the polenta in a 9x9 baking dish and set aside to cool.
2. While the polenta is setting up, add the **butter** and **olive oil** to a skillet set over medium-low heat. Add the **onions** and a sprinkle of **kosher salt** and cook, stirring occasionally until soft and golden. About 20–25 minutes.
3. After the polenta has cooled. Pour 1 tablespoon of **olive oil** in a skillet set over medium heat. Using a 3-inch round cookie or biscuit cutter, cut circles out of the firm polenta and place in the heated skillet.
4. Cook until slightly browned and crusty on one side, about 2 minutes. Then flip over and cook the other side another two minutes.
5. To assemble cakes, place on a plate and add a tablespoon of **caramelized onions** to each cake and top with about a teaspoon of **goat cheese**. Drizzle with **honey**.

CANDIED BACON

1. Preheat oven to 350°F
2. Lightly spray a cooking rack with the **olive oil** spray.
3. Place **brown sugar** in a bowl and evenly coat **bacon** with brown sugar on both sides.
4. Lay bacon on cooking rack and place the cooking sheet under it. Sprinkle additional sugar on top of the bacon.
5. Cook in the oven for 20 to 30 minutes until just crisp. Let cool and enjoy.

TO SERVE

Place the polenta cakes on the center of plate. Add a tablespoon of caramelized onions to each and top with goat cheese, a drizzle of honey, a couple of pieces of watermelon rind, one hind-quarter of rabbit on the side of the polenta cake, and top with a slice of candied bacon. Enjoy.

SEMOLINA CORN CAKE WITH CARAMELIZED ONIONS, GOAT CHEESE AND HONEY

2 Cups whole milk

2 Cups water

1 Teaspoon kosher salt

1 Cup polenta

2 Tablespoons extra virgin olive oil

1 Tablespoon butter

1 Yellow onion, halved and sliced in ¼-inch slices

2 Ounces good quality goat cheese

Honey, to drizzle

CANDIED BACON

10 Pieces of thick-cut bacon

1 Cup brown sugar

Olive oil cooking spray

Braised Wild Boar in Red Wine

BOB HURLEY

My first introduction to wild game came when I was working in Switzerland as a young cook. After the grape harvest there, wild game appeared everywhere in all the restaurants and small bistros. It was a celebrated time there that everyone looked forward to each year. When I returned to the States, and subsequently Napa Valley, it seemed natural to try and introduce wild game after the grape harvest here. I've been doing "wild game week" now at the restaurant for 20 years. The following dish has in fact become a signature dish for us all year.

3 Pounds wild boar shoulder

1 Large carrot, peeled and thick sliced

2 Ribs of celery, diced

1 Onion, peeled and diced

7 Cloves of garlic

2 Quarts veal stock, have extra on hand (substitute chicken stock)

10 Juniper berries, crushed

3 Bay leaves, broken up

Several sprigs of fresh thyme

5 Cups of red wine (syrah, zinfandel, or Cabernet sauvignon)

5 Tablespoons of olive oil

1. Combine **all ingredients except olive oil** and marinate **boar** overnight. Remove boar from marinade and set aside. Strain all solids from wine marinade and set aside reserved vegetables.
2. In saucepan, heat the strained wine marinade to a simmer and skim all the impurities from top while reducing by half.
3. Meanwhile, pat meat dry with towel, season and brown in a heavy skillet with about 5 tablespoons of **olive oil**. When browned, add the reserved vegetables to the mix to lightly caramelize them.
4. Add reduced wine marinade and additional **stock**, if necessary, to cover meat. It is important that the meat is covered with liquid during the braising. Bring to a simmer, cover and place in a 300°F oven for approximately 3 hours or until very tender (after two hours, check every 30 minutes or so.)
5. When meat is tender, remove from braising liquid. Strain all solids from liquid and discard. Place braising liquid in saucepan and reduce slowly while skimming off fat and impurities. Reduce until it reaches desired volume and flavor, generally by at least half. While sauce is in progress, take partially cooled meat and trim major fat and sinew.

TO SERVE

Thirty minutes before serving, combine meat and sauce. Re-heat gently and serve with your choice of roasted vegetables and polenta.

SUGGESTED WINE VARIETALS

RED
Cabernet Sauvignon \ Malbec \ Merlot \ Petite Sirah \ Syrah \ Zinfandel

Elk Tenderloin with Yellow Tomato Sauce

JON BONNELL

Elk is one of the sweetest flavored of all the game meats. It's very easy to like, and the wild meat tastes very similar to the commercially available meat, unless the elk comes from an area with an abundance of sage brush, which can impart a strong sage-flavor throughout the meat. Just like all other game meats, do not overcook. Anything past medium will dry out in a hurry. Recipe is for one steak, multiply as needed!

TIME: 30 minutes

1. Cut the **elk tenderloin** into 3 medallions and season on all sides with **salt and pepper**.
2. Brush lightly with **canola oil** to prevent the meat from sticking to the grill.
3. Over very high heat, grill the **elk** quickly on each side just until the meat reaches medium rare. Depending on the thickness of the elk, this can usually be done in about 1 to 1½ minutes per side. Do not overcook the meat or it will be very dry.
4. Sauté the **shallots** and **garlic** in **oil** briefly, then add in **all remaining ingredients** and simmer for 18 to 20 minutes.
5. Puree with a stick blender and strain. If the sauce appears too thin, reduce until slightly thick. If the sauce is too thick, add in a touch of **chicken stock**. The idea is to achieve a sauce with just enough thickness to coat the back of a spoon.
6. Finish with a squeeze of fresh **lemon juice**.

TO SERVE
Portion out sauce on a plate, and place **elk medallions** on top.

ELK
- 1 6-ounce cut of fresh elk tenderloin
- ½ Teaspoon kosher salt
- Pinch freshly ground black pepper
- 1 Teaspoon canola oil

YELLOW TOMATO SAUCE
- 2 Large yellow beefsteak tomatoes, roughly chopped
- 2 Teaspoons extra virgin olive oil
- 2 Shallots, minced
- 2 Cloves garlic, minced
- 1 Cup chicken stock
- 1 Pinch dried chipotle powder
- ¼ Teaspoon kosher salt
- ½ Lemon (just to finish)

SUGGESTED WINE VARIETALS
RED
Cabernet Sauvignon \ Malbec \ Merlot \ Petite Sirah \ Petit Verdot \ Rhone Blend \ Syrah \ Zinfandel

Braised Venison with Tomatillo and Poblano Peppers

JOSH DRAGE

SERVES
4-6

This is my favorite venison recipe because the neck braises up so well leaving the sauce rich but not overly gamey. The acidity in the tomatillo tempers the venison's wild flavor leaving it much more approachable to discerning palates. This dish goes great with a sweet potato gratin. The venison can be braised ahead of time.

PREP TIME: 1 hour   **COOK TIME:** 4-6 hours

1. Soak the **tomatillo** in warm water and remove one at a time and peel off the outer skin. Once all are peeled, quarter each.
2. Large dice one **onion**, dice **leeks**, and rough chop **garlic**.
3. Brown off the **venison neck** on all sides, remove from pan and add the **onions, leek,** and **garlic** with a touch more **olive oil**.
4. Deglaze pan with white wine.
5. Dice and seed the **anaheim pepper** and add to the pot.
6. Char the **poblano** over an open flame or under a broiler, turning as needed. Peel the char off the poblano, de-seed it and small dice it and add to the pot.
7. Add the quartered **tomatillo** to the pot.
8. Add the **roast** back to the pot and enough **chicken stock** to bring the level of liquid up half way around the roast. Cook over low heat about 3 to 4 hours until the bones are easily removed from the meat, pull out all bones.
9. Season with **salt, pepper,** and **lime juice**.

SWEET POTATO GRATIN

1. Caramelize the three **onions**. Start onions in a hot pan with **butter**. Season with **salt** and let cook down stirring often so they don't burn at first.
2. Once the **onions** begin to release some of their juice turn heat down to medium low and let color build up on the bottom stir and release the color.
3. Peel and slice **sweet potatoes** thinly on a mandolin.
4. Grease a casserole dish with the **olive oil**. Layer one complete layer of **sweet potatoes** on the bottom of the dish. Spoon in **caramelized onions**, add **salt** and a very, very small bit of the **red pepper**. Repeat layering until casserole is either full or you run out of sweet potatoes.
5. Top with the cotija cheese and bake at 350°F for one hour covered with foil or when potatoes are soft.

TO SERVE

Serve with fresh cilantro and cotija cheese, alongside sweet potato gratin.

FIELD NOTE: B&C staff put this recipe to the test with a roast from a black bear. Results were extraordinary. Even people who were afraid to try bear, thought it was delicious!

1 Venison neck roast, if not available, substitute with any roast cut

1 Tomatillo

1 Onion, large dice

6 Garlic cloves, roughly chopped

2 Leeks, diced

3 Anaheim peppers, seeded and diced

3 Poblano peppers

White wine

Chicken stock

Lime juice

Bay leaf

Salt and pepper

SWEET POTATO GRATIN

4 Large sweet potatoes

Butter

3 Large onions

Red chili flake

Sea salt

Cotija cheese

Olive oil

SUGGESTED WINE VARIETALS

RED
Cabernet Sauvignon \ Malbec \ Merlot \ Petite Sirah \ Petit Verdot \ Pinot Noir

French-Style Rabbit

SUSAN PRESCOTT-HAVERS

Rabbit has always been very popular in Europe, but in America it is totally underrated. Marinated and braised in red wine with prunes, and very affordable, this special dish might change people's minds. Although the list of ingredients is long, this is not a difficult dish to cook.

PREP TIME: 45 minutes, then marinate 4 hours or overnight
COOK TIME: 2 hours on stove top or 3 hours in a low oven

3 Pounds of rabbit cut into 6 pieces (without the head)

¼ Pound dried plums

½ Cup brandy, plus 2 tablespoons brown sugar

¼ Cup all-purpose flour

2 Tablespoons butter

2 Tablespoons oil

1 cup onion, finely chopped

1 Clove garlic, crushed

1 Teaspoon salt

¼ Teaspoon freshly ground black pepper

1/3 Cup dry red wine

2 Sprigs of thyme, 2 sprigs parsley, and 1 bay leaf

1/3 Cup browned pearl onions, or chopped sautéed yellow onion

¼ Cup cooked bacon bits

1/3 Cup mushrooms, quartered and sautéed

1 Tablespoon parsley, chopped

MARINADE

1 Cup dry red wine

1 Piece of orange or lemon peel

5 Whole peppercorns, cracked

5 Whole juniper berries

2 Sprigs fresh thyme, or ½ teaspoon dried

2 Whole cloves

1 Bay leaf

4 Sprigs fresh parsley

½ Cup onion, finely chopped

1. Combine **all the ingredients for the marinade** in a large plastic bag. Place the bag in a shallow glass bowl. Place **rabbit** in the bag with the marinade; close the top firmly and lay flat in the dish. Marinate the rabbit pieces, turning the bag periodically for 2 to 4 hours, or even overnight.
2. Soak the **prunes** (dried plums) in the **brandy** with the **brown sugar**.
3. Remove rabbit from marinade and wipe dry with paper towel; reserve the marinade.
4. Toss the **meat** in seasoned **flour** and drain on paper towels.
5. Strain the marinade, pressing out and reserving all liquid. Discard the solids.
6. In a large heavy saucepan or Dutch oven, melt **butter**, add **oil** and, over medium high heat, brown **rabbit**. With slotted spoon, remove rabbit and set aside. Only cook one layer at a time so as not to steam the meat and form a crust.
7. Lower the heat and gently sweat the **chopped onion** and **garlic** for about 5 minutes until translucent.
8. Deglaze the pan with the **red wine** scraping up the brown bits, and then add the **marinade liquid, chicken broth, parsley, thyme** and **bay leaf.** Return the rabbit, bring to a boil.
9. Add the **prunes** and their **soaking liquid.** Reduce the heat and simmer, partially covered for up to 2 hours or until the rabbit is tender and the sauce thickened. This last step you can also do in the oven but it will take longer. Once cooked adjust the seasoning and transfer to a heated serving bowl (or you can serve straight from the Dutch oven)
10. While the rabbit is cooking, cook separately the **onions, bacon** and **mushrooms.** Once cooked mix all these ingredients together with the **parsley.**

TO SERVE
Sprinkle onion-bacon mixture of over the rabbit as you serve. In France this dish is often served with pieces of fried bread and simply boiled baby potatoes.

SUGGESTED WINE VARIETALS

WHITE
Chardonnay

RED
Cabernet Sauvignon \ Merlot \
Pinot Noir \ Rhone Blend

Iron Cross Antelope

MICHAEL CHIARELLO

When I consider all the people, throughout centuries, who have used this method to cook, I feel like one small dot in a very long time line. This is a 30-log kind of a fire. To be safe have 3 dozen logs, each about 6 inches in diameter and each completely dry, stacked, and ready before you bring home the antelope.

The basting liquid makes enough for one antelope up to 45 pounds. I love the flavor butcher's salt adds to the basting liquid. Butcher's salt is a blend of salt and spices from France made especially for meat. In a perfect world, you'd baste the antelope while it cooks using a branch of rosemary as your brush. Silicone basting brushes—as big as you can get—do the job just fine too.

1 Pronghorn, whole, approximately
  30 to 40 pounds

BASTING LIQUID

1 Cup loosely packed fresh sage
  leaves

½ Cup fresh rosemary sprigs

½ Cup fresh thyme sprigs

4 Cups fresh flat-leaf parsley

2 Cups fresh mint

1½ Cups fresh oregano

8 Garlic cloves

1 Tablespoon kosher salt

1 Tablespoon butcher's salt (or use a
  smaller amount of black pepper)

2 Cups olive oil

2 Cups dry white wine

6 Bay leaves, fresh or dried

FOR THE BASTING LIQUID

1. In a food processor, or in a blender in batches, combine the **sage, rosemary, thyme, parsley, mint, oregano, garlic, kosher salt** and **butcher's salt or pepper**. Process to a coarse puree.
2. With the machine running, add the **oil** and **wine** and puree until smooth.
3. Transfer the liquid to a container with a lid, add the **bay leaves**, and refrigerate until the antelope goes on the fire.

SETTING UP AND ROASTING THE ANTELOPE

1. When you're ready to start cooking, clean the **antelope**, but don't tie it to the cross until you've started the fire.
2. Build your fire. When it is ready for the big logs, add them and then fasten the **antelope** onto the cross while the fire burns down a little. Look at the fires in the photo at right (I'm roasting lamb here, not antelope); the fire you need to build won't be the size of a bonfire but just big enough to provide steady, even heat for the 4 hours that the antelope will cook.
3. Have one or two friends hold the antelope up against the vertical bar, with the antelope shoulders toward the ground while you tie each of the four legs to a crossbar. The back of the antelope should be against the cross; the ribs should be facing out toward the fire. Use a heavy-gauge wire (at least 16-gauge, found in any hardware

CONTINUED...

FIELD NOTE: B&C's Assistant Director of Big Game Records Justin Spring put this recipe to a field test during Montana's 2013 pronghorn season with extraordinary results.

store) to securely tie each leg to a crossbar and then use the wire to fasten the neck to the center, vertical bar. If you have an iron cross with rings, slide each of the animal's legs through the rings. Secure each leg by twining 16-gauge stainless steel picture wire around the leg and the crossbar. **NOTE:** Don't use a wire that's too lightweight hold the animal and don't use wire with any kind of coating on it.

4. When the fire has died down slightly so it's not raging flames, maneuver the iron cross into place so it's close to the fire but not right on top of it. Use your hands to test that the antelope is close enough to the heat to cook. You'll want to allow at least 3 to 4 hours for an antelope that weighs 30 to 45 pounds.

5. Check the fire periodically. If it begins to cool, add logs but always add new wood to the edge of the fire farthest from the iron cross; you don't want flaming logs under the antelope. When the new wood glows red and is no longer emitting lots of smoke and flame, then rake it forward closer to the antelope. Don't rely on time alone to determine when the meat is done. For medium-rare antelope, it's done when the meat registers 135°F on a meat or probe thermometer. Take the antelope off the fire and let rest for 15 minutes before you begin to carve. Have a large heat-proof surface ready for the antelope. A butcher block table is ideal. Ask a friend or two to help plate the antelope as you carve.

TO CARVE

1. First untie the wire from the antelope and discard it.
2. Cut away the hind legs at the joints; the meat should be tender enough so this is easy.
3. Next, carve at the shoulder, working down toward the front legs. Cut away the front legs, and then carve the antelope one section at a time, working from the ribs toward the backbone.
4. Serve with mint pesto and chile-fennel tzatziki sauces.

SIMPLE SYRUP
½ Cup water

½ Cup granulated sugar

MINT PESTO
3 Cups fresh mint

½ Cup packed fresh flat-leaf parsley

1 Tablespoon toasted pine nuts

½ Teaspoon garlic, minced

1/16 Teaspoon ascorbic acid or finely ground vitamin C

½ Cup extra extra-virgin olive oil

2 Tablespoons simple syrup

¼ Teaspoon coarse sea salt, preferably gray salt

⅛ Teaspoon freshly ground black pepper

MINT PESTO
Makes about 1-1/4 cups

This delicious pesto has a much stronger fresh mint flavor than any store-bought jelly. You can find ascorbic acid in health food stores. It works better than anything I've found to keep this pesto bright green.

1. For the simple syrup, in a small pan over high heat bring the **water** and **sugar** to a boil. Stir until the sugar is dissolved, and then take the pan of the heat and set aside.
2. Bring about 2 quarts of **water** to a boil in a stockpot over high heat.
3. While the water heats, set up an ice bath in a large bowl full of full of ice and water. When the water boils, blanch the **mint** for 30 seconds.
4. With a slotted spoon transfer it from the hot water to the ice bath.
5. Blanch the **parsley** for 30 seconds and then transfer it to the ice bath.
6. Remove the herbs from the cold water and squeeze into a ball to remove excess moisture. Roughly chop them.
7. In a large, heavy-duty blender or a food processor, blend the **mint, parsley,**

pine nuts, garlic, and **ascorbic acid**, pulsing just until combined. With the machine running, pour in the **olive oil** very slowly.

8. Pour in 2 tablespoons of the **simple syrup**. (Refrigerate the remaining simple syrup and use for cocktails or to sweeten coffee or tea.)

9. Add **salt** and **pepper** to the pesto, taste, and season with more salt and pepper or simple syrup if you like.

CHILE-FENNEL TZATZIKI
Makes 3 cups

The rich hot antelope and the cool, creamy sauce are made for each other. I gave this an Italian twist by adding fennel, roasted lemon juice, and Calabrian chiles. Use a traditional thick Greek-style yogurt, such as Fage, and use the green fronds at the top of your fennel to give this extra flavor and color. For more flavor grate the cucumber, catching all the juices for the tzatziki, I like to make this at least an hour ahead of time so it can chill before serving.

1. Grill the **lemons** at least 1 hour before serving or the day before if you like. On a hot grill or in a cast-iron pan over a fire or on the stove, place the lemon halves cut-side down. Cook until the lemon shows some char, 4 to 5 minutes.

2. When the **lemons** have cooled, juice them and then strain the juice to get rid of some of the char.

3. Measure about 1 tablespoon of the roasted lemon juice and reserve the remaining juice.

4. Trim the **fennel**. Cut the white part into ¼-inch dice (about 1 cup); coarsely chop the green fronds (about 1 tablespoon).

5. In a medium bowl, mix the 1 tablespoon strained **lemon juice** with the diced **fennel, yogurt** and **garlic**.

6. Grate the peeled **cucumber** into a measuring cup, catching all the juice that you can. Add the grated cucumber and its juice to the bowl when you have about 1 cup. (A little less or extra is fine.)

7. Stir in the chopped **fennel fronds, chile paste, salt** and **pepper**. Taste and then add another few teaspoons of roasted lemon juice or more salt and pepper, if you like.

8. Cover with plastic wrap, refrigerate, and chill for at least an hour or overnight. Stir just before serving.

Adapted from *Michael Chiarello's Live Fire: 125 Recipes for Cooking Outdoors*, Chronicle Books 2013.

CHILE-FENNEL TZATZIKI

1 Juicy lemon, halved

1 Small bulb fennel with green fronds

2 Cups Greek-style yogurt

1 Teaspoon garlic, minced

1 Large whole peeled cucumber or 2 small whole peeled cucumbers

1 Teaspoon Calabrian chile paste, or ¼ teaspoon red pepper flakes

¼ Teaspoon coarse sea salt, preferably gray salt

⅛ Teaspoon freshly ground black pepper

Venison Pasty

DANIEL NELSON

The migrants of Cornwall spread the Cornish pasty to mining communities across the globe and the Upper Peninsula of Michigan is one area where the tradition fervently continues. This pocket of earthy flavor is as good and portable lunch as can be had, perfect for picnics, afternoons in the deer blind, or as part of a hearty winter dinner. Note: Do not substitute potatoes for rutabaga.

1. Sift **flour**, **salt**, and **baking powder** together.
2. Crumble in the **shortening** and **venison fat**, mix by hand until loosely combined. Do not over mix.
3. Mix **ice** and **water** together and stir to thoroughly chill water, measure out ¾ cup water and combine, by hand, with the dough mix. Do not over mix. Set dough in cooler for a minimum of 2 hours or up to 24 hours.
4. Place cold dough ball on well floured counter and roll out to ¼-inch thickness, cut out 5-inch diameter circles. Keep dough circles in cooler until ready to fill.

DOUGH
- 3 Cups flour
- 1½ Teaspoon salt
- ¾ Teaspoon baking powder
- 1 Cup shortening
- 2 Tablespoons venison fat
- 1 Cup water
- 1 Tablespoon apple cider vinegar
- 1 Cup ice

FILLING
- 1½ pounds venison roast
- 1 Rutabaga
- 1 Parsnip
- 1 Turnip
- ¼ Cup celery root
- 2 Cups sweet potato or winter squash
- 1 Medium yellow onion
- 4 Cloves garlic
- 2 Teaspoons each of fresh chopped rosemary, sage, oregano, and thyme
- Salt and pepper blend
- 1 Cup rendered goose or duck fat
- 2 Tablespoons butter
- 3 Tablespoons flour
- 2 Cups venison stock or beef stock
- ½ Cup Madeira wine, a dry port or sherry can also be substituted

VENISON PASTY STOCK

1. Trim the **venison roast** of all fat and sinew (reserve) and dice into ¼-inch cubes, sprinkle with **salt** and **blended pepper**.
2. Peel and dice **rutabaga**, **parsnip**, **turnip**, **celery root**, and **winter squash** into ¼-inch cubes, reserve all peelings. Do not save the rutabaga peelings if your rutabaga has been commercially waxed.
3. Dice half of the **yellow onion** and add to the venison trimmings and vegetable peelings, as well as 2 **cloves garlic**.
4. Warm ½ cup of **goose fat** in a medium stock pan and add the trimming and peeling mixture and sauté for 5 minutes or until onions become translucent.
5. Turn off flame and deglaze the pan with ¼ cup **Madeira wine**.
6. Turn flame back on to medium and continue to sauté for 2 minutes, add the **venison stock** and reduce the total liquids by half. Strain off the solids and reserve liquid.

VENISON PASTY MIX

1. Heat ¼ cup of **goose fat** in a large sauté pan until sizzling hot.
2. Add the diced **venison roast** and sauté quickly, browning but only partially cooking all meat. Remove the venison and cool.
3. Warm another ¼ cup **goose fat** over medium heat and sauté all the **diced vegetables** plus the other diced half of **yellow onion** and **garlic**. Season with **salt** and **pepper** accordingly.
4. Continue to cook for 6 to 8 minutes, stirring occasionally, do not cook vegetables completely, leave them al dente.
5. Remove and cool vegetables.

CONTINUED...

6. Turn off flame and deglaze the pan with the remaining ¼ cup **Maderia wine**, reduce.

7. Add 2 tablespoons **butter** to the pan and melt.

8. Stir in **flour** and sauté for 1 minute being sure to scrape all browned bits from bottom of pan then add the venison pasty stock, simmer and reduce until the liquids are nearly as viscous as gravy. Cool the liquids.

FILLING PASTY

1. Mix all the cooled (room temperature minimum) **venison**, **vegetables** and **demi liquids** together.

2. Take **pasty dough circles** from cooler and fill half the circle with pasty mixture.

3. Fold over the dough and pie roll the edges together. Crimp together with a fork if necessary.

4. Filled pasties can be baked immediately or frozen until needed.

BAKING

1. Preheat oven to 400°F for fresh/thawed pasties or 375°F for frozen pasties

2. Pasties can be brushed with an egg white wash for a crisper crust

3. Bake until golden brown.

      Fresh/thawed pasties for 15 to 20 minutes.

      Frozen pasties 20 to 25 minutes.

Venison Osso Buco

CHRIS HUGHES

Osso buco is traditionally made from veal shanks but we enjoy using venison. It is one of our favorites because of the deep, complex flavors that develop as the meat braises. Make it a day ahead. The flavors will blend overnight, the meat will absorb the broth, and your kitchen will already be clean for your guests. Just reheat in a 350°F oven until warmed through—about an hour.

1. Preheat oven to 275°F.
2. Combine the **ingredients of the herb rub** and rub the **meat** on all sides with the mixture.
3. Heat the **oil** in a large cast iron Dutch oven or oven proof casserole over high heat.
4. Add the **meat** and sear on all sides, about 5 to 7 minutes. Use additional olive oil if necessary to prevent the lean meat sticking to the pan.
5. Remove the meat and reduce the heat to medium. Add the **chopped cured ham, onions, carrot** and **garlic** and cook, covered, for 10 minutes, stirring often.
6. Add **remaining ingredients except salt, pepper, lemon zest,** and **parsley.** Bring stock to a boil and add meat to pot.
7. Cover and bake in oven until quite tender—this may require up to 4 or more hours. If necessary, add more chicken stock to the sauce to keep meat almost covered.
8. Remove meat to a serving bowl. Boil sauce until it is thickened slightly and add **salt** and **pepper** to taste. If necessary, add more chicken stock to the sauce to increase volume.

TO SERVE

Spoon sauce over the top of the meat then sprinkle with the **gremolata** and serve with a side of mashed potatoes or risotto.

HERB RUB
- 2 Teaspoons fresh thyme or 1 teaspoon dried thyme
- 1 Teaspoon fennel seed, crushed
- ½ Teaspoon ground coriander
- 1 Teaspoon salt
- 1 Teaspoon freshly ground pepper

OSSO BUCO
- 4 Pounds venison shanks
- 2 Tablespoons olive oil
- 1 Ounces of cured ham such as prosciutto or pancetta, chopped
- 3 Cups onions, thinly sliced
- ¾ Cup carrots, finely chopped
- 3 Tablespoons garlic, finely minced
- 1 Cup dry white wine
- 1½ Cups fresh tomatoes, seeded and chopped or canned tomatoes
- 2 Cups chicken stock
- 1 Bay leaf
- 1 Teaspoon fresh rosemary, chopped
- Salt and freshly ground black pepper to taste

GREMOLATA
- 2 Teaspoons lemon rind, finely grated
- 3 Tablespoons parsley, chopped

SUGGESTED WINE VARIETALS

RED
Cabernet Sauvignon \ Petite Sirah \ Zinfandel

Grilled Pasta with Elk Meatballs

MICHAEL CHIARELLO

This is an old-school pasta cooked in a new-school way. Grilling the pasta makes it entirely new, adding a smoky flavor and the occasional browned crunchy bit of pasta, which is delicious.

Note: It's much faster to make a meatball with a scoop than with your hands. Scoops make such quick work of certain tasks—shaping meatballs, gougeres, or cookie dough, for example—that I keep a variety of scoop sizes at home as well as at work. If you don't have a 2-ounce scoop for the meatballs, try using a ¼ cup measure instead.

1½ Pounds ground elk

¾ Pounds ground pork

2 Eggs

4 Tablespoons Parmesan cheese, freshly grated

4 Tablespoons fresh flat-leaf parsley, finely chopped

2 Teaspoons dried oregano

1 Tablespoon fresh basil leaves, finely chopped

2 Cups yellow onion, finely chopped

2 Cups finely ground dried bread crumbs

2 Large garlic cloves, minced

2 Teaspoons coarse sea salt, preferably grey salt

¼ Teaspoon freshly ground black pepper

2 Cups water, plus more if needed

5 Tablespoons kosher salt

1 Pound dried spaghetti

4 Tablespoons extra-virgin olive oil

2 Cups marinara sauce

4 Tablespoons grated pecorino cheese, substitute with Parmesan, or Asiago if necessary

1. In a large bowl, mix together the **meat, eggs, cheese, parsley, oregano, basil, onion, bread crumbs,** and **garlic,** and season with **salt** and **pepper**.
2. Add 1 cup of the **water**. Knead the water into the meat mixture with your hands. Knead and form meatballs into about 1½ inch balls with a 2-ounce scoop or with your hands.
3. Place meatballs in a large saucepan or skillet on the stove (use two pans if they don't all fit in a single pan), add enough water to fill pan about ¼ inch, and cover. Steam the meatballs over medium heat for about 25 minutes. Transfer to a platter and refrigerate until you're ready to grill them.
4. Turn a gas grill to high or ignite charcoal. When the grill is hot, for both gas and charcoal grills, clean your grill rack. Decrease the temperature to medium-high (on a gas grill only), and brush or wipe a little olive oil on the grill rack.
5. In batches, grill the meatballs in a cast-iron pan or plancha on the grill until they are well browned all the way around, 6 minutes total for the pan-cooked meatballs. Remove from the heat and reserve.
6. Fill a large pot with about 5 quarts of **water**, add the **kosher salt,** and bring to a boil over high heat on your stove.
7. Add the **pasta** and cook until al dente, just 6 to 8 minutes. Drain the pasta, reserving 1 cup of the pasta water.
8. Spread the pasta on a baking sheet and drizzle with 2 tablespoons of the **olive oil** so it won't stick together.
9. Lightly **oil** a long, flat grill basket or spritz with non-stick cooking spray.
10. With tongs, add half the **pasta** to the basket arranging it in an even layer. (If you have two grill baskets, cook both batches of pasta at once.) Place the basket on a rack over hot coals and turn frequently, until the pasta turns a golden color. You'll hear it crackling during grilling. Empty the grill basket into a long heat proof bowl.
11. Toss the pasta with 1 to 2 cups of **marinara sauce**. If it needs some moisture, add ¼ cup of the reserved pasta water and toss again.
12. Add the remaining 2 tablespoons of **olive oil** and 2 tablespoons of the **pecorino cheese**. Toss. Transfer to a serving bowl, top with the remaining pecorino cheese and serve immediately.

Adapted from *Michael Chiarello's Live Fire: 125 Recipes for Cooking Outdoors*, Chronicle Books 2013.

SUGGESTED WINE VARIETALS

WHITE
Chardonnay

RED
Cabernet Sauvignon \ Malbec \ Merlot \ Rhone Blend

Venison Quesadillas

JON BONNELL

For anyone who might not be ready to try venison all by itself, this is a great introductory dish. With an intensely-flavored marinade, grilled venison makes a perfect rich component to great quesadillas. Be careful not to overcook the venison and allow it to rest before slicing to bring out the best flavor possible.

Time: 10 to 15 minutes

FILLING

- 1 Pound venison backstrap or back leg meat
- 1 Ounce red wine
- 1 Ounce red wine vinegar
- 1 Tablespoon soy sauce
- 2-3 Shakes of hot sauce
- 2 Cloves garlic, minced
- ¼ Teaspoon brown sugar
- 2 Teaspoons olive oil

QUESADILLAS

- 5 Large flour tortillas
- ½ Cup cheddar cheese, grated
- 2½ Teaspoons butter
- 1 Jalapeño, finely diced

PREPARING THE VENISON

1. Clean the **venison** well and be sure that any connective tissue or silverskin is removed.
2. Cut the venison down to ½-inch thickness for grilling. Any size pieces will work, as long as they are not too thick.
3. Combine the **venison** with **all other ingredients** and allow to marinate for at least 2 hours in a Ziploc bag.
4. Remove the venison pieces from the bag and shake off any excess marinade.
5. Grill over a very hot fire for roughly one minute per side just until it is well seared on the outside, but still medium rare in the middle.
6. Pull the meat from the grill and allow it to rest for 8 to 10 minutes before cutting into medium-sized dice.

QUESADILLAS

1. Using ½ teaspoon of **butter** per **tortilla**, add a little butter to a preheated flat-top surface, then top with a flour tortilla and sprinkle on some of the **cheese**.
2. As soon as the **cheese** begins to melt, add in several of the **venison** pieces, a little **jalapeño** then fold the tortilla in half.
3. Continue to cook until the tortillas have nicely browned on each side, then remove.

TO SERVE

Cut quesadillas into triangles, garnish with your choice of sour cream, guacamole, salsa, and chopped fresh jalapeño.

SUGGESTED WINE VARIETALS

RED
Cabernet Sauvignon \ Merlot \
Rhone Blend \ Zinfandel

Antelope Curry

SUSAN PRESCOTT-HAVERS

The inspiration for this dish is African but the North American antelope is equally good. Long slow cooking is the secret to a tender antelope.

PREP TIME: 45 minutes   **COOK TIME:** 2 hours

1. Open the cans of **coconut** without shaking and separate the milk from the cream at the bottom of the can, keep them separate.
2. Heat a few tablespoons of **vegetable oil (or coconut oil)** in a heavy stockpot or Dutch oven over a medium high heat. Sprinkle the **meat** with **salt** and fry in batches forming a single layer so that the meat browns and does not steam. Remove with slotted spoon.
3. Reduce the heat, add a tablespoon of **oil** or **butter** and gently sweat **onions**, **garlic** and **fresh ginger** until translucent (5 minutes).
4. Add **curry paste**, **sugar**, **cinnamon**, **cardamom pods** and stir until fragrant, about 2 minutes. Add **tomatoes**, **coconut milk**, **bay leaves**, **brown sugar**, and **chicken stock**. Return the meat to the pot and bring to a boil.
5. Lower the heat to a simmer and cook covered for up to 2 hours, stirring occasionally, and add a little water or broth from time to time to prevent the pan from drying out and the coconut milk from scorching. It is done when the meat is fork tender.
6. After about 1½ hours add the **coconut cream** and the **potatoes** and cook for 15 minutes or until tender and the sauce has thickened. Adjust the seasoning to taste.

TO SERVE
Slice the **bananas** and mix with the **peanuts** and **lime juice**. Scatter over the cooked meat and serve with plain boiled rice, quinoa or couscous.

2 Cans coconut milk (or equivalent quantity of cream if you prefer)

2 Pounds antelope stew meat cleaned and cut into 1¾ inch pieces

3 Tablespoons vegetable oil, or coconut oil, 1 tablespoon of butter (optional)

3 Tablespoons curry paste (I use an Indian Madras-style paste, but Thai Red curry paste will do also)

1 Large potato cut into 1½-inch cubes

1 Yellow onion cut into 6 wedges

2 Cloves of garlic, chopped

1 to 2 inch piece of fresh ginger cut into thin strips

2 Tablespoons dark brown sugar

2 Cinnamon sticks

6 Toasted cardamom pods

3 Bay leaves

1 14-ounce can diced tomatoes

1 14-ounce can chicken broth

2 Bananas

¼ Cup peanuts

2 Tablespoons fresh lime juice

SUGGESTED WINE VARIETALS

WHITE
Sauvignon Blanc \ Rosé (dry)

RED
Pinot Noir \ Rhone Blend

Bearlognese
DANIEL NELSON

Traditional Italian bolognese is a rich, meaty red sauce with the deep savory essence of umami, making a perfect fit for game meat, especially bear. This is a perfect winter recipe, which will hold for up to 4 days and freezes very well.

½ Cup olive oil

1 Cup carrot, diced

1 Cup onion, diced

1 Cup celery, diced

1 Pound ground bear

1 Pound ground venison

½ Pound ground wild turkey

1 Tablespoon garlic, fresh chopped

1 Cup dry white wine

32 Ounces of organic tomatoes, peeled and chopped

2 Cups venison stock (see recipe on page 5)

1 Teaspoon thyme

2 Bay leaves

Salt & blended pepper

½ Cup heavy cream

3 pounds cavatappi noodles, dry

Shaved Parmesan

1. Heat 2 tablespoons of **olive oil** in a large heavy saucepan over medium heat.
2. Add the **onion, carrot, celery** and cook, stirring occasionally, until softened, 8 to 10 minutes. Remove the vegetables from the pan and set aside.
3. Reheat the pan over medium-high heat with 2 tablespoons olive oil. Add the **ground game meats**—let meat brown for 2 to 3 minute-intervals between chopping and stirring.
4. Once the meat is cooked just rare, add the **chopped garlic** and **cooked vegetables**, cook for 2 more minutes
5. Turn heat off and deglaze pan with the **white wine**. Turn heat back to medium and continue to cook, stirring occasionally, for 8 to 10 minutes or until the wine is almost all evaporated.
6. Stir in the **canned tomatoes, venison stock, thyme, bay leaves** and a tablespoon each of **salt** and **blended pepper**. Cover the pan partially with tinfoil and continue to cook over low heat for another 80 to 90 minutes.
7. Remove the **bay leaves** and store for use. Cool in refrigerator if using within a few days or freeze in heavy freezer bags.

TO SERVE

Bring 6 quarts salted water to a heavy boil and add dry **cavatappi** noodles. Cook, stirring occasionally, until al dente and drain. Warm **bearlognese sauce** in medium sauce pan. Add **heavy cream** to sauce and heat to a simmer. Toss with cavatappi noodles. Shave **Parmesan** over deep platters of Bearlognese.

Rack of Squirrel á la Forestiere

DANIEL NELSON

6 Loin racks of squirrel or rabbit

¼ Cup olive oil

¼ Cup squirrel fat or duck fat

2 Tablespoons fresh garlic, chopped

¼ Cup carrots, diced

¼ Cup onion, diced

¼ Cup celery, diced

1 Pound seasonal fresh wild mushrooms

4 Ounces dried wild mushrooms

½ Cup dry white wine

2 Tablespoons whole grain mustard

1 Cup heavy cream

1 Quart duck, goose stock or chicken stock

2 Bay leaves

2 Teaspoons thyme

Salt and blended pepper

2 Pounds fresh green beans

Package of wild rice

This is one of my favorite meals, I am a huge umami fan and this recipe is full of earthy flavor. Using full racks of squirrel or rabbit gives this sauce incredible depth, as the rendered fats and the marrow will add a bunch of savory glutamates. Rendered squirrel fat has a relatively low melting point and is a wonderful oil to work with, adding soft nutty undertones to the dish. If you ever harvest a nice plump squirrel or two, you would be doing yourself a great favor by rendering the fat. To render, simply place 3 to 4 ounces of fat in a small sauté pan with 2 tablespoons water. Slowly fry the fat tissue until it is crispy like well-done bacon. The water will have evaporated and you can pour the liquid fat into a sealable plastic bag and freeze for up to 9 months. You can break small pieces of the frozen fat off for use, while saving the rest.

1. Season cleaned trimmed **squirrel racks** with salt and **blended pepper**.
2. Heat 1 tablespoon of **olive oil** and 1 tablespoon **squirrel fat** in a heavy saucepan over medium-high heat. Sear each side of the racks for 2 to 3 minutes.
3. Remove racks from pan and add 1 tablespoon **olive oil** and 1 tablespoon **squirrel fat** on medium heat. Sauté the diced **onions, carrots** and **celery**, stirring occasionally until they are beginning to soften, 5 to 8 minutes. Then add half of the sliced fresh **mushrooms** and chopped **garlic**. Continue to cook, stirring occasionally, for 5 to 6 more minutes.
4. Remove pan from flame and deglaze with the **white wine**, return to flame and continue to cook for 6 to 8 more minutes or until wine is nearly reduced.
5. Add the **duck stock, thyme, bay leaves, whole grain mustard,** and **dried mushrooms**. Stir and add racks back to the sauce pan. Bring to a low simmer, cover and continue to cook for 90 to 120 minutes or until tender. Remove racks and let rest.
6. Add the **heavy cream** to the sauce and bring back to a simmer, reduce sauce by ¼ and season to taste.

GREEN BEANS AND WILD RICE

1. Heat 1 tablespoon **olive oil** and 1 tablespoon **duck fat** in a sauté pan over medium-high heat.
2. Add cleaned and snipped **green beans** and the other half of the fresh sliced **mushrooms**, season with **salt** and **blended pepper** and cook, stirring occasionally, until al dente, 10 to 12 minutes.

TO SERVE

Make **wild rice** by following package instructions of your favorite blend. Fill two-thirds of the plate with the wild rice and beans. Lean rack of squirrel against green beans and rice and spoon pan sauce over rack.

SUGGESTED WINE VARIETALS

WHITE
Chardonnay

RED
Merlot \ Pinot Noir \ Rhone Blend

Venison Chili with Pickled Jalapeños

SCOTT WATSON

SERVES
8-10

Venison can have a gamey yet subtle flavor, toning the spice of this chili down to let the venison and northern beans shine through was the concept in my flavor combination. I gave this venison chili an interesting profile by using a little dry vermouth instead of dark beer, which is frequently used in chili recipes. This gives it a refined flavor allowing for easier eating and a comfortable and enjoyable experience. The sweet and salty brined pickled jalapeños also add a nice pop to this dish.

PREP TIME: 30 minutes   **COOK TIME:** 1 hour

CHILI

- 2 Tablespoons extra virgin olive oil
- 3 Onions, sliced thinly
- 5 Garlic cloves, chopped
- 2 Tablespoons thyme, fresh
- 2 Tablespoons tarragon, fresh
- 2 Bay leaves
- 2 Cups dry vermouth
- 2 Pounds ground venison
- 1 Can kidney bean (10-12 oz.)
- 1 Can Northern beans (10-12 oz.)
- 1 Can chili sauce (10-12 oz.)
- 1 Can diced tomatoes (10-12 oz.)
- 2 Quarts chicken stock
- 1 Tablespoon cumin
- Chili powder, to taste
- Cayenne pepper (ground), to taste
- Salt and black pepper, to taste

PICKLED JALAPEÑOS

- 1 16 oz. canning jar
- 10 Jalapeños, sliced thinly
- 1¼ Cups water
- 1 Tablespoon malt vinegar
- 2 Tablespoons sugar
- 1 Teaspoon kosher salt
- 1 Tablespoon pickling spice
- 1 Tarragon sprig, fresh
- 1 Garlic cloves, crushed

1. Caramelize onions in **extra virgin olive oil**.
2. When the onions are caramelized add the **garlic**, cook for 5 more minutes.
3. Add the **thyme, tarragon, bay leaves** and **vermouth**. Cook until the liquid is almost gone.
4. Stir in the **ground venison** and cook through.
5. Add the **beans, chili sauce, tomatoes** and **chicken stock**. Cook for 20 minutes.
6. Add the **spices** and cook for 10 more minutes.
7. Taste and adjust seasoning. Cook until you get your desired consistency.

PICKLED JALAPEÑOS

1. Thinly slice the **jalapeños** and discard the stem. (Take care to use rubber gloves while handling jalapeños.)
2. Place **all ingredients except the jalapeños** into a pot and bring to a boil for 1 minute.
3. Strain the liquid and place the **jalapeños** into sterilized mason jar.
4. Pour the hot liquid over top the jalapeños, making sure to cover them, and then lid the jar.
5. Place a grate in a heavy-bottom pot.
6. Place the jar on top of the grate and pour cold water on it. Making sure to cover the jar with the cold water by at least 1 inch.
7. Bring to boil for 20 minutes.
8. After the time has elapsed very carefully, with tongs, pull the jar out of the water and let cool on the counter. Be careful, it will be extremely hot.

TO SERVE

Garnish with any combination of pickled jalapeños, shredded cheddar cheese, sour cream, and chive sour cream, then serve with hand-torn cornbread or pretzels.

SUGGESTED WINE VARIETALS

RED
Cabernet Sauvignon \ Petite Sirah \
Petit Verdot \ Syrah \ Zinfandel

Spinach and Ricotta Gnudi with Marsala Stewed Rabbit Ragu

ANTHONY SCANIO

This recipe combines classic Sicilian flavors—rabbit, Marsala, tomato, olives and almonds—in a fresh, modern ragu. The spinach and ricotta echoes the most traditional ravioli filling of, well, spinach and ricotta. In the case of the gnudi, however, the spinach and ricotta are not covered or "dressed" in pasta sheets, but rather they are nude and thus playfully called gnudi.

SPINACH AND RICOTTA GNUDI

1. Place **spinach**, **basil** and one quarter of the **ricotta** into a food processor. Process until the spinach is pureed and the ricotta takes on a green hue.
2. Transfer from the food processor to a large bowl and fold in the remaining **ricotta** until it is fully homogenized.
3. Add the 2 cups of **flour**, **salt** and **pepper**, and with your hands begin to work the flour into the ricotta.
4. Once the dough begins to form, transfer it to a lightly floured surface and knead it for at least 6 minutes, adding more flour as necessary to form a dough that is firm but not tacky. (With standard potato gnocchi the dough is worked as little as possible or the gnocchi become tough. However, with gnudi we need to develop the gluten so that they will hold together. Many recipes call for eggs in the dough, but it is not necessary if the dough is well worked and the protein in the flour is well developed.)
5. Once the dough is made, portion it into golf ball size pieces and roll each piece into a ½-inch thick long dowel.
6. Cut the dowels into ½-inch long pieces. Place the gnudi on a parchment-lined baking sheet and let them rest in the refrigerator for at least 30 minutes and up to 2 hours.
7. Bring a large pot of water to a boil and season well with fine salt. Drop the gnudi, about 10 at a time, into the water; they will drop to the bottom of the pot. They will rise to the top within 1 to 2 minutes and begin to float. Continue to cook the gnudi for 6 minutes longer and then remove with a slotted spoon to an oiled baking sheet. Repeat the process with the remaining gnudi.
8. Once the gnudi have cooled completely they may be used immediately or stored in an airtight container in the refrigerator for 24 hours or frozen for up to 1 month. If you plan to freeze the gnudi, place them on a baking sheet so they do not touch and once completely frozen, they can be transferred from the sheet to a resealable plastic freezer bag.

Yield: 12 servings, 10 pieces per serving

CONTINUED...

SPINACH AND RICOTTA GNUDI

1 Pound fresh spinach, blanched, drained, and squeezed well

2 Ounces fresh basil leaves

1 Pound fresh ricotta

2 Cups all-purpose flour, plus more for kneading

1 Teaspoon fine sea salt

½ Teaspoon freshly ground white pepper

SUGGESTED WINE VARIETALS

WHITE
Chardonnay \ Sauvignon Blanc

RED
Merlot \ Pinot Noir \ Rhone Blend \ Zinfandel

MARSALA STEWED RABBIT RAGU

In this recipe the rabbit is not browned because it is so lean we do not want to dry out its delicate meat. Rather, it is slowly stewed whole with the Marsala, tomatoes and basil until it is falling off the bone. The Sicilian addition of cinnamon adds an exotic depth to the dish and pairs well with the Marsala.

1. Add the **olive oil** to a large Dutch oven set over medium-high heat and when hot add the **onions, rosemary, thyme, garlic** and **red pepper flakes** and cook until the onions are soft and translucent, about 4 to 5 minutes.
2. Add the Marsala and cook until it has reduced by half, then add the **chicken stock, tomatoes, rabbit,** and **basil.**
3. Reduce the heat to medium and simmer the stew, partially covered, until the rabbit is tender and the meat is falling off the bone, about 1½ hours.
4. Once the rabbit is tender, remove it from the pot and transfer it to a plate or a baking sheet. Allow the stew to continue to cook.
5. Once the rabbit is cool enough to handle, remove the meat, discarding the skin and bones, and return it to the pot. Continue to cook the stew uncovered for 20 minutes longer. Remove the bunch of basil and stir in the cinnamon.
6. Serve the Rabbit Ragu with the Spinach and Ricotta Gnudi or with any pasta you like.

Yield: About 6 cups or 6 servings

TO SERVE

1. In a large sauté pan over medium high heat melt 4 tablespoons of the **butter.**
2. When the butter begins to foam, add the **gnudi** to the pan in small batches. It is important that the gnudi are not crowded and each touches the surface of the pan. Brown the gnudi on one side and then turn and brown them on the other side, about 1 minute per side.
3. Remove to a plate with a slotted spoon and continue with the remaining gnudi.
4. Once all the gnudi are browned, return them to the pan and add the **rabbit ragu** and **olives** and toss well to coat.
5. Fold in the remaining 4 tablespoons of **butter.**
6. Tear the **basil leaves** and add them to the pan along with the **sliced almonds.**
7. Season with **salt** and **pepper,** and serve immediately.

MARSALA STEWED RABBIT RAGU

¼ Cup extra virgin olive oil

1 Cup yellow onion, finely chopped

2 Teaspoons fresh rosemary leaves, finely chopped

2 Teaspoons fresh thyme leaves, finely chopped

2 Teaspoons garlic, minced

1 Teaspoon crushed red pepper flakes

2 Cups Marsala wine

1 Quart chicken stock

2 28-ounce cans whole plum tomatoes (hand crushed, with juices)

1 2 to 2 ¼ Pound whole rabbit

1 Bunch fresh basil, tied with butcher twine or string

½ Teaspoon ground cinnamon

SERVING

8 Tablespoons (1 stick) unsalted butter

60 Pieces Spinach and Ricotta Gnudi, recipe follows

6 Cups Marsala Stewed Rabbit Ragu, recipe follows

24 Pitted green olives (Cerignola or Castelvetrano recommended), sliced in half lengthwise

6 Large basil leaves

1 Cup toasted sliced almonds

Salt and pepper to taste

Teriyaki Bear

DANIEL NELSON

Bear has a fatty meat composition with a pungent, yet delicious, smell and flavor. A digital thermometer is a must when cooking bear. It will allow you to hit the target 165°F perfectly, because every degree above is useless and only dries the meat out further. Using the meat preparation in this recipe will give you thin, easily cooked, yet tender petite filets, suitable for many recipes.

Total Time: 35 minutes

- 2 Pounds whole muscle bear loin
- 2 Pounds fresh firm vegetables such as snap peas, asparagus, broccoli, or zucchini

    Fresh chopped garlic, to taste
- ½ Cup yellow onion, minced
- 2 Tablespoons olive oil
- 2 Cups venison stock, or beef stock
- 2 Cups low sodium teriyaki sauce
- 2 Teaspoons lime juice
- ¼ Cup mirin, rice cooking wine

    Arrowroot, enough to make a slurry

1. Whole muscle bear meat can be taken from many areas on the animal, including round, sirloin, and even parts of the hip and chuck. You are looking for solid continuous muscle fiber that has no sinew running through. Most cuts, outside of the backstrap loin, will be no more than 2 inches thick and are ideal for the hot searing cooking of stir-fry. I also cut the meat for kabobs this way, as it greatly reduces toughness. I prefer to have the bear meat slightly frozen as it aides in making thin, clean cuts.
2. Slice slightly frozen **bear loin**, across the grain of the muscle into $1/8$-inch thin filets.
3. Once all meat is sliced, toss it with the **teriyaki sauce**, **venison stock**, **lime juice** and **mirin**, for a quick 10 minute marinade.
4. Clean and trim fresh **vegetables** into bite-size pieces
5. Strain the meat from the marinade. Reserving liquid and meat.
6. Warm, to searing hot, a large wok or frying pan.
7. Coat the wok with **olive oil** and add the sliced bear, quickly searing the meat for 2 to 3 minutes. Remove the bear from the wok and set aside to rest.
8. Return wok to heat and cook the **vegetables**, **onion**, and **garlic** similarly for 2 to 3 minutes.
9. Add as much of the marinade liquids as you will want for the sauce. Finish cooking vegetables in sauce for another 2 to 3 minutes.
10. Add **Arrowroot** slurry to thicken and bring to simmer
11. Mix in cooked bear meat and warm thoroughly to 165°F.

TO SERVE
Prepare rice or quinoa and serve bear piled on top.

SUGGESTED WINE VARIETALS

RED
Cabernet Franc \ Cabernet Sauvignon \
Malbec \ Petite Sirah

Grilled Marinated Caribou Sirloin

SCOTT LEYSATH

It sounds far-fetched, but suppose that you don't have caribou sirloin in your freezer. What then? This simple marinade is great with any antlered game, although it's hard to beat the delicate flavor and texture of caribou. A marinade should enhance, not disguise the flavor of game meats. Too often, home chefs go to great lengths to mask the rich, vibrant taste of wild game.

This marinade has a hint of Asian flavors with both sweet and sour components. Marinated meat can be skewered or simply grilled alongside peppers and onions. If skewered, consider placing vegetables like peppers and onions on separate skewers to better control the cooking temperatures of both meat and vegetables.

2½ Cups caribou sirloin, trimmed and cut into 2-inch cubes

MARINADE

¾ Cup olive oil

½ Cup honey

¼ Cup red wine vinegar

⅓ Cup low-sodium soy sauce

1 Tablespoon garlic powder

1½ Teaspoons ground ginger

1½ Teaspoons kosher salt

1 Tablespoon coarse ground pepper

1. Combine **all marinade ingredients** in a tight-fitting jar and shake vigorously. Can be stored in the refrigerator for several weeks.
2. Place **caribou** in a non-reactive container or zipper lock bag. Add **marinade**, toss and refrigerate for 1 to 6 hours.
3. Remove from marinade, drain and place on a medium-high, well-oiled grill and brown on all sides, but preferably not past medium-rare (130°F to 135°F internal temperature).

SUGGESTED WINE VARIETALS

RED
Cabernet Sauvignon \ Merlot \
Pinot Noir \ Syrah

48

Wild Boar Pozole

CHRIS HUGHES

Pozole is a pork and hominy stew that has been served for centuries in Mexico and the American Southwest. In this version, the nutty flavor of wild boar nicely complements the earthy flavors of the chilis and hominy.

TOTAL TIME: 3 hours

3 Pounds wild boar stew meat

Flour

3 13 Ounce cans hominy, drained (white, yellow, or mixed)

3 Quarts chicken or pork broth

1 Medium onion, chopped

8 Cloves garlic, minced

3 Dried New Mexico (Anaheim) chilis, ground (or 2 tablespoons chili powder)

½ Teaspoon dried oregano

½ Teaspoon black pepper

2 Poblano peppers, roasted, peeled, seeded, and chopped (or one 7 oz can diced green chilis)

Salt

Sour cream (optional)

Green onions, chopped (optional)

1. Lightly coat **stew cubes** with **flour**. Stew cubes can be seasoned with salt and pepper when browning, if desired, but lightly as it can be easy to over salt if you are using store-bought broth.
2. Knock off any excess flour and brown stew cubes over medium-high heat in small batches, preferably using the pot you will be cooking the stew in.
3. Once all stew cubes are browned, deglaze the pot/pan with a small amount of **broth**, scraping up all the bits, and add this mixture to your cooking vessel. If you are using the same pot/pan for the whole recipe just set it aside, off heat, while you work on the next step. If you are using canned green chilis, skip to step 7.
4. Meanwhile, roast the **poblano peppers**.
5. Broil the peppers 2 to 3 inches below the coils in a rimmed baking pan or roasting pan until the skins are nicely charred, about 7 minutes. Flip the peppers over and broil about 5 minutes longer until the other side is also charred.
6. Remove from oven and drape foil over the peppers for about 10 minutes. (This will make skinning the peppers much easier.) Pull off skin, stems and seeds. Discard. Rinse peppers and then chop.
7. In the large pot/pan you used to brown the meat (or new pot if you prefer), add the **browned stew cubes, hominy, onion, garlic, ground New Mexico chilis, roasted poblano peppers, oregano, pepper,** and **broth**.
8. Bring mixture to a boil then cover and gently simmer until wild boar is fork tender, about 2 hours. Add **salt** to taste.

TO SERVE

Serve in bowls garnished with **sour cream** and **chopped green onions**.

SUGGESTED WINE VARIETALS

RED
Cabernet Sauvignon \ Malbec \
Petite Sirah \ Petit Verdot \ Syrah

Elk Carpaccio

JORGE MORALES

Traditionally carpaccio is an Italian dish made of very thin slices of raw beef that is usually served as an appetizer. However, in this day and age many other types of meat and fish are being used. Note: To make the vinaigrette foamy use a whip cream dispenser with a nitrous oxide charger that can be purchased at most kitchen/household stores.

ELK CARPACCIO

- ¼ Cup fresh flat leaf parsley
- ¼ Cup, plus 2 tablespoons neutral oil, like canola or peanut
- 2 Cloves garlic, peeled
- ½ Teaspoon grated orange zest
- 1 Tablespoon kosher salt
- ½ Teaspoon pink peppercorn
- ½ Teaspoon truffle oil
- 1 10-ounce piece of center cut elk tenderloin

GARNISHES

- 4 Hard cooked eggs, peeled
- 1 Tablespoon trout roe
- 1 Radish, thinly sliced (reserve leaves)
- 1 Lemon, juiced

PICKLED RADISHES

- ¾ Cup apple cider vinegar
- ¼ Cup water
- 1 Tablespoon sugar
- 1 Tablespoon honey
- 1 Teaspoon dried oregano
- 2 Teaspoons kosher salt
- 2 Cloves garlic, crushed
- 1 Bunch of radishes, thinly sliced

RIESLING VINAIGRETTE

- 1 Egg yolk, large
- 1 Tablespoon Riesling
- 1 Tablespoon apple cider vinegar
- ¼ Cup neutral oil, like canola or peanut
- ¼ Teaspoon truffle oil
-   Pinch of salt

1. Using a mortar and pestle, combine the **parsley**, ¼ cup of the **oil**, **garlic**, **orange zest**, **salt**, **peppercorns** and **truffle oil** to make a paste.
2. Rub the paste all over the **elk** and allow to marinate in the fridge for at least 5 hours and up to 24 hours.
3. In a heavy sauté pan over high heat, heat the remaining 2 tablespoons of **oil** until it begins to smoke.
4. Add the **elk** to the pan and sear for 10 seconds on each side. You don't want to cook the meat, but create a delicious crust with the rub.
5. Remove the **elk** from the pan and refrigerate until very cold, about an hour. (The elk can sit like this for up to 3 days as long as it is tightly wrapped.)
6. Using a very sharp knife, cut the elk across the grain into very thin slices, almost like beef sashimi. Divide among four chilled plates. Squeeze **lemon juice** and sprinkle **kosher salt** on top to taste.
7. Spoon **pickled radish** (recipe follows) next to elk. Carefully cut the hard cooked **eggs** in half and place the two halves on top of the radishes.
8. In a small bowl, gently stir the **trout roe**. Top the egg with the trout roe.
9. Spoon the **riesling vinaigrette** (recipe follows) generously around the plate. Top with fresh radish slices and garnish with radish leaves.

PICKLED RADISHES

1. In a small sauce pan over high heat, combine the **vinegar, water, sugar, honey, oregano, salt** and **garlic** and bring to a boil, stirring to dissolve the sugar and salt.
2. In a heatproof bowl, pour the pickling liquid over the **sliced radishes**.
3. Let cool to room temperature and serve with elk carpaccio.

RIESLING VINAIGRETTE

1. In a bowl whisk together the **egg yolk**, **riesling** and **vinegar** well.
2. Whisk in both the **neutral oil** and **truffle oil** in a thin steady stream to create an emulsion.
3. Season with **salt** as needed.

SUGGESTED WINE VARIETALS

WHITE
Chardonnay \ Rosé (dry)

RED
Cabernet Franc \ Cabernet Sauvignon \ Malbec \ Merlot \ Pinot Noir \ Zinfandel

Wild Boar Porchetta

CHRIS HUGHES

Is there anything better than roasted wild boar shoulder? Only if it's stuffed with sausage and herbs!

TIME: 3 hours

1. Wild boar will often come wrapped in netting. Cut one end of netting and remove **wild boar**. Keep the netting to rewrap the wild boar after stuffing it. Unroll the wild boar so that you have a flat piece of meat and set aside.
2. Heat **olive oil** in a large sauté pan over medium-high heat.
3. Add sliced **onion** and **fennel**. Cook until onion is soft and translucent.
4. Add **Italian sausage**, **fennel seeds**, **ground pepper**, **rosemary**, and **garlic**. Cook about 10 minutes, stirring frequently so garlic does not burn.
5. Allow mixture to cool then mix in chopped **fennel leaves** and **beaten eggs**.
6. Preheat oven to 350°F. Spread mixture over one side of the wild boar then roll it up. If possible, stretch original netting back over wild boar and secure cut end with butcher's twine. Otherwise, tie the roll with a truss of butcher's twine.
7. Spread **chopped vegetable mixture** on bottom of roasting pan. Use a mix of sturdy vegetables to keep wild boar off of the bottom of the pan and that will taste good when roasted. Set wild boar on top of vegetable mix. Roast in oven until internal temperature reaches 150°F, about 2 to 2½ hours, basting every 20 to 30 minutes with **melted butter** and **olive oil** mixture.
8. Let meat rest for 15 to 20 minutes, slice thickly and serve.

4 Pounds wild boar shoulder roast or rolled & tied leg

4 Tablespoons olive oil

1 Onion, thinly sliced

1 Fennel bulb, thinly sliced

Fennel leaves, chopped

1½ Pounds wild boar Italian sausage, cut from casings

2 Tablespoons fennel seeds

2 Tablespoons ground pepper

2 Tablespoons fresh rosemary, chopped or ½ tablespoon dried rosemary

6 Cloves garlic, chopped

2 Eggs, beaten

Salt and pepper, to taste

4 Cups coarsely chopped mixed vegetables (onion, celery, carrots, parsnips, etc.)

4 Tablespoon butter, melted

4 Tablespoon olive oil

SUGGESTED WINE VARIETALS

RED
Cabernet Sauvignon \ Merlot \
Petite Sirah \ Zinfandel

Venison Rib Roulettes

DANIEL NELSON

Venison rib meat, despite being the most flavorful cut of venison, is often underutilized; most toss it into the grinding pile for burger and sausage. Rib meat of all types has a unique and palatable combination of fat and sinew, that when roasted properly, yields a sweet and earthy meal. I often find that bone in venison ribs are too cumbersome for the amount of meat available and have the tendency to dry out quickly. This recipe uses the intra rib strip of meat cut free from the bones during processing. These roulettes make a phenomenal appetizer as well. I use slightly larger bamboo sticks when skewering the meat and then cut in half for service. To truly appreciate the great flavor of venison rib meat, serve the BBQ sauce on the side.

PREP TIME: 3 hours

12 Intra-rib meat strips from venison

12 Thick-cut smoked bacon strips

2 Large yellow onions, julienne

2 Tablespoons garlic, fresh chopped

1 Tablespoons yellow mustard seed

1 Teaspoon celery seed

3 Tablespoons tomato paste

1 Cup apple juice

1 Cup venison stock

½ Cup apple cider vinegar

Kosher salt and blended pepper

4-inch wood picks

1. Lay **venison rib strips** flat on cutting board, sprinkle with **salt** and **blended pepper**, and top each with 1 slice of **bacon**
2. Pinwheel roll each rib strip and bacon. Skewer twice or more to ensure the roulette does not unroll.
3. Warm a heavy braising dish over medium-high heat. Sear rib roulettes for 2 to 3 minutes on each side. Remove and set aside roulettes
4. In the same dish, over medium-high heat, sauté the **julienne onions** for 5 minutes, stirring occasionally.
5. Mix **tomato paste**, **venison stock**, **apple cider vinegar** and **seasonings** in the braising pan with the onions.
6. Add the roulettes, cover the braising dish and cook at 250°F for 2 to 3 hours until very tender.

TO SERVE
Serve hot with your favorite BBQ sauce and fresh fries.

Coniglio Bianco, Italian Braised Rabbit

HANK SHAW

You will want at least two cottontail rabbits for three people, although two bunnies will serve four in a pinch. One snowshoe hare feeds two easily, and a domestic rabbit will feed two to three people. Still, this dish is so good, and it reheats as leftovers so well, that I'd suggest you make more than you think you will need.

I use my preserved garlic for this recipe, but you can also simply roast a head of garlic. Nothing else in this recipe is hard to find.

PREP TIME: 90 minutes, mostly for breaking down the rabbit and making stock
COOK TIME: 2 hours

QUICK RABBIT STOCK

Ribs, neck and belly flaps from the rabbits

2 Bay leaves

½ Teaspoon fennel seeds

1 Teaspoon coriander seeds

10 Juniper berries, crushed (optional)

1 Teaspoon cracked black peppercorns

Salt

BRAISED RABBIT

2 to 4 cottontails, 2 to 3 snowshoe hares or 2 domestic rabbits

Salt

⅓ Cup olive oil

1 Medium yellow or white onion, sliced root to stalk

1 Teaspoon dried thyme

½ Cup white wine or vermouth

1 Cup quick rabbit stock (see above)

5 to 6 Cloves, roasted or preserved garlic

10 to 20 green olives, pitted and cut in half

3 Tablespoons chopped fresh parsley

1. First you must break down your **rabbits**. Save the stray bones in the pelvis, ribs, belly flaps and neck for the stock.
2. To make the stock, place all the rabbit pieces—not just the stray ones—into a pot and cover them with cool water by about ½-inch. Bring this to a boil, then turn off the heat. Skim off any sludgy stuff that floats to the top. Fish out all the good pieces of rabbit—legs and saddle—and put them in a bowl in the fridge. Add the **remaining stock ingredients**, return everything to a bare simmer and cook for 1 hour. Strain and set aside.
3. Now find a heavy, lidded pot such as a Dutch oven and heat the **olive oil** over medium heat. When it is hot, add the sliced **onions** and cook until soft and translucent. Do not brown them. Add the **white wine**, 1 cup of the **stock**, the **rabbit pieces** from the fridge, **thyme** and **garlic cloves**. Bring to a simmer and add **salt** to taste. Turn the heat down to low, cover the pot and cook until the meat is tender, about 90 minutes to 2 hours.
4. Finish the dish by adding the **green olives** and fresh **parsley**. Cook for 2 to 3 minutes,

TO SERVE

Serve with mashed potatoes, white polenta or rice. A green thing alongside is always nice, too.

SUGGESTED WINE VARIETALS

WHITE
Chardonnay

RED
Merlot \ Pinot Noir \ Rhone Blend

Braised Elk Chuck Roast with Puttanesca Sauce

JOSH DRAGE

I first made this on the North Fork of the Flathead River with venison steaks seared over an open flame in a cast iron pan. I have since cooked a variation of such on rivers between there and the San Juan in southern Utah. I adapted the recipe to use a shoulder or chuck roast off of an elk. I served this at the Pebble Beach Food and Wine festival in 2011. Both the elk and the puttanesca sauce can be done ahead of time and held properly for days before serving. Use good anchovies and lots if you like, the elk can handle it.

BRAISING ELK: 6 to 8 hours   **PREP TIME:** 45 minutes

BRAISED ELK ROAST

- 5 **Pound elk roast, chuck or shoulder**

   Half bottle red wine

- 2 **Onions, medium**
- 3 **Carrots**
- 6 **Pepper corns**
- 6 **Garlic cloves**
- 2 **Bay leafs**
- 6 **Fresh thyme twigs**

   Veal stock, amount variable, see cooking instructions

BRAISED ELK ROAST

1. In a Dutch oven brown the sides of the **roast**, remove and deglaze with **red wine**.
2. Add the **roast** back to the pot along with **everything else except the stock**.
3. Fill the Dutch oven with stock until the level of liquid reaches two thirds of the way up. Cover and cook for about 6 hours in the oven on a very low heat of 250°F degrees. Roll the roast every so often plus check the level of liquid readjusting the level if necessary so the pot does not dry out. Uncover and cook for another hour rolling the roast in the pot. When the meat easily pulls apart it is done, even if that happens before six hours.

ROAST TOMATO BASE

1. Toss **all the ingredients** in a bowl, leaving the tomatoes whole. Add to a baking dish and roast at 400°F for about 30 to 45 minutes.
2. Remove from the oven and leave to cool then run through a food mill removing the skins.

PUTTANESCA SAUCE

1. Put the **olive oil** in a broad sauce pot and add the chopped **shallots, garlic,** and **onion**. Cook over high heat just to soften the flesh but not to really brown, add the **anchovies**, stir in allowing them to melt, about two minutes.
2. Add the **tomatoes** to pan and continue cooking for about a minute, deglaze with **white wine** and reduce by half.
3. Add the **tomato base, olives, capers, roast red peppers** and **chili flake**. Simmer over a low heat for 30 minutes, turn off the heat, chop and mix in the **fresh herbs** and serve.

CRISPY EGGPLANT

1. Make an egg mixture by whisking the **eggs** and **milk** together. Standard breading procedure is to take the item being breaded first into flour then into the egg/milk mixture and then into the bread crumbs. In this case do so with slices of the **eggplant** about a ½ inch thick.
2. Once you have all of your eggplant breaded, brown the outside in a pan with a fair bit of **olive oil** in the bottom. If you apply color on a medium heat it will be richer and also cook the eggplant all the way through. Season with **salt** and **pepper**.

TO SERVE

Remove the elk from the cooking liquid and let cool, tear meat apart into about 3 to 4 ounce pieces, removing any unwanted parts. Reduce cooking liquid until it gets thick and rich. Add a portion of this to the puttanesca melding the flavors. In a large straight-sided sauté pan bring to temperature the puttanesca and lay the servable elk portions in the puttanesca to bring to temperature. Once all is hot and the eggplant is done, layer on a plate the eggplant and the puttanesca sauce topping it with the elk, shred a bit of Parmesan reggiano and add more fresh parsley, marjoram, or basil

ROAST TOMATO BASE
- 12 Whole Roma tomatoes
- 1 Head of garlic
- ½ Cup olive oil
- Pinch of salt
- Pinch of red chili flakes

PUTTANESCA SAUCE
- 3 Tablespoons olive oil
- 2 Shallots
- 3-6 Garlic cloves
- 1 Onion, medium
- 12 Anchovies
- 6 Roma tomatoes
- 1 Cup pinot grigio
- 2 Cups roast tomato base, recipe above
- 1 Cup Kalamata olives
- 2 Tablespoons capers
- 2 Roasted red peppers
- 1 teaspoon chili flakes
- ½ Cup Italian parsley leaves, fresh
- 6 Basil leaves, fresh
- 1 Teaspoon marjoram, fresh

CRISPY EGGPLANT
- 2 Eggs
- 2 Cups milk
- 1 Eggplant
- 1 Cup flour
- 4 Cups panko bread crumbs
- Salt and pepper

Fish

Abalone with Rustic Caper-Lemon Beurre Blanc

HOLLY PETERSON

Like a truly great steak, the most important aspect of great abalone is the abalone itself. Then cook it right! As my dive buddies have taught me, you cannot have great abalone, unless it is killed right away, quickly. The best way to do this is right on the beach when you come out of the water with your fresh bounty. Pop the mollusk out of the shell, wrap it in a kitchen towel, set it on a nearby rock and thump it hard with a flat surface (like a 2x4 board—no kidding.) I am giving you the ab-divers secret, which is paramount. At this point, you can wrap and save it on ice or freeze it. Abalone is best sliced thinly so you do not need to pound it much. This is true when you kill the abalone properly, the mussel will immediately relax, and tenderness will be your reward. You will be able to enjoy the natural texture of abalone, and yet it will be tender—a rare thing. One last recommendation is to cook over an open fire, perhaps at the beach with a sky full of stars if you are lucky. In Northern California it is cold at the beach around dinner time, but we bundle up and have a bonfire.

1 Abalone (the size will vary, so adjust the sauce quantities if needed)

1 Meyer lemon, zested and segmented

1 Cup sauvignon blanc

4 Branches of young fresh marjoram (or lemon thyme)

1 Clove fresh garlic, thinly sliced

3 Ounces organic butter (keep it cold)

1 to 2 Ounces virgin olive oil

2 Ounces of capers

Fleur de Sel (Sea Star Sea Salt is my favorite of course)

Flour for dusting (you can use egg and panko if you like a thicker coating, but I like it delicate with flour)

1. In a cast iron skillet heat **olive oil**, but don't burn it. Sprinkle the **abalone** with **Fleur de Sel**, and press each slice on to a plate of **flour**.
2. Cook the **abalone** on medium heat, cover with half of the of **marjoram** (save some to add to the sauce), sliced fresh **garlic**, Meyer **lemon zest**, and turn to cook the other side golden brown. Remove the abalone, and keep it warm while you make the sauce.

SAUCE
1. Wipe out the iron skillet to remove some of the black bits from the flour, heat your pan until the cooking juices bubble, then deglaze the pan with **white wine**, and reduce for a few minutes.
2. Whisk in the cold **butter** to taste and finish by adding the **capers** to the sauce. Add some of the reserved **marjoram** leaves, and season to taste with **Fleur de Sel**.

TO SERVE
Place a spoon of light, fluffy, mashed potatoes on each plate, top with perfectly cooked abalone, and pour the sauce over your abalone and garnish with a pretty lemon segment. You will be happy to have the mashed potatoes for the sauce. Enjoy with a crisp shaved garden salad.

SUGGESTED SIDE DISHES
Light, fluffy mashed potatoes

Crisp shaved garden salad with mustard red wine vinaigrette

SUGGESTED WINE VARIETALS

WHITE
Chardonnay \ Marsanne \
Pinot Blanc \ Pinot Gris \
Riesling (dry) \ Sauvignon Blanc

RED
Grenache \ Pinot Noir \ Rhone Blend

Edwards' Surry-ano Ham Wrapped Salmon Filet Mignon

TRAVIS BRUST

Salmon recipes can be very repetitive and lackluster at times so we wanted to give this dish a unique look and flavor. Edwards of Surry, Virginia, makes Surry-ano Ham—a beautiful, dry-cured Virginia ham smoked for 7 days with hickory and aged for 400 days, producing one of Virginia's most flavorful Serrano-style hams. We wrap the salmon with the Surry-ano ham to impart the true flavor of Virginia into the protein. The plate finishes with incredible recipes of garden fresh vegetables.

PREP TIME: 35 minutes **COOK TIME:** 25 minutes

- 2 Tablespoons olive oil
- 4 5-ounce fresh salmon filets
- 4 Slices Edwards' Surry-ano ham, (Prosciutto will work as well)
- ½ Tablespoon black pepper, freshly ground
- 1 Teaspoon kosher salt
- 2 Tablespoons butter
- 2 Cloves garlic, minced
- 1 Shallot, minced
- 1 Tablespoon chives, minced
- 1 Tablespoon tarragon, minced

CHARD-LEMON PUREE
- 1 Bunch green Swiss chard
- 1 Lemon, juiced
- ½–1 Cup olive oil
- ¼ Teaspoon black pepper, freshly ground
- ½ Teaspoon kosher salt

1. Roll the **salmon filet** into a circle and wrap with the **ham**, use a bit of twine to hold the proteins together.
2. Place a large skillet on the stove with the **olive oil** over medium high heat and begin to sear one side of the **salmon**, cook for 2 to 3 minutes.
3. Flip the salmon over to the other side and add the **butter**, **garlic** and **shallots** to the pan and begin to baste the fish with the oil and butter mixture. See example at right.
4. Add the **herbs** after about 2 minutes and continue to baste for 2 more minutes.
5. Place the pan into a 300°F oven for 6 to 8 minutes to finish the fish. Be sure to remove the twine before eating.

SWISS CHARD-LEMON PUREE

1. Remove the stems from the **Swiss chard** and reserve for another recipe.
2. Blanch the **chard** in boiling **salted water** for 30 seconds then strain and allow to drip dry for 2 minutes.
3. Place the **chard** and **lemon juice** into a blender and puree while drizzling in the **olive oil** until a nice thick, yet spreadable consistency is achieved.
4. Finish by seasoning to your preference.

CONTINUED...

SUGGESTED WINE VARIETALS

WHITE
Chardonnay \ Riesling (dry) \ Rosé (dry) \ Sauvignon Blanc

RED
Grenache \ Merlot \ Pinot Noir \ Rhone Blend

THE PERFECT TOMATO

6-12 Large fresh cherry tomatoes

Extra virgin olive oil, as needed

6-12 Fennel fronds for garnish

6-12 Tarragon leaves

Fresh ground black pepper, to taste

Kosher salt, to taste

CUCUMBER, RADISH AND STRAWBERRY SALAD

1 Shallot, minced

½ Cup cucumber, sliced thin

½ Cup radish, match stick cut

½ Cup fresh strawberries, sliced thin

¼ Cup fennel tops

2 Tablespoons olive oil

1 orange, juiced

Ground black pepper, to taste

Kosher salt, to taste

THE PERFECT TOMATO

1. Remove the stem core of the **tomato** and make a small "X" on the bottom of the tomato.
2. Place the tomatoes into **salted boiling water** till the skin starts to pull back. Remove from the boiling water and shock in **ice water** to stop the cooking process.
3. Remove the skins of the tomato. Drizzle with the **extra virgin olive oil**.
4. Season with the **kosher salt** and **pepper**. Garnish with the **fennel tops** and **tarragon leaves**.
5. Serve the tomato at room temperature for the final presentation.

CUCUMBER, RADISH AND STRAWBERRY SALAD

1. Toss the **first five ingredients** together.
2. Whisk **olive oil** and **orange juice** together, season to taste with **salt** and **pepper**.
3. Pour dressing over salad and serve.

Great Lakes Chowder

DANIEL NELSON

Eight years hosting the bi-annual Western Michigan Collegiate Steelhead Tournament gave me ample opportunity to pack as many local Great Lakes ingredients into this chowder as possible. The smoked duck tongue has been my favorite. It not only makes a near perfect replacement for clams, but also adds that special uniqueness, cherished by the nose-to-tail food movement, which helps make a meal unforgettable. The tongue flesh in duck is rich, soft and chewy, not tough and grainy like deer. I've included the recipe to make your own duck tongue, or you find them at specialty markets, or order on-line.

COOK TIME: 60 minutes

- 8 Ounces steelhead, thawed, skin and pin bones removed, ½-inch chop
- 8 ounces whitefish fillets, thawed, skin and pin bones removed, ½-inch chop
- 4 ounces smoked duck tongue, recipe follows
- 2 Ounces bacon, diced
- 1 Bunch green onions, chopped
- ½ Cup yellow onion, diced
- 3 Medium potatoes, peeled and diced
- 1 Teaspoon salt
- ⅛ Teaspoon white pepper
- 1 Cup dry Sherry
- 1 Quart fish stock
- 1 Quart whole milk
- ¼ Cup butter, softened
- ¼ Cup flour, sifted
- 1 Cup cream

  Sourdough croutons

1. In a large heavy pot, sauté **bacon** and **yellow onions** together over medium heat, stirring occasionally, until onions are soft and bacon is crisp. Turn off the heat, deglaze with **Sherry**, turn the heat back on and reduce to nearly all Sherry has evaporated.
2. Add **fish stock**, bring to a boil, and par-cook all cubed fish to medium-rare, drain reserving liquids, set cubed fish, bacon, and onions aside to cool.
3. Bring stock back to a boil, and add **potatoes**—cook until fork tender, drain and reserve potatoes and stock.
4. Add **milk** to stock and warm to a near boil.
5. Prepare a roux: In a small saucepan, heat **butter** until melted, add **flour** all at once and mix well.
6. Stir 1 quart of stock liquids into butter/flour mixture and mix until a smooth paste is formed. Mix roux paste into the remainder of **milk** stock and heat over low flame until thick.
7. Add **cream** and heat through without boiling. If ready for service, fold in all par-cooked ingredients including **duck tongue**, portion into individual bowls and top with **croutons** and **green onions**.

SMOKED DUCK TONGUE

- 8-16 Duck tongues
- 2 Cups fish stock
- ¼ Cup Mirin, rice cooking wine
- 3 Tablespoons oyster sauce
- 1 Tablespoons Sriracha sauce
- 1 Tablespoon soy sauce

SMOKED DUCK TONGUE

1. On its own duck tongue is not very flavorful, so a long marinade is necessary to add flavor. Harvesting **duck tongue** is easy with a small sharp knife or processing scissors. Feeling the bottom of the tongue, towards the back, you will find a boney structure. Cut under this bone, back and up towards the base, until the tongue is free.
2. Remove the small bone near the back and the thin bone that runs from there up through the middle of the tongue. Rinse tongues thoroughly under cold running water for 10 to 15 minutes. Drain them. **Combine all marinade ingredients.** Add tongues to the marinade, wrap and store in refrigerator for 24 hours.
3. Remove the tongues from marinade and drain off excess. Lay them out in a single layer of the smoking rack and slowly smoke in 180°F. I prefer to use hickory chips. Once smoked, they can be held under refrigeration for a week or in the freezer for several months.

SUGGESTED WINE VARIETALS

WHITE
Chardonnay \ Pinot Blanc \
Pinot Gris \ Riesling (dry) \ Rosé (dry) \
Sauvignon Blanc

RED
Grenache \ Merlot \ Pinot Noir

Clams in a Cataplana with Chicken-Apple Sausages

MICHAEL CHIARELLO

Go to a trattoria or taverna in any little seaside town where people support themselves by what they catch in the ocean, and you'll find clams and sausages together on the menu. To cook this in the hearth on a cataplana—a hinged copper pan resembling a clam shell—is to give a nod to those fishermen who realized how good fresh clams can be with some chopped sausage. I set my cataplana right on hot coals in the fireplace. If you are a cataplana fan who prefers to keep their copper bright and shining, don't do this. Personally, I like rustic kitchen utensils and pans that show some battle scars, but I get it when people want to keep their cookware looking new. A big cast-iron pan set on the coals will serve just fine but have something ready to cover it with when it's time for the clams to steam.

1. Build a fire in a Tuscan grill set in your fireplace or directly on the floor of your fireplace. Allow the fire to burn until the flames have died down and the glowing wood provides a steady, even heat.

2. On a cast-iron pan or a plancha set on the Tuscan grill rack, directly over the coals, or on the stove, brown the **sausages**. Transfer to a platter to cool, and set aside.

3. Line a heat-proof plate with paper towels. Set the cataplana on the coals in the hearth or use a cast-iron pan with a lid. Pour the **olive oil** into the cataplana or the pan and when it's hot add the **sage leaves**. When they're crispy, transfer the leaves to the towel-lined plate and set aside.

4. Add more **oil** to the cataplana if needed. When it's hot, add the **garlic** and cook until it begins to turn golden, about 3 minutes.

5. Add the **bell pepper** to the pan and cook for 2 to 3 minutes. Add the **thyme, clams, parsley,** and **white wine**.

6. With a lemon peeler (the type used for a lemon twist for drinks), peel the whole **lemon** into several long strips, each about 3 inches long, adding it to the cataplana just as it comes off the fruit. Set the peeled lemon aside for another use.

7. If using a cataplana, close it. If using a cast-iron pan, cover it. The wine and juices released from the shellfish will begin to simmer inside the cataplana. The shellfish will open in about 5 to 7 minutes.

8. Carefully remove the pan from the heat and open the top. Discard any clams that haven't opened. Cut the sausages diagonally into ½-inch slices and add them to the pan.

9. The cataplana can be separated into two pieces. Use the bottom as a serving bowl and the top as a place to put empty clam shells. If using a pan, have a bowl on the table to collect the shells.

Adapted from *Michael Chiarello's Live Fire: 125 Recipes for Cooking Outdoors*, Chronicle Books 2013.

6 Chicken-apple sausages (such as Aidells)

2 Tablespoons extra-virgin olive oil, plus more if needed

4 Perfect whole sage leaves

2 Garlic cloves, minced

½ Cup red bell pepper, finely diced

3 Long sprigs fresh thyme

2 Pounds Manila or cherrystone clams, scrubbed

⅓ Cup fresh flat-leaf parsley, chopped

1½ Cups white wine

1 Lemon

SUGGESTED WINE VARIETALS

WHITE
Chardonnay \ Pinot Blanc \ Pinot Gris \ Riesling (dry) \ Rosé (dry) \ Sauvignon Blanc

RED
Grenache \ Merlot \ Pinot Noir \ Rhone Blend

Crispy Fried Fish, Hmong Style

HANK SHAW

2 to 4 Plate-sized bass-like fish, scaled and gutted

Salt

1 Cup peanut or other vegetable oil

3 to 5 Garlic cloves, smashed

Freshly ground black pepper

1 or 2 Lemons, cut into wedges

4 Green onions, sliced on the diagonal

Cilantro, torn into 1-inch pieces, for garnish

DIPPING SAUCE

3 to 5 Small hot chiles, such as Thai, or 1 habanero

1 Tablespoon lemongrass, white part only, minced

3 Tablespoons cilantro, minced

3 Tablespoons green onion or chives, minced

Juice of a lemon

Grated zest of a lemon

A pinch of salt

1 Teaspoon sugar

2 Tablespoons fish sauce

This recipe work with any bass-like fish. I mostly use Pacific rock cod (rockfish), but perch, large- or smallmouth bass, walleyes, black seabass, croakers, puppy drum, porgies, large crappies or bluegills would all work. The ideal length for the fish is about the size of a big dinner plate. You can use larger fish, but you'll probably want to split one fish for two people, and that's not quite as fun as getting to tear into a fish of your own.

Everything here should be pretty easy to find, with the possible exceptions of the lemongrass and the fish sauce. Both are readily available in larger supermarkets now, and any Asian market will have them. If you can't find it, go 50-50 with soy sauce and water. It's definitely not the same, but it's better than nothing.

PREP TIME: 20 minutes   **COOK TIME:** 30 minutes

1. Take the **fish** out of the fridge and rinse it under cold water, checking for any remaining scales. Remove the gills if they are still there. You can snip off the fins with kitchen shears if you want. Use a sharp kitchen knife to slash the sides of the fish perpendicular to the backbone. Make the slices at an angle, from the tail end toward the head end. This opens up the fish to the hot oil and makes it cook faster. **Salt** the fish well and set aside.

2. Make the dipping sauce by combining **all the ingredients** in a bowl. Make sure everything is chopped fine. Set aside.

3. A wok is the best thing to use for cooking these fish, unless you have a deep fryer. I have both, and still prefer the wok. A large frying pan will work, too. Heat the oil until it is between 330°F and 350°F. Fry the crushed **garlic cloves** until they are a lovely brown and remove.

4. Gently put one or two **fish** into the hot oil. It's OK if the tails and heads are not submerged. It will sizzle violently, so watch yourself. Use a large spoon to baste the fish with the hot oil as it cooks. Fry like this a solid 6 to 10 minutes, depending on how thick the fish is. You want it very crispy and golden brown. Carefully flip the fish—I use two spatulas to do this. Fry another 5 to 8 minutes. Repeat with any remaining fish. If you do have to do this in batches, let the cooked fish rest on a rack set over a baking sheet in a 200°F oven.

TO SERVE

Lay the fish down on plates and grind a healthy portion of black pepper over them. Black pepper is a signature flavor in this dish so be generous. Arrange the fried garlic and the remaining garnishes alongside. Serve with the dipping sauce and white rice.

SUGGESTED WINE VARIETALS

WHITE
Chardonnay \ Pinot Blanc \ Riesling (dry) \ Rosé (dry) \ Sauvignon Blanc

RED
Grenache \ Pinot Noir \ Rhone Blend

Fresh Caught Trout Cooked in Foil

MICHAEL CHIARELLO

4 Trout, about ¾-pound each (see headnote)

3 Tablespoons extra-virgin olive oil

2 Lemons, thinly sliced

4 Tablespoons fresh flat leaf parsley leaves, stemmed

4 Teaspoons fresh tarragon

Coarse sea salt, preferably grey salt

Freshly ground black pepper

Optimally, your trout will weigh about ¾ pound each, but this recipe works no matter how big or small your fish ends up being. Just remember to add a few inches when you tell people how big the fish were. If you are buying fish, ask your fishmonger to clean and debone them for you.

1. Start a campfire, ignite charcoal, or turn the gas grill to high.
2. Scale the **fish** and lift out the bones. Leave the tail intact but cut off the fins. Rinse the fish inside and out with cool water and pat dry with paper towels.
3. Have ready 12 sheets of aluminum foil, each 16 inches long. For each fish, stack two sheets of aluminum foil and have a third sheet ready for the top. Drizzle about 1 teaspoon **olive oil** on the top sheet of foil and place the fish skin side down. Open the fish and arrange three to five thin **lemon slices** inside—enough to that the trout has lemon from end to end. Drizzle on another 1 teaspoon of **olive oil** and sprinkle with 1 tablespoon of **parsley leaves** and 1 teaspoon **fresh tarragon**. Sprinkle with **sea salt** and **pepper**. Place the third sheet of foil on top of the fish, then neatly fold each side into a packet, using the bottom layers of foil to close and seal the top sheet of foil in place (see photo).
4. When the coals are more grey than red, put the packets right on top of the coals (or cook on a gas grill set to medium). Shovel some coals from the edge of the fire over the packets to cover them or fill a grill basket with hot coals and rest the grill basket on top of the fish packets.
5. Roast the fish for about 4 minutes.
6. Take one of the packets out of the fire and open it to see if the fish is done—when it's opaque and more white than pink. If it's still pink inside, rewrap the fish and put it back on the coals for another 2 to 3 minutes.
7. Take the packets out of the coals, let them cool for at least 2 minutes and then let each person unwrap their own fish.

Adapted from *Michael Chiarello's Live Fire: 125 Recipes for Cooking Outdoors*, Chronicle Books 2013.

Fish and Shrimp Cakes

SCOTT LEYSATH

If you like crab cakes, you'll really like these fish and shrimp cakes. There are two things to remember when making fish cakes. First, they have to be just moist enough to hold together, but not so moist that they fall apart when cooked. Second, you can't mess with them when they're in the pan or they'll break apart. Now that we've got that straight, let's get started. I use any light white fish that will flake easily, like crappie, halibut, rockfish, etc. It's also a great way to use up leftover cooked fish.

8 Large shrimp, tail-on, peeled, deveined and butterflied

2 Tablespoons butter

½ Cup onion, finely diced

1 Jalapeño pepper, seeded and finely diced

¼ Cup fresh cilantro, chopped

4 Cups fish fillets, flaked and pressed dry with paper towels (really important!)

1 Tablespoon red pepper flakes

2 Garlic cloves, minced

2 Tablespoons flour

3 Tablespoons Japanese breadcrumbs (or any breadcrumbs)

½ Teaspoon salt

⅛ Teaspoon pepper

1 Teaspoon Old Bay Seasoning

3 Tablespoons mayonnaise

2 Egg whites, beaten

   Oil for frying

1. Heat **butter** in a medium skillet over medium heat. Add **onion** and **pepper** and sauté for 4 to 5 minutes.
2. In a large bowl, add **cilantro, fish, pepper flakes, garlic** and **cooled onion/pepper** from pan. Make sure that fish has been patted dry thoroughly with paper towels.
3. Sprinkle remaining **flour, breadcrumbs salt, pepper** and **Old Bay Seasoning** over while tossing, making sure to coat fish evenly.
4. Fold in **mayonnaise** and **egg whites**. Take some of the mixture and form into a ball, about 3 inches in diameter. If it holds together, you're in business. If it's too dry and flaky, add some more breadcrumbs. It should be moist, but not soggy.
5. Form mixture into 8 equal-sized patties. Dust **shrimp** thoroughly with **flour**. This will enable the fish cake to more readily stick to the shrimp. Hold shrimp flat and build the fish cake around the shrimp. The idea is to have a normal looking fish cake with a shrimp tail sticking out of the side.
6. Add enough **oil** to just cover the bottom of a large skillet and heat over medium heat. When oil is hot, add cakes and cook until medium brown on one side, about 5 to 6 minutes. Carefully flip over and brown other sides, about 5 minutes more. When cakes are just cooked, remove from pan and top with your favorite sauce.

Zuppa d'Great Lakes

DANIEL NELSON

2 Pounds firm-meat fish, cubed, such as walleye, carp, salmon, steelhead, and/or bass

8 Ounces smoked duck tongue, substitute clams

10-12 walleye cheeks, substitute scallops

1 Pound crawdad tails, carapaces can be added while simmering for added flavor, substitute shrimp

2 Pounds cajun roasted leg of bear, venison, or bison, pulled

SAUCE

3 Green peppers

2 Large yellow onions

3 Stalks celery, chopped

2 Tablespoons fresh garlic, chopped

3 Quarts chopped, cooked tomatoes in juice

1 Tablespoon Sriracha sauce

2 Tablespoons blended pepper

1 Tablespoon kosher salt

1 Teaspoon each of fresh basil, oregano, and thyme

6 Bay leaves

2 Tablespoons rendered duck or goose fat

1 Quart thin venison bordelaise sauce or venison gravy

This Great Lakes twist on a Tuscan staple is perfect for the first cool nights of fall, or whenever you have a lot of firm-flesh fish scrap in the freezer. Try adding more Great Lakes flavor by adding crawdads and duck tongue (see page 67 for recipe).

The freshwater crawfish is an unbeatable ingredient to deep, rich, satisfying Zuppa. First, trapping or night-netting live crawfish is a thoroughly enjoyable and easily accessible activity for young and old alike. Keep your harvest alive by bringing a pail large enough to carry your catch and some of their local water whenever you check your traps or wade the evening away, under headlamp, chasing them backwards into a net. I usually steam and freeze my 'dads within a few hours of catching them.

TOTAL TIME: 5 hours. Can be done ahead of time and re-heated for service.

1. Rub **bear leg** (inside round) liberally with cajun seasoning and braise at 250°F until falling off the bone, 3 to 4 hours. Pull meat and roughly chop any long or large pieces. Set aside.
2. Prepare crawdads. Instructions below.
3. In heavy sauce pan warm the **duck fat** over medium-high heat, sauté the **green peppers**, **onions** and **celery** for 3 to 4 minutes, then add the **garlic** and continue to sauté, stirring occasionally for another minute. Add the pulled **cajun bear meat** and sauté for 5 more minutes.
4. Add the **tomatoes** and **remaining spices**, bring to a simmer and cover to let simmer for 20 minutes
5. If serving the same day, add the prepared **crawdad tails, fish, smoked duck tongue, and walleye cheeks** only 4 to 5 minutes before service to ensure they are not over cooked. If serving the following day, simmer the sauce for only 10 minutes and cool as rapidly as possible in a shallow pan on the bottom of your refrigerator.

TO SERVE

Reheat sauce to a simmer and again only add the fish 5 minutes before service. Best served with fresh baked sourdough or foccacia bread.

STEAMING CRAWDADS

1. You must use live, fresh **crawdads**. Rinse your harvest thoroughly, scrubbing lightly with a soft bristle toothbrush. Discard any that are dead.

2. Bring water, **Old Bay seasoning** and the juice of the two **lemons** to boil, in a large pot which can suspend your strainer in the steam. Place the **crawdads** in the strainer and the strainer onto the pot, cover and steam until they turn a deep red color, 8 to 15 minutes. Steaming, and not boiling, your crawdads will help keep the flavor and juices locked in the meat.

3. If serving hot and fresh, toss the cooked 'dads in a few small pinches of Old Bay seasoning, pick and enjoy. Pinch 'dads where carapace meets the tail and twist to remove. Be sure to suck the juices from the carapaces! The tails can be peeled by cutting down the middle of the topside on the tail with a pair of scissors, pulling apart and removing the tail meat. Serve with clarified butter, lemon wedges and cocktail sauce. Reserve the carapaces and use in savory stews.

4. If processing and storing, remove the strainer and cool crawdads in the refrigerator, where they can keep for up to a week. For freezing, reserve and cool the brine. Place cooled crawdads in a heavy-duty freezer bag, cover with cool brine, remove air and seal. Label and freeze. Thaw under refrigeration when needed.

5. To be the center of attention at the next crawdad boil, bring precooked and cooled crawdads and sauté in salted garlic lemon butter over high heat for 5 to 7 minutes, until heated through. Pile next to boiled crawdads and enjoy the steady stream of compliments.

Crisp Soft-Shell Blue Crab with Corn Grits, Fennel and Radish Pod Salad

TRAVIS BRUST

The soft-shell blue crab is the quintessential secret of our southern waters. Simply succulent and sweet, any crab connoisseur wouldn't make it through the soft-shell season without enjoying this southern delicacy. The simple treatment of the crab is best as to not mask its flavor. Pairing the crab with a play on an ol' southern classic, grits, with a fresh new twist is fun to enjoy alongside the salad of fennel and radish pods. The radish pod is an often overlooked part of the radish plant. They appear after the plant bolts to seed and sends up the flowering stalk. The pods form on the stems as a means for seed development. They have a flavor of light radish without being spicy.

PREP TIME: 20 minutes   **COOK TIME:** 30 minutes cooking

- 4 Fresh, cleaned soft-shell blue swimming crabs
- ½ Cup all-purpose flour
- ½ Tablespoon freshly ground black pepper
- 1 Teaspoon kosher salt

Frying oil of choice, such as peanut oil

FRESH CORN "GRITS"
- 1 Tablespoon butter
- 1 Shallot, minced
- 3 Fresh ears of corn on the cob
- 1 Cup chicken stock
- 1 Cup heavy cream
- 1 Tablespoon chives, minced
- 1 Tablespoon tarragon, minced
- ¼ Cup cheddar cheese, grated
- ½ Cup fresh peas, blanched
- ¼ Teaspoon fresh ground black pepper
- ½ Teaspoon kosher salt

FENNEL AND RADISH POD SALAD
- 1 Fennel bulb, shaved thinly
- ¼ Cup fennel tops
- 1 Shallot, sliced
- ½ Cup fresh radish pods, sliced
- 2 Oranges, segmented
- 1 Lemon, segmented
- 2 Tablespoon olive oil
- Fresh ground black pepper, to taste
- Kosher salt, to taste

1. Place a large skillet on the stove with about 1 inch of **oil** and heat to about 350 to 370°F.
2. Combine **flour, salt** and **pepper**. Dredge the **crab** with the seasoned flour.
3. Fry the **crabs** for 2 to 3 minutes on each side.

FRESH CORN "GRITS"
1. Remove the kernels from the **corn** and scrape the knife against the cob to "milk" the corn juices, chop the corn roughly to break up the kernels into smaller bits.
2. In a large skillet lightly sauté the **shallot** in the **butter** for 2 to 3 minutes.
3. Add the **corn** and sauté over medium-high heat for 3 to 4 minutes. Add the **chicken stock** and cook to reduce the stock by three quarters.
4. Add **cream** and reduce the volume while stirring to release starches and thicken.
5. Fold in the **fresh blanched peas**.
6. Finish with stirring in the **herbs** and **cheddar cheese** and season to your preference.

FENNEL AND RADISH POD SALAD
1. Toss **all ingredients** together and allow to marinate for one hour.
2. Garnish with fresh nasturtium flowers and leaves or other edible flowers such as marigolds, chive blossoms or radish flowers.

SUGGESTED WINE VARIETALS

WHITE
Chardonnay \ Pinot Blanc \ Riesling (dry) \ Rosé (dry) \ Sauvignon Blanc

RED
Granache \ Merlot \ Pinot Noir \ Rhone Blend

Gravlax

KATHY SIMPSON

Gravlax is similar to lox, however gravlax literally translated means "buried salmon." It was traditionally cured with the salmon encased in salt and sugar allowing the juices released to brine the fish. Your gravlax will keep from 1 to 2 weeks if it is well wrapped and refrigerated. Serve as an appetizer with a variety of accompaniments like thin slices of dark bread (dense rye or pumpernickel), pickled or fresh cucumber ribbons, capers, chopped red onions, or a mustard sauce. Any leftovers can be frozen for up to a month.

PREP TIME: 20 minutes   **CURING TIME:** 12 to 18 hours

3 Pounds salmon filet, deboned

3 Large white onions, peeled

1 Cup kosher salt

¾ Cup sugar

1 Teaspoon white pepper

2 Cups fresh dill, roughly chopped

1. Chop **onions** roughly and blend in a food processor into a liquid.
2. Strain and squeeze through a cheese cloth to create 2 cups of onion juice.
3. Mix the **onion juice, salt, sugar, pepper,** and the **dill** to dissolve.
4. In a large Ziploc bag, lay the **salmon filet** flat and add the **onion mixture** to cover all the salmon surface.
5. Place the closed Ziplock on a sheet pan and cover with another sheet pan.
6. Add 7 pounds of weight evenly to the top and refrigerate for 12 to 18 hours. Flip the bag with the salmon filet once. The salmon flesh should be firm to the touch.
7. Rinse the filet and refrigerate.

SUGGESTED WINE VARIETALS

WHITE
Chardonnay \ Sauvignon Blanc

RED
Pinot Noir

Grilled Sturgeon

JON BONNELL

Sturgeon is an incredible fish for the grill, almost meat-like in texture. I sometimes refer to sturgeon as the pork chop of the sea. You can literally see yellow fat layers marbling the meat of sturgeon which may seem odd for fish, but don't let that put you off. Although many species of sturgeon are highly protected, and deservedly so, there are sustainable sources of domestic sturgeon in the United States that produce very high quality fish every year such as those coming out of the Columbia River.

PREP TIME: 50 minutes, 30 inactive   **COOK TIME:** 10 minutes

2 6-8 Ounce sturgeon filets

½ Teaspoon Waters fish spice, substitute with Old Bay fish spice if necessary

1½ Teaspoon olive oil

1 Clove garlic, minced

1 Teaspoon fresh thyme, chopped

½ Teaspoon fresh rosemary, chopped

1 Teaspoon Dijon mustard

1 Tablespoon dry white wine

Vegetable oil for the grill

1. Clean and rinse the **sturgeon filets** thoroughly with cool water.

2. Combine the **mustard, wine, olive oil, fish spice, garlic** and **herbs** in a mixing bowl, then coat on all sides of the sturgeon.

3. Allow to marinate in the fridge for at least 30 minutes.

4. Heat a wood burning grill ahead of time until the wood is burning orange and white coals. Brush the grill bars well with a wire brush to ensure that they are clean.

5. Brush the grill bars lightly with a towel soaked in **vegetable oil** just before grilling the fish to keep it from sticking.

6. Place the sturgeon over the grill on medium heat with the lid closed. Cook until the fish reaches an internal temperature of 145°F (approximately 4 minutes on each side).

TO SERVE
Remove from the grill and serve on top of herbed risotto.

SUGGESTED WINE VARIETALS

WHITE
Chardonnay \ Pinot Blanc \ Sauvignon Blanc

RED
Pinot Noir

Halibut Braised in Olive Oil with Leeks and Mushrooms

DANIEL BOULUD

Hon Shimeji (brown beech) mushrooms have burlap colored, smooth petite globular caps and ivory white slender stems. They have piquant, umami aromas, sharp flavor when fresh, mild and nutty when cooked and a firm chewy texture that softens with cooking. If you don't have access to Shimeji mushrooms, substitute with sliced fresh shitake mushrooms or enoki mushrooms.

SORREL SAUCE

1 Egg in the shell

1 Bunch sorrel, stems removed

½ Cup peanut oil

5 Ice cubes

VEGETABLES

2 Tablespoons unsalted butter

4 Celery stalks, cut into 3" segments and thinly sliced lengthwise

2 Leeks, white and light green parts only, thinly sliced lengthwise

½ Cup heavy cream

1 Pound Yukon gold potatoes, peeled, and cut into 1/4-inch thick slices

1 Clove garlic, peeled and crushed

1 Sprig thyme

2 Cups unsalted chicken stock or low sodium chicken broth

HALIBUT AND MUSHROOMS

4 Ounces Hon Shimeji (beech) mushrooms

4 6-ounce center-cut halibut fillets, bone and skin removed

Salt and freshly ground pepper

2 Cups extra-virgin olive oil

1 Garlic clove, peeled and crushed

1 Sprig thyme

SORREL SAUCE

1. Bring a small pot of water to a boil. Gently slip in the **egg** and cook for 4 minutes. Remove the egg from the pot and let the egg cool under cold running water for 2 minutes. Gently peel the egg.
2. In a blender, whirl together the **soft-poached egg**, **sorrel leaves**, **oil** and **ice cubes** until smooth. Set aside until needed.

VEGETABLES

1. Melt 1 tablespoon of the **butter** in a large sauté pan over medium heat. Add the **celery** and **leeks** and cook, while stirring, for 2 minutes.
2. Add the **heavy cream** and continue to cook until the vegetables are tender and the cream has reduced to 2 tablespoons, about 10 minutes. Season with **salt and pepper**. Transfer the vegetables to a plate and keep warm.
3. Wipe the inside of the sauté pan clean with a paper towel; melt the remaining 1 tablespoon **butter** over medium-high heat. Arrange the **potatoes** in an even layer and top with the **garlic, thyme**, and **chicken stock** and cook until the potatoes are tender, about 10 minutes.
4. Using a slotted spoon, transfer the potatoes to a plate.
5. Combine the sorrel cream with any remaining liquid in the pan. If there is not enough liquid or the sauce is still too thick, add some water or chicken stock to thin. Season with **salt** and **pepper**. Set aside, keep warm.

HALIBUT AND MUSHROOMS

1. Center a rack in the oven and preheat the oven to 350°F.
2. Trim the **mushroom** bases to separate the stems and pull apart.
3. Season the **halibut** with **salt** and **pepper**. Heat the **olive oil** in a Dutch oven or large casserole to 200°F as measured on a deep-fat thermometer. Slip in the **halibut, mushrooms, garlic**, and **thyme** to the oil. Loosely cover with aluminum foil, slide the pan into the oven, and bake for 8 minutes.
4. Using a slotted spoon, carefully lift the fish and mushrooms out of the oil and onto a plate lined with a double thickness of paper towels. Pat off any excess oil and season with salt and pepper, if necessary.

TO SERVE

Reheat the vegetables and sorrel cream, if necessary. Divide the vegetables evenly among four warm dinner plates. Top each with a halibut filet and garnish the fish with the Hon Shimeji mushrooms. Spoon the sorrel sauce around the plates.

Adapted from *Chef Daniel Boulud: Cooking in New York City*, Daniel Boulud and Peter Kaminsky, Assouline 2002.

SUGGESTED WINE VARIETALS

WHITE
Chardonnay \ Pinot Blanc \ Riesling (dry) \ Sauvignon Blanc

RED
Pinot Noir

Marinated Blue Crab Claws

EMERIL LAGASSE

Save the claws the next time you have a crab boil at your house, or purchase them already peeled from a local seafood market. However you go about getting your crab claws, this simple, toss-together dish makes for a festive party hors d'oeuvre. Make it a day or two ahead of time and pull it out of the fridge just in time for the party. Now that's what I'm talking about!

PREP TIME: 20 minutes

1. Combine **all the ingredients except the crab claws** in a large nonreactive bowl, and whisk to mix well.
2. Add the **crab claws** and toss to coat.
3. Cover, and refrigerate for at least 6 hours or as long as overnight.

TO SERVE
Serve chilled or at cool room temperature in individual serving bowls or allow guests to serve themselves from a large bowl.

½ Cup extra-virgin olive oil

2 Tablespoons red wine vinegar

1 Tablespoon freshly squeezed lemon juice

¼ Cup green onions, white and green parts chopped

2 Tablespoons shallot, minced

2 Tablespoons celery, minced

2 Tablespoons fresh parsley leaves, chopped

1 Tablespoon fresh basil leaves, chopped

2 Teaspoons garlic, minced

2 Teaspoons Worcestershire sauce

1 Teaspoon fresh oregano leaves, chopped

¼ Cup pimento-stuffed green olives, thinly sliced

1 Teaspoon salt

½ Teaspoon freshly ground black pepper

½ Teaspoon hot pepper sauce

1 Pound cooked blue crab claws, outer shells removed

SUGGESTED WINE VARIETALS

WHITE
Chardonnay \ Riesling (dry) \ Sauvignon Blanc

RED
Grenache \ Pinot Noir

Smoked Trout with Arugula and Fried Green Tomatoes

JOSH DRAGE

AVOCADO VINAIGRETTE
- ¼ Avocado
- ⅓ Cup white balsamic vinegar
- ⅔ Cup olive oil
- Pinch salt
- 3 Large basil leaves
- Splash of white wine or water to adjust consistency

HORSERADISH VINAIGRETTE
- ½ Cup olive oil
- 1¼ Cup Champagne vinegar
- 1 Shallot
- Fresh thyme, chopped
- 1 Tablespoon prepared horseradish
- Salt and pepper, to taste

FRIED GREEN TOMATOES
- 1-3 Green tomatoes, depending on size
- 2 Cups flour
- 2 Eggs
- 2 Cups milk
- Panko bread crumbs
- Olive oil, for shallow frying
- Salt and pepper, for seasoning

SMOKED TROUT AND ARUGULA SALAD
- 1 Smoked trout
- A handful of arugula
- 1 Red onion, julienned
- 1 Avocado, sliced

SUGGESTED WINE VARIETALS

WHITE
Chardonnay

RED
Pinot Noir \ Rhone Blend

Trout, arugula and green tomatoes are all Montana summer staples. The avocado vinaigrette gives it a more healthy touch rather than a mayonnaise. One tip when frying the green tomatoes, if you brown the tomatoes too quickly and they are not warmed through, finish them in the oven.

PREP TIME: 1 hour   **COOK TIME:** 20 minutes

AVOCADO VINAIGRETTE
1. Add **all ingredients except the olive oil** to a blender. Blend and slowly add the **oil** until smooth.

HORSERADISH VINAIGRETTE
1. Mince **shallot**, pick fresh **thyme leaves**, add **all ingredients except oil** to a small bowl. Pour in **oil** slowly, whisking to combine. This vinaigrette will not be emulsified, so re-whisk just before using.

FRIED GREEN TOMATOES
1. Whip the **egg** and **milk** together.
2. Slice the **green tomatoes** and dredge in **flour**, dip in the egg mixture and then coat in the **panko bread crumbs**, pressing them down on each side.
3. Fry in a sauté pan on a medium heat with **olive oil** in the bottom. Cook until crispy and deep brown, pull out of pan and season with **salt** and **pepper**.

TO SERVE
Sear off the fried green tomatoes, cool slightly and place two of them to the side of the a plate. Toss the arugula lightly in the horseradish vinaigrette. Place in a small pile on the opposite side of the plate. Fleck the smoked trout on the arugula and garnish with the red onion. Place one slice of avocado on the fried green tomatoes and garnish with the avocado vinaigrette.

Tiger Abalone with Cauliflower and Caviar

DANIEL BOULUD

I always love cauliflower with caviar, a combination perfected by Joel Robuchon in the 1980s. Before you cure them in salt, let your abalone rest in the refrigerator for two days, covered in a damp cloth—it makes for a more tender result.

Back in its vessel, cooked and mixed with cauliflower puree, the mollusk now reads both briny and rich. Under a sprinkling of caviar, another briny salty touch, and hard-boiled eggs, a vodka beurre blanc finishes this Russian-themed appetizer. Alongside the abalone on the plate are the different cauliflower preparations: pureed, pickled, in florets, and in crispy tempura. The mixed lettuce on the dish mirrors delicate seaweed moving with the tide—a delicious underwater landscape.

TIGER ABALONE

- 16 Tiger abalone, in their shell
- ½ Cup kosher salt
- 1 Quart chicken stock
- ¼ Quart cream
- 3 Tablespoons Dijon mustard

CAULIFLOWER PUREE AND CONCASSÉE

- 2 Heads cauliflower
- 2 Cups milk
- 1 Cup chicken stock
- 1 Sachet (1/4 piece bay leaf, 1 sprig thyme and 1 teaspoon black peppercorns wrapped in cheesecloth and secured with butcher's twine)
- 2 Tablespoons crème fraîche
- 1 Teaspoon lemon juice
- Tabasco sauce, to taste
- Salt and ground white pepper

1. Rinse the **abalone**, and with a stiff brush, scrub the shells to remove the black ink around the flesh.
2. Using a spoon, remove abalone from their shells, reserve shells. Place in a non-reactive container with the **salt**, toss to coat, and cover. Refrigerate for 12 hours.
3. Meanwhile, bring a large pot of water to a boil and add the **shells**. Boil for ½ hour, strain, wipe clean and reserve.
4. Combine **chicken stock**, **cream**, and **Dijon mustard** in a large saucepot and bring to a light simmer.
5. Rinse **abalone**, pat dry and add to the sauce. Cover, and cook at a low simmer for 1½ hours. Remove from the heat and cool the abalone in the liquid.
6. Strain; and slice the **abalone** into diagonal pieces 1 mm thick, arrange back into their original shape. Reserve, chilled.

CAULIFLOWER PUREE AND CONCASSÉE

1. Trim and reserve 32 small-sized **florets** and 3 large **florets** from the head of cauliflower.
2. Roughly chop the remaining **cauliflower** and combine with the **milk**, **chicken stock** and **sachet** in a saucepot. Season with a pinch of **salt** and bring to a simmer. Cook, stirring occasionally, until tender, about 20 minutes.
3. Strain **cauliflower** and transfer ¾ of it to a blender with the **crème fraîche** and **lemon juice**. Puree until smooth and season with **Tabasco**, **salt** and **pepper** to taste.
4. Coarsely chop the remaining ¼ of cooked cauliflower into a concassée; and season with salt and pepper. Reserve puree and concassée warm.

CONTINUED...

GLAZED CAULIFLOWER AND ROMANESCO FLORETS

1 Head romanesco cauliflower

16 Small cauliflower florets, reserved from Cauliflower Puree and Concassée

3 Tablespoons butter

¼ Cup chicken stock

Salt and ground white pepper

CAULIFLOWER AND ROMANESCO PICKLES

16 Small cauliflower florets, reserved from cauliflower puree and concassée

16 Small romanesco florets, reserved from glazed cauliflower and romanesco

½ Cup distilled white vinegar

1 Teaspoon salt

10 White peppercorns

2 Tablespoons sugar

CAULIFLOWER TEMPURA

3 Large florets cauliflower, reserved from cauliflower puree and concassée

$^2/_3$ Cup rice flour

1 Tablespoon cornstarch

1 Teaspoon baking soda

1 Cup soda water

Vegetable oil, for frying

Salt

GLAZED CAULIFLOWER AND ROMANESCO FLORETS

1. Trim **romanesco** into small florets, reserve 16 for pickles, and discard the core.
2. Bring a large pot of salted water to a boil and place a bowl of ice water on the side.
3. Boil the **romanesco** florets and **cauliflower** florets in separate batches until tender, and chill in the ice water.
4. When ready to serve, bring **butter** and **chicken stock** to a simmer, reduce to a glaze, add florets and toss to heat through.
5. Season to taste with **salt and pepper.**

CAULIFLOWER AND ROMANESCO PICKLES

1. Place **florets** in a heat-proof container.
2. Combine **vinegar, salt, white peppercorn** and **sugar** in a small saucepot and bring to a simmer.
3. Cover, and rest for 10 minutes. Pour over the florets and chill in the liquid.

CAULIFLOWER TEMPURA

1. Fill a heavy-bottomed saucepot $^1/_3$ with **vegetable oil** and heat to 350°F.
2. Using a mandoline, slice the **florets** into (at least 16) $^1/_{16}$-inch slices.
3. In a medium bowl, combine the **rice flour, cornstarch,** and **baking soda** and make a well in the center. Pour in the **soda water** and combine by whisking from the center outwards, slowly incorporating the flour to make a smooth tempura batter.
4. When ready to serve, dip cauliflower slices into the batter to coat; and fry in batches until crisp and golden. Strain onto a paper-towel lined plate and sprinkle with **salt.**

VODKA BEURRE BLANC

1. In a small saucepan, combine the **shallots** and ¾ of the vodka. Simmer until almost dry, and stir in the **cream**.
2. Over low heat, whisk in the **butter** piece by piece (the mixture will thicken), being sure not to bring to a boil to avoid separation.
3. Add remaining **vodka** and **salt** to taste. Reserve warm.

TO SERVE

Preheat oven to 350°F and arrange a rack on the top shelf. Place **abalone shells** face up on a baking sheet and divide the warm **cauliflower concassée** into the bottoms. Top each with a piece of **abalone**, slightly fanning the slices. Cover with foil and bake for 5 minutes, or until the abalone is heated through. Remove and set oven temperature to broil. Spoon the **vodka beurre blanc** onto the top of the **abalone**, about 1 tablespoon per shell. Broil until the sauce is shiny, about 3 to 4 minutes. Sprinkle with crushed black pepper, chives, and hard boiled eggs. Top each abalone with a 4-gram spoonful of caviar. For each serving, spoon a line of sauce in the center of a warm plate. Arrange 2 each **glazed romanesco and cauliflower florets** around the sauce. Place 2 **cauliflower tempura pieces** on top and garnish with 3 pieces of **baby lettuce**. Place two **abalone** on opposite sides, and serve hot.

VODKA BEURRE BLANC

1 Shallot, finely minced

¼ Cup vodka

2 Tablespoons heavy cream

¼ Cup chilled butter, diced

Salt

TO SERVE

32 Pieces baby mixed lettuce

3 Tablespoons crushed black pepper

¼ Cup chopped chives

½ Cup hard-boiled egg, finely chopped

80 Grams golden Oscetra caviar

Vermouth Baked Arctic Char in a Lettuce Shirt

SUSAN PRESCOTT-HAVERS

This dish can be made with salmon or trout if Arctic char is not available, but it works best with an oily fish rather than a white fish. This is a classic French inspired dish and you can substitute any large lettuce leaf for the romaine and if you do not have vermouth handy, use a dry martini or white wine.

PREP TIME: 30 minutes   **COOK TIME:** 15 to 20 minutes

1. Blanch **lettuce leaves** in boiling water then plunge into ice cold water to keep color. Remove and pat dry once cold.
2. Heat a skillet low to medium, add one tablespoon of **vegetable oil**, season the **fish** with **salt** and **pepper**, and then gently color both sides in the pan. Set aside.
3. Preheat oven to 450°F.
4. **Butter** a baking dish big enough to hold all 4 filets, pour in the **broth**, **vermouth** and **chopped shallots**.
5. Lay a **lettuce leaf** on the chopping board, place one tablespoon of **butter** in the middle, place a **fish filet** face down on the lettuce leaf and then wrap the whole into a little parcel. Place fold side down in the baking tray. Repeat with the next 3 filets.
6. Cover the baking dish with foil and bake for 15 to 20 minutes or until the internal temperature of the fish is 145°F, if you have a thermometer. Remove from the oven.

TO SERVE
Drizzle any remaining juices over the fish. Serve with sautéed carrots and wild rice.

- 4 6 ounce filets of arctic char, skinned, substitute salmon or trout
- 4 Large leaves of romaine lettuce (enough to completely wrap each filet)
- 1 Large shallot, finely chopped
- ½ Cup dry vermouth
- ½ Cup chicken broth
- 4 Tablespoons butter

Walleye Cheek Ceviche

DANIEL NELSON

Walleye cheeks are the scallops of the Great Lakes. Their cheeks are deeper than most other fish and they are made of the softest flesh. Treat them similarly to scallops and you will enjoy every recipe you use them in.

Note: Serving raw or undercooked fish always exposes the consumer to the risks, but if you freeze the flesh to -4°F for 7 days, you will kill any potential parasites. If you pack you fish very well, take care to remove all air from the package, and thaw under refrigeration for 12 to 24 hours, you will not notice any significant change in taste or texture.

TIME: 20 minutes

6 Ounces walleye cheeks (cut in half if cheeks are large)

6 Ounces walleye fillet, sliced to similar size of the cheeks

6 Limes, squeezed

½ Lemon, squeezed

½ Orange, squeezed

2 Medium vine ripened tomatoes, diced

¼ Cup garlic scapes, diced, or 1 tablespoon fresh chopped garlic with ⅛ cup diced chive

⅛ Cup red onion, diced

2 Tablespoons fresh cilantro, chopped

½ Fresh jalapeño, diced

1 English cucumber, peeled and diced

1 Large avocado, diced

2 Teaspoons Sriracha

Salt and blended pepper

1. Dry the **walleye** with paper towel and place in a glass bowl. Mix the juice of the **limes, lemon,** and **orange**. Make sure the juice completely covers the walleye. Marinate the fish in the refrigerator until it has turned opaque (4 to 12 hours).
2. Drain the **walleye**, saving the **citrus juice**. Add all the **remaining ingredients** and toss gently to incorporate. Flavor with the reserved **citrus juice** and season to taste

TO SERVE
Portion into tall chilled cocktail glasses and serve immediately.

Fowl

CHUKAR | DOVE | DUCK | GOOSE | GROUSE | PHEASANT | QUAIL | TURKEY

© Holly A. Heyser

Duck Soup with German Riebele Dumplings

HANK SHAW

You can make this with the roasted or smoked carcass of any animal—I just prefer it with ducks and geese. There's no reason this would not work with wild pigs, pheasants or turkeys, venison, elk, pronghorn or rabbits. Feel free to play with it! The broth will keep for several days in the fridge, or you can freeze it. The dumplings are best made early in the day you make the soup, but you can store them in the fridge for a couple days if need be.

PREP TIME: 15 minutes   **COOK TIME:** 2 to 3 hours

DUMPLINGS

- 1 Egg
- A pinch of salt
- 2 Tablespoons water
- 1 Cup flour

SOUP

- 1 Duck carcass, preferably with its wings
- 2 Quarts water
- 2 Cups onion, sliced
- 2 Tablespoons duck fat or butter
- 1 Bay leaf
- 1 Teaspoon coarsely ground black pepper
- 1 Teaspoon crushed juniper (optional)
- ½ Ounce dried mushrooms (about a handful)
- 1 Carrot, chopped
- 1 Celery stalk, chopped
- 2 Cloves garlic, chopped
- ¼ Cup parsley, chopped
- Salt

1. Make the dumplings first, as they need to dry. Mix the **egg, salt** and **water** together. Put the **flour** into a bowl and pour the egg mixture in. Mix well until a dough forms, then knead it for 5 minutes. Shape the dough into a ball and then flatten it out somewhat to make a fat disk. Let this dry while you start the soup.
2. Chop the **duck carcass** into chunks using kitchen shears or a large knife or cleaver. Put it into a large pot with the water and turn the heat to medium. It is important to never let this soup boil, or it will turn very cloudy and can get bitter.
3. Heat the **duck fat** in a sauté pan and cook the **onions** over medium heat, stirring occasionally. You want to caramelize the onions here, so as you cook them you may need to drop the heat to medium-low and cover if need be. Take your time doing this, as the flavor of the caramelized onions is important. You want the onions to be well browned.
4. Make the dumplings by running the dough against the large edge of a box grater. Hold the dough in one hand, the grater in the other over a tea towel or other clean cloth, and be sure to move the grater so all the dumplings don't land on each other and make a doughy mess. You will need to flip the dough a lot so you have a good edge that will grate properly. They should look like raggedy spaetzle. Let the dumplings dry on the cloth as the soup cooks.
5. Add the **bay leaf, black pepper, juniper** and **dried mushrooms** to the soup. Let this cook gently while the onions finish caramelizing. When the onions are ready, move them to the soup and add the remaining soup ingredients. Let this simmer very gently, uncovered, for 90 minutes.
6. Turn the heat off the soup and strain it. Start by fishing out all the big pieces of duck and vegetable with a slotted spoon or a Chinese spider skimmer. Then strain the soup through a fine-mesh strainer into another pot. If you want to get fancy, strain this again through the fine-mesh strainer, only this time with cheesecloth or a plain paper towel set inside the strainer; this filters out much of the fat, and very fine debris. You may have to change the paper towel midway through: It blots up a lot of fat, and this can stop the soup from straining. Add **salt** to taste and set the strained soup in a pot over low heat to keep warm.
7. Bring a large pot of salted water to a boil. Drop the dumplings in a few at a time and boil until they float on the top, then for another minute. Skim them out and lay the cooked dumplings on a baking sheet while you finish cooking the rest.

TO SERVE
Put some dumplings in each person's bowl and ladle over the soup.

SUGGESTED WINE VARIETALS

WHITE
Chardonnay \ Rosé

RED
Cabernet Sauvignon \ Petite Sirah \
Pinot Noir \ Syrah \ Zinfandel

Grilled Quail with Jalapeño Sauce

JON BONNELL

The secret to this recipe is to start with the best quail in the world, then treat them simply and enjoy their naturally good qualities.

TIME: 30 Minutes

1. Remove the stems from **all herbs** and chop.
2. Mix the **herbs, garlic, seasonings** and **oil** together and coat the **quail** with this marinade both inside and out.
3. Allow to marinate overnight in the fridge.
4. Grill over medium heat with a light sprinkle of **creole seasonings** until cooked through.
5. Serve hot with jalapeño and garlic cream sauce.

JALAPEÑO SAUCE

1. Sauté the **jalapeños** and **garlic** in **butter** just until it bubbles, but do not let the garlic brown.
2. Deglaze the pan with **white wine** and reduce until the pan is almost dry.
3. Add in the **cream** and season with a pinch of **salt** and **pepper**.
4. Reduce the sauce until it thickens to a nice rich coating sauce consistency and pour over the quail.

QUAIL

- 2 Semi-boneless large quail
- 2 Tablespoons olive oil
- 4 Sprigs fresh thyme
- 2 Sprigs fresh rosemary
- 2 Cloves fresh garlic, chopped
- ½ Teaspoon creole seasoning blend

JALAPEÑO SAUCE

- ½ Teaspoon butter
- 1 jalapeño, seeds removed and chopped
- 1 Clove garlic, chopped
- 1 Ounce dry white wine
- ¼ Cup heavy cream
- Pinch of Kosher salt
- Pinch Freshly ground black pepper

SUGGESTED WINE VARIETALS

WHITE
Chardonnay \ Pinot Gris \ Rosé (dry) \ Riesling (dry) \ Sauvignon Blanc

RED
Merlot \ Pinot Noir

Sweet and Spicy Goose Summer Sausage

SCOTT LEYSATH

Goose meat, especially from an old Canada goose, can be a bit of a challenge to prepare. The breast fillets are tough, the legs and thighs are even tougher and roasting a whole wild goose just doesn't make any sense at all. This isn't the Christmas goose you see in cookbooks. With infinitely less fat than their domestic counterparts, wild geese need some help to get to the dinner table. Turning goose meat into summer sausage is a great way to make more room in the freezer and create a flavorful snack that will taste very much like the store-bought variety. Feel free to add your own seasonings, cheeses and herbs to create your own signature sausage.

Once you prepare your first batch of summer sausage, you'll realize just how simple it is to make something that you have been paying way too much for at the store. The process is simple. You grind or process game meat, add some seasonings and cure, refrigerate for a day or two and then cook in an oven or smoker. Don't think that the process requires any special equipment. A food processor and some heavy-duty aluminum foil will get you there. If, after a batch or two, you decide that sausage making suits you, consider buying a decent meat grinder and a package of sausage casings. Outdoor retailers carry easy sausage kits that include cures, seasonings and casing to transform your game meats into delicious bologna, bratwurst, summer sausage and more. I highly recommend the Cracked Pepper N' Garlic from Hi Mountain Seasonings!

- 4 Pounds ground boneless, skinless goose breast fillets (about 8 cups, firmly packed)
- 1 Pound ground pork or beef, 20% fat
- 2 Tablespoons Morton® Tender Quick®, measured precisely!
- ⅓ Cup fresh garlic cloves, minced
- 4 Jalapeño peppers, seeded and minced
- 2 Tablespoons coarse ground black pepper
- 2 Tablespoons water
- 1 Tablespoon red pepper flakes
- ⅔ Cup honey
- 2 Teaspoons mustard seed
- 2 Teaspoons kosher salt

1. Combine **ground meats** in a large glass, stainless steel or plastic bowl (not aluminum). Sprinkle **cure** over meat, add **remaining ingredients** and mix very well. Cure must be evenly distributed. When mixed thoroughly, meat should be a little sticky.
2. Cover bowl and place in the refrigerator. Every 12 hours, mix again thoroughly, cover and refrigerate.
3. After 48 hours, divide meat mixture into 5 equal portions and roll into logs, about 2-inches thick. Place each on a square of heavy-duty aluminum foil, shiny side up, and wrap snugly with foil. Pierce each log 3 or 4 times with a fork.
4. Arrange foil logs on a rack above a baking sheet (to catch any drippings). Place in a preheated 200°F oven or smoker until the internal temperature at the center of the sausage reads 160°F, about 6 to 8 hours. Do not allow the internal temperature to go past 170°F.
5. Allow meat to thoroughly cool before slicing. Summer sausage can be re-wrapped in butcher paper or vacuum-packed and refrigerated for up to 2 weeks or frozen for up to a year.

SUGGESTED WINE VARIETALS

WHITE
Chardonnay \ Riesling

RED
Barbera \ Cabernet Sauvignon \ Merlot \ Pinot Noir \ Rhone Blend \ Zinfandel

Hoisin Glazed Quail

CHRIS HUGHES

SERVES
4

Quail were originally domesticated 1,000 years ago in East Asia so there is a nice historic tie to these Asian flavors. This recipe is simple enough for weeknight dinners and elegant enough for a dinner parties.

TIME: 15 minutes   **COOK TIME:** 15 to 20 minutes

1. Preheat the grill to medium-hot.
2. Season **quail** with **oil, salt** and **pepper**.
3. In a small bowl, mix the **glaze ingredients**.
4. Grill **quail** starting breast down for 5 to 6 minutes. To get good grill marks start the quail at an angle to the grill grates then rotate 90° halfway through cooking. Flip the quail.
5. Brush or spoon the **glaze** on both sides of each bird and grill another 5 minutes or until done. When done the breast will be plump and firm to the touch.

TO SERVE
Serve with additional glaze drizzled over the top or on the side for dipping.

4 Semi-boneless, whole, boneless breasts, or breast-split quail

2 Tablespoons olive oil

Salt and ground black pepper to taste, about 1 teaspoon each

HOISIN GLAZE

3 Tablespoons hoisin sauce

1 Teaspoon fresh ginger, grated

1 Garlic clove, minced

1 Teaspoon soy sauce

1 Teaspoon rice vinegar

½ Teaspoon sesame oil

¼ Teaspoon red pepper flakes

SUGGESTED WINE VARIETALS

WHITE
Chardonnay \ Rosé (dry) \ Sauvignon Blanc

RED
Grenache \ Pinot Noir \ Rhone Blend

107

Hickory Cider Glazed Wild Turkey

DANIEL NELSON

The bark of a shagbark hickory tree (*Carya ovata*) is very distinctive and once shown it is easily recognizable, they like to live in the flood plains of the Midwest. The nut of a shagbark hickory is sweet and delicious, but very hard to harvest from the tough shells. It is however, very easy to collect the bark from these trees and it can often be found on the ground under the canopy, simply wiggle loose-looking pieces until you find ones that are ready to fall off.

Hickory cider syrup is best made using a clean percolator, a percolator is important because runs the cider through the bark at hot but not boiling temperatures. If you boil shagbark hickory bark the tannins will release from the wood fibers and turn the juice bitter. I use a 90-cup percolator for a double batch of this recipe. If shagbark hickory trees are not available in your region, you can crush whole hickory nuts or even acorns and use this nut/shell meal in the drip tray of the percolator.

PREP TIME: The several percolation cycles will take several days. Marinate 12–48 hours.
COOK TIME: 20 minutes

HICKORY CIDER SYRUP
- 1 Gallon apple cider
- 2 Quarts Shagbark Hickory bark broken into small pieces
- 2 Quarts sugar

GLAZED TURKEY
- 1 Wild turkey breast

  Salt and blended pepper
- 6 Cups hickory cider syrup, divided

HICKORY CIDER GLAZE: YIELD 4 QUARTS
1. Add the **cold cider** to the percolator and the **bark** pieces to the filter.
2. Turn on percolator and run a complete cycle. Remove the liquids and remove the filter chamber of bark, keep separate and cool in refrigerator.
3. Once cooled, set the percolator back up and run the liquids through again. Repeat this process 5 to 10 times.
4. After the last run you will need to strain the liquids; the finer the strain the clearer the resulting syrup. I will often put a layer of coffee filters between two china caps and filter the liquid through.
5. Once strained, mix the 2 quarts of **sugar** into the hickory cider and bring to a near boil. Cool hickory cider syrup and store in refrigerator. If air tight the syrup can be stored for several months. The syrup can re-crystallize but a quick heat through in the microwave will dissolve any crystals.

FOR THE HICKORY CIDER GLAZE WILD TURKEY
1. Turkey breast has long very grains of muscle fiber, running in three distinct manners. Trim and divide the breast following these long running grains, removing the inner silverskin as well. I typically cut my turkey breasts into 3 to 5 smaller portions for grilling.

CONTINUED...

SUGGESTED WINE VARIETALS

WHITE
Chardonnay \ Riesling (dry) \ Rosé

RED
Pinot Noir \ Rhone Blend \ Syrah \ Zinfandel

2. Season the raw, trimmed **turkey breast** with **salt** and **pepper** and add to a heavy plastic bag, cover with 4 cups **hickory cider syrup**, remove all air and set in refrigerator to marinate for 12 to 48 hours, turning every 12 hours.
3. Remove turkey breast sections from marinade and drain.
4. Preheat grill to 500°F being sure to create a cool zone for slower grilling. Have a basting brush with 2 cups of the **hickory cider syrup** available for basting. Grill for 3 to 4 minutes on all sides, basting between sides, if turkey breast hasn't reached 145°F, move it to a cooler section of the grill to finish slowly. Once the breast has reached 145°F in the center of the mass, remove it from direct heat to rest.
5. Rest for 20 minutes. To serve tender pieces of turkey it is important to thinly cut these sections, across the long grain of the muscle fiber. The shorter the fiber pieces of each slice cut from the loin, the more tender the meat will be to the palate.

TO SERVE

Serve in a variety of ways such as on a toasted hickory nut and apple spinach salad; with roasted sweet potatoes and sautéed fiddleheads; or on toasted baguette with sliced apple and Brie cheese.

Curried Pheasant Wontons

DANIEL NELSON

This is a great recipe for using the tougher leg meat of upland game, waterfowl, small game, even wild boar. I will often use leftover pulled game meat from a previous dinner. These creamy wontons are a perfect appetizer for wild game stir-fry, served with a crisp white wine or Riesling.

PREP TIME: Roasting 3 to 4 hours   **COOK TIME:** 45 minutes

BLOOD ORANGE MARINADE AND DIPPING SAUCE

- 1 Quart pheasant stock or chicken stock
- 1 Cup brown sugar
- ¼ Cup honey
- 3 Tablespoon red pepper flakes
- 4 Teaspoons Chinese 5 spice
- 2 Tablespoons garlic
- 2 Tablespoons paprika
- 1 Cup rice wine vinegar
- 4 Cups blood orange juice
- 2-4 tablespoons cornstarch slurry (equal amounts of cornstarch and water)

WONTONS

- 25-30 Wonton skins of your desired thickness
- 8 Pheasant thighs and backs or roughly 1 ½ lbs
- ¾ cup curry powder, preferably yellow
- Salt and blended pepper
- 3 Green onions
- 1 Pound cream cheese
- 2 Eggs beaten with ½ cup water

1. In a sauce pot combine the **pheasant stock, brown sugar, honey, red pepper flakes, Chinese 5 spice, garlic, paprika, rice wine vinegar** and **blood orange juice**, then bring to a boil.
2. Remove ⅓ of this hot liquid and slowly add **corn starch slurry** until you have a nice smooth dipping sauce. Set in refrigerator to cool.
3. Add a ½ cup **curry powder** to the remaining liquid for a marinade and set in the refrigerator to cool.
4. Once cool, mix with **pheasant thighs and backs** in a large plastic bag, taking care to remove all air, and keep in refrigerator for 12 to 48 hours.
5. Place pheasants and marinade in a braising dish, cover and cook at 300°F until meat is tender and falling off the bone, 2 to 4 hours. Pull and cool pheasant meat.
6. Blend room temperature **cream cheese** with ¼ cup **curry powder, 1 teaspoon Chinese 5 spice, sliced green onion** and the **pulled pheasant**.
7. Place small dollop of mixture in the center of the **wonton square**, brush **egg wash** on all four edges of wonton and then fold corner to corner making a triangle, take two corners of the triangle and fold onto center.
8. Fry or freeze wontons within a couple hours of making.

TO SERVE

Serve as an appetizer with blood orange dipping sauce.

SUGGESTED WINE VARIETALS

WHITE
Chardonnay \ Pinot Blanc \ Pinot Grigio \ Riesling \ Rosé (dry) \ Sauvignon Blanc

RED
Cabernet Sauvignon \ Charbono \ Merlot \ Pinot Noir \ Syrah \ Zinfandel

American Heritage Chocolate Dusted Duck Breast

TRAVIS BRUST

4 Young duck breasts

Freshly ground black pepper, as needed

Kosher salt, as needed

4 Tablespoons American Heritage Chocolate Powder

ROASTED ROOTS AND BULBS

4 Tablespoons butter, melted

4 Whole shallots

4 Whole green onions

8 Tri-color carrots, peeled

12 Whole fingerling potatoes

1 Tablespoon chives, minced

1 Tablespoon tarragon, minced

¼ Teaspoon fresh ground black pepper

½ Teaspoon kosher salt

PORT SOAKED CHERRIES

1 Cup dried cherries

1½ Cup port wine

¼ Cup light brown sugar

1 Cinnamon stick

1 Orange, zested and juiced

Fresh ground black pepper, to taste

Kosher salt, to taste

SUGGESTED WINE VARIETALS

WHITE
Chardonnay

RED
Cabernet Sauvignon \ Merlot \ Zinfandel

This delicious recipe for duck may seem a little different however the ingredient choice of American Heritage 18th Century Chocolate, produced by Mars, brings a unique flavor profile from the mixture of spice notes in the chocolate such as cinnamon, orange peel, annatto seed and chili pepper. For a substitute for the American Heritage Chocolate, you may use a dark chocolate cocoa powder for a similar, less-spiced version of this recipe.

1. Clean any excess fat and silverskin from the **duck breasts**. Then lightly score the fat of the breast with a knife to allow more surface area for the fat to render.
2. Season the **duck breasts** with **kosher salt** and fresh ground **black pepper**.
3. Place a large skillet on the stove over medium heat; place the **duck breasts** skin side down to render.
4. Render for 8 to 12 minutes or till the skin is very crispy, then place into a 325°F oven until an internal temperature of 140°F is achieved inside the duck breast.
5. Remove from the oven and set aside.
6. Dust the breast with the **chocolate powder** and allow to rest at least 6 to 8 minutes before slicing.

ROASTED ROOTS AND BULBS

1. Toss **all the ingredients** together and ensure they are well coated in **butter**.
2. Spread the ingredients onto a sheet pan and place into a 350°F oven and roast till fork tender.
3. Toss the vegetables occasionally throughout the roasting process; this should take about 20 to 28 minutes.

PORT SOAKED CHERRIES

1. Place **all ingredients** into a small sauce pot and place on a stove over medium heat.
2. Cook the **cherries** till the raw alcohol flavor has gone away.
3. Remove the **cinnamon stick** and cool to room temperature. Serve alongside duck and roasted roots and bulbs.

TO SERVE

Place the sliced duck breast alongside of the roasted potatoes and vegetables, then spoon the port soaked cherries over and around the sliced duck.

114

Indian Style Quail In Beet, Apricot, And Tomato Chutney

DANIEL BOULUD

Quail is elegant, refined and delicate, yet this version also has a nice spicy element. When it comes to the best dishes for entertaining at home, braised recipes are ideal as they can be made ahead, enabling you to spend time with your guest(s).

Note: Garam masala is a blend of ground spices common in North Indian and other South Asian cuisines. You should be able to find it at your local store.

2 Medium yellow beets

12 Dried apricots

½ Cup packed mint leaves

3 Tablespoons unsalted butter

1½ Cups onion, coarsely chopped

2 Tablespoons ginger root, finely grated

4 Teaspoons garam masala

2 Teaspoons crushed coriander seeds

1 Teaspoon turmeric

½ Teaspoon saffron

4 Whole star anise

1 Hot green chile pepper (such as serrano), split and seeded

8 Plum tomatoes, blanched and peeled, if desired, seeded and chopped

 Freshly squeezed juice of 2 oranges

 Coarse sea salt or kosher salt

¼ Cup vegetable oil, plus additional

2 Red apples (such as Rome), peeled, cored, and quartered

8 Jumbo quail, boneless breast and bone-in legs

 Freshly ground pepper

1 Tablespoon black mustard seeds

SUGGESTED WINE VARIETALS

WHITE
Chardonnay \ Riesling (dry) \
Sauvignon Blanc

RED
Cabernet Sauvignon \ Merlot \
Petite Sirah \ Pinot Noir \
Rhone Blend \ Syrah \ Zinfandel

1. Put a rack in the lower third of the oven and preheat the oven to 350°F.
2. Wash the **beets** and wrap in aluminum foil. Place in a baking pan and roast until they are easily pierced with a paring knife, 1½ to 2 hours.
3. Remove the beets from the oven. When they are cool enough to handle, peel and cut them into ½-inch cubes.
4. Meanwhile, bring 1 cup of water to a boil. Add the **apricots** and **mint leaves**, remove the pan from the heat, and let cool to room temperature. Purée mixture in blender or food processor.
5. Lower the oven temperature to 300°F. In a large roasting pan over medium heat, melt 2 tablespoons of the **butter**. Add the **onions**, **ginger root**, **garam masala**, **coriander seeds**, **turmeric**, **saffron**, **star anise**, and **chile pepper** and sweat until the onions are lightly colored, about 5 minutes. Add the **tomatoes**, toss, and cook 4 minutes more. Pour the **orange juice** and **apricot purée** into the pan, and stir to combine. Add the diced **beets**, bring to a simmer, and season to taste with **salt**. Bake for 60 minutes.
6. While the sauce is cooking, in a large nonstick sauté pan over medium-high heat, melt the remaining 1 tablespoon of **butter**. Add the **apples** and cook until golden brown, 3 to 5 minutes.
7. When the apples are cool enough to handle, stuff each **quail** with an apple piece, and run a skewer through both legs, just below the knee, fitting two quails to a skewer. Alternatively, you can skip the skewers; if a piece of apple pops out of a quail cavity, simply pop it back in.
8. In a large nonstick sauté pan over medium-high heat warm the **vegetable oil**. Season the **quail** with **salt** and **pepper** and press the **mustard seeds** evenly all over each quail. Add 4 quails to the pan and sear on all sides until golden brown, about 7 to 8 minutes. Repeat with the remaining 4 quails, adding more oil to the pan if needed.
9. Put the quails, skin-side down, over the tomato-beet chutney, pressing them into the mixture. Return the pan to the oven and braise, uncovered, for 60 minutes. Serve with the salad. Recipe follows.

CONTINUED...

FENNEL, APRICOT AND TOMATO SALAD

1 Teaspoon saffron threads

¼ Cup extra-virgin olive oil

Finely grated zest and freshly squeezed juice of 1 lime

1½ Teaspoons white wine vinegar

6 Fresh mint leaves, julienned

Coarse sea salt or kosher salt and freshly ground pepper

2 Small bulbs fennel, trimmed and thinly sliced lengthwise (preferably on a mandoline)

2 Apricots, pitted and thinly sliced lengthwise

1 Cup cherry tomatoes, halved

FENNEL, APRICOT AND TOMATO SALAD

1. In a small pot on the stove, or in a small bowl in the microwave, warm 2 tablespoons water until hot. Remove from the heat, add the **saffron**, and let infuse until the water turns bright yellow, about 10 minutes. Strain through a fine-mesh sieve, discard the saffron threads, and set the liquid aside.

2. Whisk together the **olive oil**, **lime zest and juice**, **vinegar**, **mint leaves** and **saffron water**. Season to taste with **salt** and **pepper**.

3. In a salad bowl, toss the **fennel**, **apricots**, and **tomatoes** together with the vinaigrette and season to taste with **salt** and **pepper**.

Adapted from *Braise: A Journey Through International Cuisine*, Daniel Boulud and Melissa Clark, Ecco, 2006

Turkey Moose Drool Molé

JOSH DRAGE

1 Whole turkey, quartered

White wine

Chicken stock

MOLÉ

1 Spice pack, including:
Whole cloves, star anise, bay leaf, fennel seed, caraway seed, thyme, sage

1 Onion

3 Garlic cloves

3 Tablespoons olive oil

½ Cup pumpkin seeds

½ Cup salted cashews

3 Dates

5 Dried figs, Calimyrna recommended

⅓ Cup huckleberries, fresh or frozen

Orange zest from two oranges

4 New Mexico chiles, dried

4 Ancho chiles, dried

2 Small red chiles, dried

1 Bottle Moose Drool beer, or any brown ale

1 Pint turkey stock

Salt and pepper

½ Cup apple caramel, or reduced apple juice. (If you don't have apple caramel available, reduce a gallon jug of natural apple juice, like Knudsens, to one cup or until syrup consistency

4 Ounces dark chocolate

¼ Cup maple syrup

This is a wonderful way to highlight this year's harvested wild turkey. Molé is a traditional preparation for turkey in Mexico, and soon with the addition Big Sky's Moose Drool ale and a wild Montana turkey it will be traditional in the Treasure State. Moose Drool is a brown ale from Missoula, Montana-based micro-brewery Big Sky Brewing Company. Brown ales range in color from copper to dark brown and are not typically roasty, burnt, bitter like most Porters and Stouts.

TOTAL TIME: 6 hours

MOOSE DROOL MOLÉ

1. Make a sachet enclosing the **herbs** and **spices** with cheese cloth and tie around the top with butcher twine, set aside for later.
2. Chop both the **onion** and the **garlic**, add to a sauce pot with a bit of **olive oil**, add the **dried chili pods** with the stems and seeds removed.
3. Over medium heat cook **onions** until translucent, add the **pumpkin seeds** and **cashews**, plus the **dates, figs**, and **orange zest**.
4. Cook for a few more minutes toasting the nuts and letting the flavors develop.
5. Add the **rest of the ingredients**, as well as the **spice sachet**.
6. Bring to a simmer and cook on low temperature for two hours, reducing the level of the liquid.
7. Blend smooth in your blender. You will want to let the blender go on high until the color gets a bit creamy looking.
8. Push through a basket strainer.

TURKEY

1. To braise the **turkey**, brown all sides, deglaze with a bit of **wine**, add 2 cups of **molé sauce**, a bit of **chicken stock** to get the level of the liquid right.
2. Cook on low heat for about 2 hours, replenishing the level of the liquid when it needs it.

TO SERVE

Serve the turkey, either whole pieces or with the bones picked out, with the molé sauce and white rice.

SUGGESTED WINE VARIETALS

WHITE
Chardonnay \ Pinot Blanc \ Rosé (dry)

RED
Cabernet Sauvignon \ Charbono \ Pinot Noir \ Rhone Blend \ Syrah

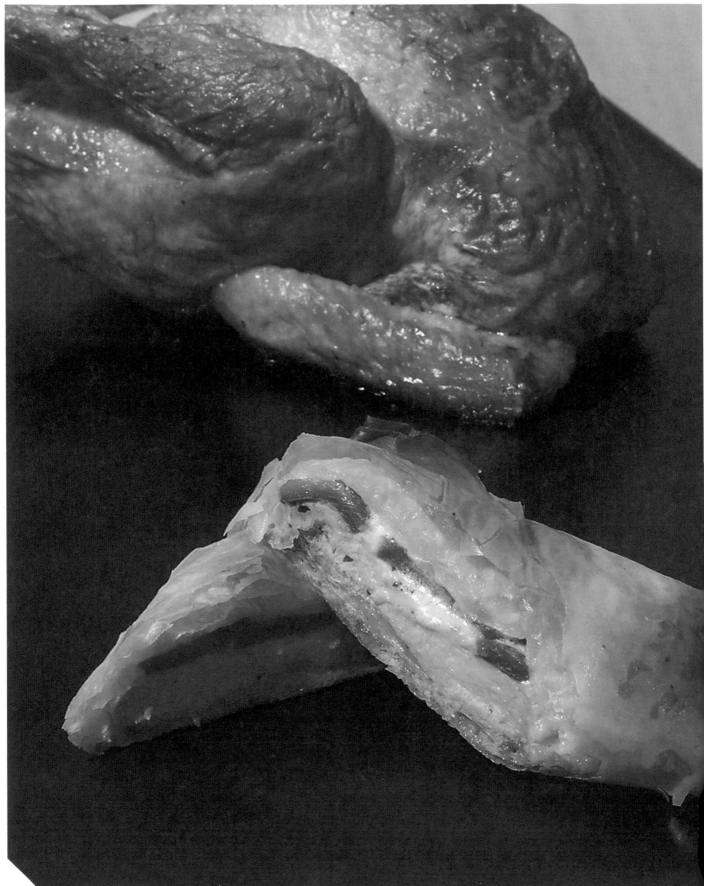

Pheasant, Goat Cheese and Herbs in Phyllo

JON BONNELL

This is an easy dish to make a day ahead and will keep very well in the fridge. Bake at the last minute and be sure to get the outer phyllo pastry golden brown and flaky. The cooking time may vary quite a bit, depending on the size of the pheasant, but it's easy to check the internal temperature with a thermometer without having to cut in to see if it's done. When the middle reaches 140°F to 145°F, it's ready.

TIME: 30 to 45 minutes

2 Pheasant breasts

3 Ounces fresh goat cheese

2 Sprigs thyme

2 Leaves sage

2 Tablespoons shallot, chopped

¼ Teaspoon rosemary, chopped

2-3 Strips roasted red pepper

Pinch Kosher salt

Pinch Freshly ground black pepper

8 Sheets phyllo dough

3 Ounces butter

1. Combine the **goat cheese**, **shallots** and **herbs** in a mixing bowl and season with a pinch of **salt** and **pepper**.
2. Remove the skin from the **pheasant breasts** and pound them down to a thin and uniform thickness.
3. Smother the entire surface of the pheasant with the goat cheese mixture.
4. Place one or two strips of **red pepper** in the middle, then roll the pheasant breasts up into a roulade (like a jelly roll).
5. Melt the **butter**.
6. Lay one sheet of **phyllo dough** on a smooth counter surface, then brush well with melted butter. Lay down a second sheet on top and brush again. Repeat until four layers of the phyllo have been buttered.
7. Place one pheasant roulade on the dough and roll from one end to the other, folding in the ends to create a somewhat sealed package. Be sure there is enough butter to help keep the dough together and refrigerate. Repeat for the second pheasant breast as well.
8. Preheat an oven to 400°F, and cook the stuffed pheasant on parchment paper or a nonstick surface for approximately 15 to 18 minutes. The time may vary, depending on the thickness of the pheasant and the type of oven being used. The outside should become golden brown and the pheasant should be cooked just through.
9. Remove from the oven and allow to cool for 2 to 3 minutes before slicing. Cut on a bias and serve hot.

SUGGESTED WINE VARIETALS

WHITE
Chardonnay \ Pinot Blanc \ Pinot Gris \ Riesling (dry) \ Rosé

RED
Merlot \ Pinot Noir \ Rhone Blend

Pan-Seared Chukar Breast with Lemon Vinaigrette

SCOTT LEYSATH

Harvesting a limit of chukars is a daunting task, considering the work that goes into chasing these elusive birds up and down ankle-twisting rocky hills. Fast fliers and runners, chukars are very low in fat and will dry out if overcooked. The cure for dry and chewy upland birds is not to drown them in a slow-cooker with cream of mushroom soup until they fall off the bone. A medium-hot skillet, a spirited vinaigrette and proper cooking time will insure a moist, tender and tasty bird.

Don't discard the legs and carcasses of upland birds. Roast along with celery, carrots and onions before placing into a stock pot and covering with cold water. Heat until almost boiling, then reduce heat to a low simmer and leave the uncovered pot alone for several hours, overnight is fine as long as the heat is low and there is plenty of water in the pot. Cool and strain through a cheesecloth-line colander for an incredible stock or broth.

LEMON VINAIGRETTE

1. Whisk together **garlic, lemon juice, vinegar, Dijon mustard** and **sugar** in a medium bowl. While whisking, add **olive oil** in a thin stream until emulsified. Whisk in **basil** and **green onions**. Season to taste with **salt** and **pepper**. Divide vinaigrette in half.

CHUKAR

1. Season **chukar** liberally with **salt** and **pepper**. Place in a non-reactive container or heavy-duty zipper-lock bag and toss with one-half of the **vinaigrette**, reserving the other half for later. Refrigerate for 2 to 3 hours, tossing to coat evenly every hour or so.
2. Remove chukar from vinaigrette. Heat a thin layer of **oil** in a large skillet over medium-high heat. Add **chukar breasts** and brown evenly on both sides. Just before removing from the skillet, baste with reserved marinade.
4. Serve over vegetables, pasta or rice. Spoon warm pan sauce over the top.

8 Whole chukar breasts, skin on or off

Kosher salt and freshly ground black pepper

LEMON VINAIGRETTE

3 Garlic cloves, minced

¼ Cup freshly squeeze lemon juice

3 Tablespoons white wine vinegar

1½ Teaspoons Dijon mustard

¾ Teaspoon granulated sugar

⅔ Cup extra virgin olive oil

¼ Cup fresh basil leaves, chopped

2 Green onions, chopped

Kosher salt and pepper, to taste

SUGGESTED WINE VARIETALS

WHITE
Chardonnay \ Sauvignon Blanc \ Viognier

RED
Merlot \ Pinot Noir \ Zinfandel

Duck With Green Picholine Olives

DANIEL BOULUD

4 to 6 Duck legs (about 3 pounds)

Coarse sea salt or kosher salt and freshly ground black pepper

2 Tablespoons extra-virgin olive oil

3 Carrots, peeled and chopped

¼ Pound sliced bacon, cut into ¼-inch pieces

2 Small onions, peeled, trimmed, and chopped

2 Small turnips, peeled and diced

½ Cup green picholine olives, pitted

2 Sprigs fresh thyme

1 Bay leaf

2 Cups chicken stock or low-sodium canned broth

This duck recipe is almost a cross between a braise and a confit, since I leave all the fat under the skin during the cooking, then take it off the next day when it's hardened on the surface of the contents of the pot. The fat gives a lot of flavor to the sauce and keeps the duck legs extremely tender. This is an ideal dish to make ahead for a dinner party, since you do all the heavy lifting the day before.

Picholines are green, torpedo-shaped olives that are brine-cured. Those made in Provence are marinated with coriander and herbes de Provence, while American picholines are soaked in citric acid. They are available at well-stocked or high-end markets and are also available on-line.

Cooking duck with olives has been a classic method ever since olives became fashionable in France about 100 years ago. Their brininess and acidity work well with the richness of the duck meat. Serve this with crusty bread, because there will be plenty of good sauce for mopping up.

ACTIVE TIME: 30 minutes **TOTAL PREPARATION TIME:** 1 hour and 45 minutes.

1. The night before you plan to serve the dish, place a rack in the lower third of the oven and preheat the oven to 350°F.
2. Season the **duck** with **salt** and **pepper**. Heat the **olive oil** in a medium cast-iron pot or Dutch oven over medium-high heat. Add the **duck legs** and sear until golden brown on all sides, 7 to 10 minutes.
3. Transfer the duck to a platter. Pour off the excess fat from the pot.
4. Return the duck to the pot along with the **bacon** and cook, stirring, over medium-high heat for 5 to 6 minutes. Spoon out any fat out of the pot.
5. Add the **carrots, onions, turnips, olives, thyme,** and **bay leaf,** and pour in the **stock.** Transfer the pot to the oven and braise, covered, for 2 hours, until the duck is tender.
6. Chill overnight.
7. Preheat the oven to 350°F. Remove the layer of fat from the top of the sauce and heat the duck in the oven for 30 minutes. Remove the thyme sprigs and the bay leaf and serve.

Adapted from *Braise: A Journey Through International Cuisine,*
Daniel Boulud and Melissa Clark, Ecco, 2006

SUGGESTED WINE VARIETALS

WHITE
Chardonnay \ Riesling (dry) \ Rosé (dry)

RED
Cabernet Sauvignon \ Malbec \ Merlot \
Petite Sirah \ Petit Verdot \
Pinot Noir \ Syrah \ Zinfandel

Quail with Apple and Sausage Stuffing

CHRIS HUGHES

This recipe makes great use of fall's fresh apples and sage. My mom requests this every October for her birthday dinner.

It doesn't matter what type of bread you use for the stuffing—the quality is the main thing. Use any neutral flavored, white bread loaf from a good baker. Challah is nice, rich option.

PREP TIME: 30 minutes   **COOK TIME:** 20 minutes

1. Cut **bread** into ½-inch cubes and place on a baking tray. Toast bread in 400°F oven until it is lightly toasted, about 5 to 10 minutes.
2. Remove **sausage** from casing and cook in a large pan over medium-high heat until it is just starting to turn golden but not yet crisp, about 10 to 12 minutes. Remove sausage from pan and reserve. Drain fat from pan until about 1 tablespoon remains.
3. Return pan to heat and add **butter, apple** and **sage**. Sauté about 5 minutes.
4. Deglaze pan with ¼ cup of **chicken broth**. Add **toasted bread** and **sausage**.
5. Gently mix the stuffing and add broth ¼ cup at a time until the bread is moist but not soggy. Season to taste with **salt** and **pepper**.
6. Remove from heat and allow stuffing to cool until it can be handled.
7. Pat the **quail** dry with a paper towel. Stuff each quail generously with the **stuffing**. Lightly coat the outside of the breast with **olive oil** then season with **salt** and **pepper**.
8. Grill over medium heat. Start with breast side down and cook about 5 to 7 minutes. Flip and cook another 5 minutes. Quail meat is done when it feels firm to the touch. (For oven: Cook 8 inches under broiler starting with meat side down. Cook about 5 minutes, flip and cook another 5 minutes until skin is golden brown and meat is firm to the touch.)

4 Semi-boneless quail

1 6-Ounce link wild boar Italian sausage

1 Tablespoon butter

1 Cup apple, diced but not peeled (recommend Honeycrisp Apples)

2 Tablespoons fresh sage, chopped

1 Cup chicken broth

2 Cups bread, cubed

   Olive oil

   Salt and pepper

SUGGESTED WINE VARIETALS

WHITE
Chardonnay \ Rosé (dry)

RED
Grenache \ Merlot \ Pinot Noir \ Syrah \ Zinfandel

126

Roasted Dove with Polenta and Gremolata

SUSAN PRESCOTT-HAVERS

This is a reasonably simple roast you can do with any game bird, but you will have to adjust the cooking time to suit the age of the bird (e.g. pigeon will take longer than squab or quail). They all need a rich side like polenta, garlic mashed potatoes, or similar.

PREP TIME: 15 minutes   **COOK TIME:** About 1 hour.
Polenta and gremolata can be prepared while bird is cooking. Once bird is cooked and resting, you can reduce the remaining sauce to a thicker consistency if desired.

1. Preheat oven to 375°F.
2. Bring **broth, milk** and **salt** to a boil. Slowly whisk in the **polenta**. Turn heat to low and continue to whisk for about 10 minutes or until the mixture is smooth and creamy (it should look like oatmeal).
3. Oil a small 6x6 baking dish and spread the polenta evenly, set aside to cool.
4. Season the **birds** inside and out and stuff a ¼ **lemon** and a **bay leaf** into each cavity.
5. Push a tablespoon of **butter** under the skin of the breast and place in the baking dish breast side up, making sure the birds do not touch. Drape a piece of **bacon** over each bird.
6. Combine **wine/sherry** and **broth** and pour into the baking dish. Place uncovered in the hot oven and cook for about an hour or until the juices of the leg run clear. Baste occasionally to keep moist, but not in the last 15 minutes to crisp up the skin. You can also remove the bacon and crisp that separately, then crumble it for serving with the bird.
7. Remove the birds and keep warm for 10 minutes. Meanwhile combine the **ingredients of the gremolata** and set aside.
8. Cut the **polenta** into 4 pieces or use a cookie cutter to cut 3 inch disks. Dust with a little **corn flour** for a crisper finish, otherwise heat a skillet to medium hot with 1 tablespoon of oil and fry the polenta until brown and crispy on one side, turn and cook the second side the same (each side should take about 2 minutes). Drain on paper towel.

TO SERVE

Place the **polenta** in the middle of the plate place the **bird** on top. Drizzle the **sauce** and the **bacon bits** around the outside and sprinkle the **gremolata** over the whole dish. You can also add a layer of sautéed spinach.

4 Whole doves, or any game bird

4 Bacon strips

4 Tablespoons of unsalted butter at room temperature

½ Cup of white wine or Sherry

1 Cup of water or chicken broth

4 Bay leaves

1 Lemon cut into quarters (use the same lemon that you used making zest for gremolata)

POLENTA OR GRITS

1 Cup whole milk

1 Cup chicken stock or water

½ Teaspoon kosher salt

½ Cup polenta

1 Tablespoon extra virgin olive oil

GREMOLATA

½ Cup parsley, chopped

⅓ Cup fresh oregano, chopped

3 Garlic cloves, chopped

2 Tablespoons grated lemon zest

Freshly ground black pepper

SUGGESTED WINE VARIETALS

WHITE
Chardonnay \ Pinot Gris \
Riesling (dry) \ Sauvignon Blanc

RED
Grenache \ Pinot Noir \ Rhone Blend

Grilled Duck Breast with Raspberry Relish

JON ASH &
SID GOLDSTEIN

It's important to remember that duck doesn't remotely resemble chicken and your approach to cooking should reflect that difference. Duck is completely dark, red meat and is best served medium rare.

PREP TIME: 15 minutes, plus 2 to 4 hours inactive time   **COOK TIME:** 10 minutes

1. In a glass bowl combine **all the ingredients for the relish** and mix thoroughly.
2. In a separate bowl, mix **all the ingredients for the marinade**, add $1/3$ cup of the **relish mixture** to the marinade and stir well.
3. Marinate the **duck breasts** for 2 to 4 hours, refrigerated, and turning occasionally. Refrigerate remaining relish.
4. Grill the **duck breasts** skin side down over a hot heat for 5 to 7 minutes. Duck should be served medium-rare.

TO SERVE
Slice duck breasts on bias and arrange on individual serving plates. Garnish each serving with 2 raspberries and a mint sprig. Dollop relish over the duck.

Recipe courtesy of John Ash and Sid Goldstein's *American Game Cooking*

---

4 Duck breasts, boned

RASPBERRY RELISH

2 Cups chopped raspberries, you could also use frozen

¾ Cup sweet onion, chopped

4 Teaspoon raspberry vinegar

2 Teaspoon fresh lemon Juice

1 Tablespoon chopped sage, or ½ tablespoon dried sage

½ Teaspoon crushed red pepper flakes

3 Tablespoons Creme de Cassis

MARINADE

¼ Cup olive oil

½ Teaspoon freshly ground pepper

½ Teaspoon salt

1 Clove garlic, minced

1 Teaspoon chopped fresh or dried sage

SUGGESTED WINE VARIETALS

WHITE
Chardonnay \ Rosé (dry) \
Sauvignon Blanc

RED
Cabernet Sauvignon \ Merlot \
Petite Sirah \ Pinot Noir

Skewered Quail with Grape Salad and Citrus-Rosemary Salt

MICHAEL CHIARELLO

- 5 Quail, each about 5 ounces (ask a butcher to bone them)
- 3 Tablespoons of extra virgin olive oil for rubbing

  Citrus-rosemary salt for seasoning

CITRUS ROSEMARY SALT
- 1 Tablespoon fresh rosemary leaves, chopped
- 2 Tablespoons lemon zest
- ½ Cup coarse salt

GRAPE SALAD
- 2 Tablespoons extra-virgin olive oil, plus ¼ cup
- 2 Heaping tablespoons fresh rosemary leaves
- 3 Cups red grapes, halved
- 1 Teaspoon citrus-rosemary salt (make your own, or order on-line from www.napastyle.com)
- ¼ Teaspoon freshly ground black pepper
- 1 Teaspoon grated lemon zest
- 1 Tablespoon freshly squeezed lemon juice

Hot, smoky, crisp-skinned quail served with a salad of cool, juicy grapes—the contrast is fantastic. You have two options for holding the quail near the fire. You can use green branches to skewer the quail or use wooden skewers and then stand the quail in heat-proof pots filled with sand placed close to the fire. If you opt to cook your quail on branches, choose branches at least 2 to 3 feet long. Make sure they're green, not dry wood—to be sure, cut them off the tree rather than gathering them from the ground. Use a sharp knife to strip off the bark before placing the birds. You can stand the tree branches upright on your hearth beside the fire or jam the ends of the branches in pots filled with sand. If you want to be more precise, you can drill holes in a big log that can hold the branches in place. Move the tree branches to shift the quail closer or farther from the fire. Check the birds during cooking to make sure they're browning evenly all the way around. If your quail is skewered and set in pots, rotate the pots every once in a while. Boned quail are called for here. There's a cool machine that removes the quail bones from the inside. But you can make this with bone-in quail too, if that's what you have.

CITRUS ROSEMARY SALT
In food processor, process all the ingredients. Pulse until well blended.

GRAPE SALAD
1. In a cast-iron pan or plancha set on the rack of a Tuscan grill or set directly on the fire, heat the 2 tablespoons of **olive oil**. (You can also do this in a sauté pan on your stove.) Line a platter with paper towels.
2. When the oil is hot, add the **rosemary leaves** and sauté until crisp, about 30 seconds. With a slotted spoon or spatula, transfer the leaves to the paper-lined platter and set aside to cool.
3. In a medium bowl, toss the **grapes** with the 1 teaspoon of **citrus-rosemary salt**, **black pepper**, **lemon zest**, **lemon juice** and the remaining ¼ cup of **olive oil**.
4. Add the crisp rosemary leaves and toss. Chill salad until quail is ready.

QUAIL
1. If using wooden skewers, soak 12 skewers in cool water for 30 minutes while you work on the birds.
2. Prepare the **quail** by removing the wing at the first joint (or have your butcher do this for you). Leave the drumstick portion of the wing.

CONTINUED...

SUGGESTED WINE VARIETALS

WHITE
Chardonnay \ Pinot Blanc \
Pinot Gris \ Rosé (dry) \
Riesling (dry) \ Sauvignon Blanc

RED
Grenache \ Merlot \ Pinot Noir \
Rhone Blend

3. If using green branches, skewer the **quails** using at least two thin sharp branches per bird to hold it firmly above the fire. If using skewers, use two skewers per bird, and form a criss-cross with the skewers by inserting one from the quail's right wing to the left leg and the other from the left wing to the right leg. Work so that the skewers are held in place by the legs and wing joints.
4. Rub each bird with **olive oil**, about 1 teaspoon per bird and season with the **citrus-rosemary salt**.
5. Stand the ends of the skewers in pots of sand next to the fire. Cook for about 3 minutes on each side, or until the juices run clear when you cut into a thigh (just as you'd chicken).
6. Allow the quail to cool for a few minutes and then take them off the branch or remove the skewers, twisting them slowly so they don't tear the meat.

TO SERVE
Place one quail on each plate and spoon some of the grape salad beside it.

Adapted from *Michael Chiarello's Live Fire: 125 Recipes for Cooking Outdoors*, Chronicle Books 2013.

Braised Grouse with Bacon and Sage

WILD HARVEST TABLE

Ruffed grouse have been called "Wild Chicken of the Adirondacks" or "road chicken" and indeed you can substitute wild caught grouse in most chicken recipes. Grouse roasts nicely and can also be sautéed (think Grouse Marsala). Keep in mind that grouse has less fat than domesticated chicken and is smaller, so cooking time may vary from a chicken recipe. Chicken recipes that cook with liquid (braising or sauces) are often a good way to cook grouse to insure moistness. The following recipe brings out all of the delicious flavor of grouse.

1. Preheat oven to 325°F.
2. In a large, oven-proof skillet (i.e. cast iron fry pan) fry the **bacon** until almost crisp but not overly browned, over medium-high heat. Remove bacon and set aside. Leave 1 to 2 tablespoons of the bacon drippings in the pan and discard the rest.
3. Place the **grouse breasts** in the pan and brown them quickly, about 2 minutes per side. Remove the grouse from the skillet and wrap each grouse breast with 2 pieces of bacon, securing them with a toothpick if necessary.
4. Add the **remaining ingredients**, except the flour, to the pan and scrape up any bits off the bottom of the skillet with a wooden utensil. Remove from heat and add the grouse back to the pan. Place the oven-proof skillet in the preheated oven and roast uncovered for 45 minutes. When done, remove the grouse from the pan and keep warm on a separate plate loosely covered with aluminum foil.
5. Put the skillet on a burner over medium heat and whisk the flour into the pan juices, stirring constantly until thickened.

TO SERVE
This dish tastes excellent over wild rice. Serve the pan gravy over the grouse breasts.

4 Grouse breast halves, boneless and skinless

8 Slices of bacon

1 Cup chicken broth

1 Cup white wine

½ Cup shallot, chopped, or ¼ cup red onion, chopped

4 Cloves garlic, chopped

½ Teaspoon salt

1 Tablespoon fresh sage, chopped

Ground black or white pepper, to taste

3 Tablespoons flour

SUGGESTED WINE VARIETALS

WHITE
Chardonnay \ Pinot Blanc \ Marsanne \ Viognier

RED
Cabernet Franc \ Merlot \ Pinot Noir \ Zinfandel

Processing

Wild Game Processing, Preparation and Cuts

CHEF DANIEL NELSON

PHOTOGRAPHS BY MATTHEW WESENER

I have always loved being in the kitchen. And coming from a hardworking two-income home, my mother was more than willing to share the cooking duties. I can remember standing on a stool so I could reach the stovetop to cook spaghetti—and the joy I got from making it as good as my mother did. My father and I would watch some TV while my brothers did the dishes; he would look over from his satisfied recline to say, "Dan, you're going to make a great wife some day." He wasn't prone to compliments, and they were always similarly hidden within some patronizing sarcasm, but it meant a lot to me and certainly inspired me more than he knows.

I got my first kitchen job at 14. I didn't stay in the dish tank long, though I never really considered being a chef as a profession. The old adage that the most rewarding careers come from working in a field which you are passionate about rarely crosses the mind of the college-bound. I came close to making the choice to go to culinary school the summer after high school graduation. I took a job working in the kitchen of Master Chef Dave Minor. His restaurant, Old Dixie Inn, featured exotic wild game and was a destination for hunters across the state. Chef Minor was a generous man, taking the time to teach and refine my technique by letting me eat off the menu every work day—great meals of zebra, lion, ostrich, snake, and of course, venison. But the allure of cooking wild game for a living was overshadowed by the millions I planned to make as a corporate lawyer, so I left for Michigan State University to study liberal arts. However, I never left the kitchen, quickly finding a job at a small French bistro, and in my junior year, with Columbus restaurant mogul Cameron Mitchell. As I approached graduation and began looking into law school, the thought of stretching my student loan debt into the six-figure mark during the worst economic conditions in decades was quickly eroding my desire to chase white-collar fortunes.

Fortunately, restaurant work is one of the last few vestiges of true meritocracy; hard work and attention to detail often shine brighter than a well-framed culinary degree. I was in line to become an executive chef and happy enough with my situation to decide to take a sabbatical from school to reassess my goals. I took a second part-time job at Eagle Eye Golf Club, hoping that if I worked a couple doubles a week I could golf for free on my one day off. Eagle Eye had just opened and was being touted as one of the best public upscale golf clubs in the country, and the 65,000 square-foot banquet facilities overlooking this well-manicured landscape proved to be a perfect combination for success. The course had a single family proprietorship, which was a welcomed reprieve from the high-stress, profit- and loss-driven world of corporate restaurants. The owners, the

Processing, Preparation and Cuts

Kesler family, had been in the community for generations and had run a successful building and excavating company for decades. They were also exceptionally avid hunters and leaders in many conservation groups. When first meeting them, I mentioned that I, too, loved to hunt—and especially cook—wild game, and after some good conversation, I was given permission to hunt some prime spots of their land. I quickly realized the opportunity I had before me and jumped at the offer to become the director of food and beverage when it was offered. The Kesler's generosity towards conservation groups quickly made Eagle Eye the home to nearly every hunting banquet in the county. Every year for the last decade I have had the pleasure and fortune to host multiple wild game dinners for groups as large as 700, as well as dozens of conservation fundraisers. This consistent association with groups such as Michigan Duck Hunters, Pheasants Forever, Safari Club International, Whitetails Unlimited, National Wild Turkey Federation, and many others, has instilled in me a passion for new hunter recruitment, and I have found no better tool for that than exposing the non-hunters in the healthy, local and sustainable food movement to just how delicious wild game can be.

Chefs are quite often asked, "What is your best/favorite recipe?" or "What is the best meal you have ever had?" I often give them some rendition of the following:

One unseasonably warm Thanksgiving, after a final serving of my grandmother's perfect pie, as my uncles lazed, sleeping through afternoon football, my cousins and I soaked up the last warm rays the sun was going to offer for the next few months. I was 16, so nearly everything I could need in life was in my powder blue '81 Monte Carlo. Popping the trunk, digging under my hunting gear, I found a few shag balls, grabbed a few clubs and started rifling them into the cornstalk-studded field.

Suddenly, a shotgun blast thundered across the empty farmland, frantically followed by two more. After a short pause, one final desperate discharge rang out. Hurrying back to my open trunk, with hopeful thoughts of a distracted buck fleeing in my direction, I unzipped the faded brown soft case of my 870, slid it out and filled the chamber. I looked up to find a bewildered four point standing broadside a mere 20 yards away. Aiming well, I squeezed the trigger tighter and tighter. It wasn't until the deer had grasped my lethal intention that I realized my safety was still on. "Shoot!" screamed the steady stream of uncles and cousins now pouring from the front door. I clicked the safety off and wrestled the sights back towards the center mass of the now quartering-away buck. The blast buried into both our shoulders, and my first buck tumbled down in a dusty cloud. Now, in the days before cell phone photos and the ease of gloating through social media, if weather permitted, and sometimes when it didn't, country boys drove their trophy, tailgate down, at least until the end of the following school day where parking lot revelry could not be beat. But weather was not permitting, and before I could ask my dad for his keys, grandpa had came up from the barn with his hatchet and blade, handles worn from the countless meals they carved from bone in the first half of the century. Placing the sharp blade in my hand, and his critical eye over my shoulder, surrounded by the chaos of nieces and nephews clamoring about, we field dressed the young buck and had it to the butcher before the evening's leftovers were served. The German butcher in nearby Frankenmuth did wonderful things with that venison *and everything I made with it was likely one of the best meals of my life.*

Every recipe in this book has the opportunity to be the best meal you have ever made, if you can connect it to your personal narrative through hunting and harvesting. However, our culture has for generations been removed from this connection to land and meat. The years of ignorance with which we have consumed our meat, void of any end-user processing and with an apathy to the life conditions in which it was produced, have left many without the skill set— or desire—to harvest and prepare their own meat. Thankfully there is a social renaissance of the hunter-gatherer or farm-to-table food paradigm of generations past. Consumers are demanding healthy, local, and sustainable foods, especially foods that are raised organically or ethically, and they are willing to pay much more to obtain them. This surge in concern for the quality of life of our groceries has been strong enough to transform the food production industry and change the menus of the most successful restaurants in the world. I remember the first time, probably around the turn of this century, a major food service company brought in a market representative for a chief beef producer touting their new line of "natural beef." I was quite sure of what "natural" meant to me and just as certain that any commercial beef was far from it. I asked the enthusiastic salesman to explain what made his particular beef natural and set it apart from the "unnatural" competitors. He quickly handed me the company's glossy colored brochure, pointing out the organic grass-fed diet and hormone-free raising of their top-quality beef. I wasn't persuaded.

Do the cows graze on natural prairie grasses? Are they left to fight the pangs of hunger if the dry heat of summer turns their grass to dust? Are they left to sexually mature as nature intended it? What becomes of the male calves? Are they free of antibiotic injections? If so how do they fight disease, when centuries of domestication and decades of antibiotic use have left major breeds without any natural immunity?

Don't get me wrong, I understand the necessity of corporate commodity production, and it is hard to imagine what prices and availability would be if the industry wasn't so efficient, but I couldn't let this salesman leave my kitchen thinking he was selling truly natural meat. I was amazed over the next five or so years, as "natural" products kept finding their way to market shelves, but finally consumer knowledge caught up with the "natural" marketing campaign and corporations could no longer trick us into believing that "less synthetic" could justly be defined as truly natural.

Truly natural protein lives unabridged in nature, suffering and thriving with times of famine and bounty; it has undergone no domestication and overcomes or succumbs to nature's law every single day. Hunters bear witness to this struggle, and when they decide to take nature's law into their own hands and harvest a wild animal, the solemnity is only truly justified by ensuring that the meat goes to good use. Fortune and circumstance were mostly responsible for my first buck, but the warm temperatures of that harvest season could have easily sent the meat on a bacterial journey towards a 120-pound pile of inedible protein. Thankfully, the familial knowledge I had around me helped ensure I field dressed that deer successfully. I am deeply indebted to my uncle for his tip to quickly take the dressed deer to the butcher's cooler. Not only did it ensure the meat was processed cleanly and packaged correctly, but the two weeks' pay I owed the butcher encouraged me to learn to do it myself. I offered as often as I could to help friends, family, and neighbors process their deer, and it was most often cheerfully accepted. Learning to process large game in the school of hard knocks was quite enlightening; and often disheartening. The volunteer butcher is often compensated with hop pops (beer) and a few pounds of venison steaks, which is quite helpful in tasting for the best methods of processing. The sad thing was, bad-tasting wild game seemed more common than good.

I can remember only managing a few bites of a deer from the harvest of a neighbor who felt that aging wasn't complete until a good film of mold developed. I still shudder thinking of the rancid smell emanating from his deer which hung in front yard trees. Unfortunately, foul-tasting game meat is often consumed by non-hunters, given to them by an uncle or friend looking to clear some space in their deep freezer, as it is often so poorly processed and freezer burned that their family hasn't been able to consume it all. Luckily, if you are willing to get your hands dirty and can manage a few key factors from field to freezer, fetid-tasting wild game doesn't have to be your lot. I will share with you my favorite wild game recipe—a recipe for success. I have found that this recipe consistently produces clean, palatable game meat that your entire family is sure to enjoy.

What is Success? Success is that rewarding guttural satisfaction a hunter gets from sharing delicious game with their family and friends at the dinner table, bringing together the joy of conservation and consumption. Far too often I hear stories of outdoor enthusiasts who, after their first few successful hunts, eventually stopped, because time and again they were wasting meat. Choosing to give up an enjoyable hobby because one feels so regretful for wasting the food it produces shows how deep our personal connection is to the animals we hunt. In the same manner, if a hunter and family are avid consumers of the meat they hunt, it always seems to drive them to a deeper more meaningful relationship with conservation. Choose to make dinner one of your core connections to hunting, and with time and experience you will begin to serve some of the best stories of your life.

My Favorite Recipe: Success for MEAT
MICROORGANISMS
EXPOSURE
FAT
TEMPERATURE

Successful field processing starts by going into each hunt prepared to care for your harvest from the moment you take its essence until the moment you consume it.

There are four main ingredients to proper care that you must consider in the first moments after you harvest your game: microorganisms, exposure, fat, and temperature. Mistakes in these first crucial hours can irreparably affect the taste and safety of the entire animal. Much of what you need to do in the field will depend on the length of time before you can get your harvest to your final processing area. If you are a short walk away from your vehicle and plan to return to your home for processing in a short time span, then you should keep the work done in the field to a minimum, as it is much more difficult to control the variables of success in the open field. The further you have to travel from your hunting area, the more difficult your field processing will be. I always have, at minimum, the necessary tools to gut my quarry. For me, this is a sharp knife, preferably with a skinning hook; three to six plastic bags for keeping offal, protecting meat from exposure, and collecting trash; a stack of paper towels; several pairs of vinyl gloves; a good length of rope.

I have found that a properly assembled field-processing tool kit is the best measure you can take to ensure you are prepared for success. If you take this gear bag on all your hunts, the worst you will be is over-prepared. I have separate totes for each of my favorite game to hunt. If weight of gear is a concern, try packing in only the essentials for gutting and removing your game to your finish processing area. When scent control is a concern, I will pack these essentials in a carbon scent bag and leave it a safe distance downwind.

MICROORGANISMS

Your first care after finding your harvest is to check the integrity of the meat. The safety of your harvest can be jeopardized by two major factors: length of time the carcass was at a temperature higher than 45°F and a break in the guttural integrity. Both of these factors are crucially controlled by the kill shot on the animal. When you have a quick, clean kill, not only have you been witness to the final moments of life, but typically the wound path is no where near the guttural area, so it is in your best interest to choose only the best of kill shots.

I will try to take the temperature of any harvest that has been left to expire for any length of time over six hours. Harmful bacteria, parasites, and other microorganisms thrive at temperature above 70°F and will continue to survive until 40°F; some parasites even require deep freezing below −10°F. It is easy enough to bring a small digital thermometer when you go back to track. Once you find your harvest, you want to take the internal temperature of the meat in the deep thigh; this is the thickest part of the animal and will be the last to cool completely. The colder it is outside, the longer you can wait before tracking, but don't be fooled by mild temperatures. The hide of large game is especially prone to retaining warmth, and I have measured core muscle temperatures above 70°F four hours postmortem even in zero-degree conditions.

The contents of the alimentary canal, running from mouth to anus, should never be allowed to come in contact with the flesh of your game. There are many bacteria and parasites that live in the nether regions of the bowel, and they can ruin your harvest in no time. I gut all of the animals I harvest in the field, even fowl and small game. Gutting your quarry removes a large quantity of hot organs as well as the main source of bacterial contamination. It also creates a large cavity to aide in cooling your game.

FIELD PROCESSING TOOL KIT

- Skinning knife, boning knife, game shears, knife sharpener, hand-held zip/bone saw
- Digital thermometer
- Disposable vinyl gloves, disposable plastic aprons
- Box of paper towels that can be individually drawn out like tissue—this helps ensure you are not contaminating a whole roll of towels when trying to remove a sheet
- Several sizes of thick, plastic bags (black preferred, because exposure to light, especially ultraviolet light, can brown out the color of flesh and accelerate the development of rancidity in fat)
- Zip ties, rope, hanging pulley, gambrel
- Heavy drag-out bag designed for hauling large game from woods
- Adequately sized coolers, hard plastic freezer bricks, dry ice
- Collapsible shovel

Processing, Preparation and Cuts

FIELD DRESSING YOUR ANIMAL

1. Begin by closing off the anus. To do this, you will need to cut the flesh around the end of the large intestine.
2. Once the intestine is free of connective tissue you can pull out the end and seal it tightly with a zip tie or piece of string.
3. With the animal on its side and in the cleanest area you are near, start at the base of the sternum, cut through just the skin of the stomach and work back towards the rear of the animal. With a little experience, you will be able to tell when enough of the dermal layers have been cut.
4. Work the forward portion of the offal onto the ground and cut the diaphragm open.
5. Work a knife high onto the esophagus and cut it through. Grabbing the top of the lungs and heart, pull diligently until all organs pull from the chest cavity and can be pulled out your stomach incision. With the anus cut free and closed off, you should be able to pull the intestines and all the organs of the rear out as well.
6. Clean all the offal you can use for dinner or give to a friend to use and put each into its own dark, heavy, plastic bag, remove all the air from the bag, and tie shut. It is best to dispose of unwanted offal by digging a small hole and burying it. If the area you are in is remote private land you may consider leaving it for scavengers. I prefer to bury mine to avoid affecting future hunting by myself or others from the presence of scavenger scent.
7. Once your animal is gutted, wipe dry the inside of the cavity. Do not wash out with water! Bacteria thrive only in wet conditions and it is best to simply dry the cavity out to prevent the bacteria from spreading.

EXPOSURE

Now that you have removed the major sources of contamination that exist within the animal, you must address the possibility of contamination from outside. There are innumerable sources of contamination in nature, from bugs, dirt—even air. I always do my best to close off the chest cavity from these bacteria sources. For large game, I prefer to put the entire animal in a body bag. These heavy-duty, sealable bags are great for keeping out contaminants and they really help make dragging large game easier. I will often stuff the cavity of smaller game and fowl completely with rags to help prevent any buildup of moisture and guard against dirt and germs.

As soon as the last heartbeat thumps from the chest of your harvest, the natural process of decay begins, and the only way to slow it is by bringing the core temperature down. Again, heat only travels from areas of high concentration to areas of low concentration, so the ice packs do not necessarily cool the meat; rather heat leaves the muscle to warm the ice packs. This means that you want to remove any barriers to heat energy and reduce the distance needed to travel to reach the ice packs. The empty chest cavity is an excellent place to begin to cool your game. I prefer to use hard-frozen ice packs. The dense material in these ice packs lasts much longer than ice, and the hard protective plastic makes them easy to clean and reuse. I often have a small cooler loaded with these frozen packs and topped off with a couple pounds of dry ice. The extreme cold of the dry ice will sink down into the cooler keeping the packs hard frozen. If you have a very efficient cooler, you can even put in a completely thawed pack and refreeze it. Keep these packs pressed against the flesh of the cavity as the contact with muscle will aid in the transfer of heat. If I have a few hours' time before I begin processing the animal, I will put an ice pack in the armpit of each leg and between the thighs to help cool these muscle-dense areas more rapidly. If you are hunting in high temperature conditions (55°F and above) you should make every effort possible to get to your harvest quickly and begin removing heat as rapidly as possible.

Once you have taken control of the microorganisms, exposure, and temperature, your game is ready to drag out of the woods. You don't necessarily want to process the animal any further until you are in a cleaner, more controlled environment. If you have a lot of demands on your time and cannot finish butchering the animal in a timely manner, then I suggest you are always knowledgeable of a close and reputable butcher. If you can get your game to the butcher within the next few hours, you are all set! This is the point at which I handed my first deer over to a butcher and the quality and usefulness of the meat changed my life. Any trustworthy butcher will take great care of your game and deliver the exact cuts you ask for. Take the time to talk to your butcher and let him know what your family will find most useful. Perhaps it will be a lot of ground venison for quick family meals, large muscle roasts for special occasions or a big pile of jerky to snack on for the next year. Many deer processors are also quite capable and willing to handle your other game meats as well. It may be the first time they have been asked to process squirrel, pheasant, or duck, but if you talk to them, establish a relationship and are clear with what you want, I am sure that you will find most eager to help you.

FAT

Wild game fat is not something that I used to give much thought, but as I began to delve deeper into the components of quality tasting wild game, I found that not all fat is created equal. Fat quality is a major contributor to the resulting "gameyness" of wild meat. The best wild fats come from non-diving ducks and geese; some of the worst fats are in cervids

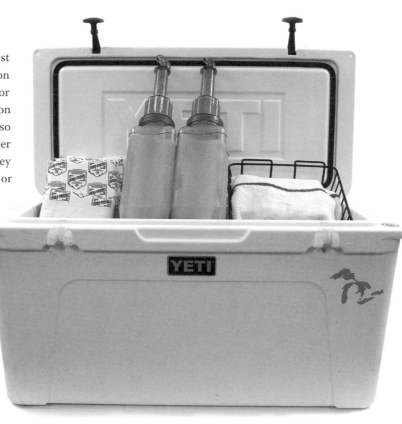

(venison) and mammalian males. Adipose tissue or fat stores many of the minerals and hormones in the body, and in nature, these flavors can be quite overwhelming. It is important to know the quality of fat specific to the game you are harvesting. If you are dealing with the high quality fat of ducks and geese—even squirrel, rabbit, bear, or wild boar—then it will be in your interest to keep the fat on the animal (as long as it is kept cold) until you process it. If you are dealing with poor quality fats like venison and elk, or the high hormone-laden fat of mammalian males, it is important that you remove as much of the fat as possible as quickly as possible. I am not suggesting that you throw this fat away; keep it. It still has useful and delicious capabilities, and splitting the fat and flesh will give you more control over the flavor of your dishes.

I always skin my venison and mammalian males. The skin of all game is covered in a thin layer of adipose and until that fat completely hardens (40°F) the flavor profile is constantly seeping into the flesh. Even the energy from sunlight is sufficient to thaw dermal fat enough that flavor transfer quickens. The strong glands of male animals is particularly pungent and this scent can be off-putting enough to make some unwilling to eat the meat.

It is best to leave the hide on while in the field as the damage from microorganisms is worse than the detriments of fat. But once you are in a clean and manageable environment, remove the hide from these animals as quickly as possible. Keep the flesh from drying out by covering the muscle with plastic wrap or plastic bags. If I am deep in the heart of Michigan's Upper Peninsula, far from the clean sanctuary of my processing room, I will break the carcass into manageable sections, usually consisting of the neck, chuck/grinding meat, plates/

Processing, Preparation and Cuts

Both at 180°F
Both fats are thin and clear.

Both at 95°F
Elk fat begins to coagulate.

Duck Fat at 85°F vs. Elk Fat at 95°F
The congealed elk fat will lose heat more slowly than the liquid duck fat.

Duck Fat at 80°F vs. Elk Fat at 94°F
Even as the duck fat continues to cool it thickens only slightly,
while the elk fat continues to solidify with each degree of cooling.

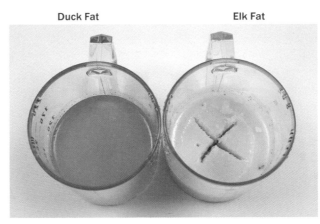

Duck Fat at 70°F vs. Elk Fat at 85°F
The elk fat has become solid enough to cut.

flanks, rib meat, loins, rounds, shanks/bones. I place each group into large black plastic bags (remove all the air) and seal, then layer in a large cooler with hard frozen ice packs. No buck-pole sunlight is going to taint the quality of the flesh this animal worked so hard to produce; my delicious dinner will age just beautifully tucked away in the cold, dark cooler.

Wild game does not often suit traditional consumer butchering, cutting whole muscle groups into the individual steaks and roasts we see in grocery isles. Domestic meats are better suited for whole roasts or large crosscuts of complete muscle groups or individual steaks because they have a much higher and more palatable fat content. This added fat helps negate the toughness of intramuscular sinew and keeps the mouth moist while chewing. It also makes for a much more forgiving meat, which can be cooked well-done and still be reasonably tasty. Without this fat, the connective tissue can easily become a rubber band and if the meat is overcooked; it becomes stuck in an arid and burdensome oral desert.

Fat, temperature, connective tissue, and muscle grain must always be under constant care when cooking and serving wild game, so it is necessary to understand them before processing your game. Using this information, we can better cut and package meat in a manner which will produce the best quality cuts that you are confident in using.

The high quality fat with which our culinary world is so familiar only exists because centuries of domestication have selected for it. We have fats and oils uniquely favored for every sumptuous quality this delicious ingredient has to offer. Because all fats are not created equal, each has its own particular qualities which will dictate its best use.

The first quality of fat I look for is its melting point. The higher the melting point, the higher the amount of heat the fat is capable of withstanding. However, these high melting-point fats, particularly with wild game, will remain thick and solid at room temperature. When these fats are served in your game dishes, the liquid fat will congeal in the mouth and leave a heavy, gamey, fatty taste which can ruin the whole meal. Lower melting-point fats cannot withstand high heat, but are generally light and soft on the palate at room temperature.

DUCK FAT VERSUS ELK FAT

High-temperature cooking fats, like venison, are best suited for frying and searing. Using these fats at the right time and temperature can add an incredibly deep savory flavor to your favorite dish. I love to use two parts vegetable oil and one part venison fat for frying French fries. I also keep a solid block of venison or bear fat in the freezer and use it to slick the grates on a searing hot grill. Lower-temperature fats, like those from the non-diving duck, goose, squirrel, rabbit, young female bear and wild boar are perfect for adding the wet, juicy qualities back into any game dish. The best fats from duck and goose can even be used for cold cooking applications like salad dressings.

TEMPERATURE

Most wild game, unless it is being braised in liquids, should be cooked to rare or medium-rare (110°F to 135°F). Heat is obviously very damaging to protein, so we must do all we can to avoid using too much. We have all seen the affects of

Processing, Preparation and Cuts

Roasting at too high a temperature or beginning at a raw core temperature below 40°F can significantly diminish the percentage of perfectly cooked meat (left); whereas proper roasting temperatures and a raw core temperature from 55°F to 70°F will yield much better results (right).

Large grilled steaks have much longer grains of muscle fiber and will yield a much smaller amount of perfectly cooked meat (A), than a large grilled loin which is carved for service (B).

heat on muscle fibers—each time you add a steak to a hot frying pan you see the surface tighten and contract. Overcooking your venison will create an excessive amount of tension, which in turn, pushes the juices right out of the steak. There are several things you can do to avoid overcooking your game.

Rest your meat before you cook it. Pulling your roast from refrigeration an hour or two before cooking will allow the internal temperature to rise from 40°F to a more manageable 55°F to 70°F. A smaller range of temperature travel to 110°F will allow you to make a larger percentage of rare meat. Only the red portion of the roast has been cooked to rare; all the brown meat has been overcooked.

Reduce the amount of meat exposed to the heat of the oven, pan or grill. Heat must travel from the outer edges of the meat into the center, so the outer edges essentially get overcooked while you raise the internal temperature. This is

good reason to avoid cooking individual steaks of venison; all the exposed sides of the steak are being overcooked, limiting the total amount of rare meat. However, if the muscle is left intact and cooked whole, you can greatly reduce the exposed surface area of the meat.

Rest your meat after you cook it. Heat energy will always travel from areas of high concentration to areas of low concentration. Since the surface and first few centimeters of meat are overcooked (165°F, plus), that heat will continue to travel inward towards the cool center. In most instances, this heat travel will continue to cook the roast and raise the internal temperature another 5°F to 15°F. I recommend pulling 2- to 3-inch roasts at 105°F. Help the heat dissipate into the roast by keeping it in a warm area (120°F) or by placing a tinfoil tent over the roast. If you have overcooked your roast (140°F), you can avoid further cooking by letting it rest in a cool place where the heat will disperse out into the cool air and not inward. Resting your roasts after cooking also allows the built-up tension in the muscle fibers to diminish. If you cut into a roast fresh from the oven, that tension will squeeze all the juice from the meat and onto the cutting board. A well-rested roast can be completely carved without any significant liquid lost.

The cutting board with the roast that was rested stays dry while, the roast stays moist (top). The un-rested cutting board is drenched in the savory juices being squeezed from the roast (bottom).

Even when you want to slowly braise or stew game in liquids, you must be careful to avoid overcooking your game. Generally braising and stewing are cooking methods used on the tougher cuts of meat, like chuck or shank, which are heavily laced with sinew and fat. The objective is to raise the temperature of the meat over 170°F and hold it there for one to two hours. This time and temperature combination begins to break down the tougher connective tissues into shorter, more savory protein chains like glutamates. Domestic cuts of chuck and shank can handle being cooked at much higher temperatures because the meat is comprised of 15 to 30 percent fat. Wild meat, with its incredibly lean nature, is not so lucky. Take care to rest these meats prior to cooking to pull some of the chill out of it. Cook them very slowly at temperatures no greater than 225°F to help warm the entire dish evenly. Watch your internal temperature closely. I would even suggest buying a remote thermometer which will show you exactly where you are at, and once you have maintained the magical 170°F for 90 minutes, stop cooking. Pull the pot from the oven and let rest for another hour.

Processing, Preparation and Cuts

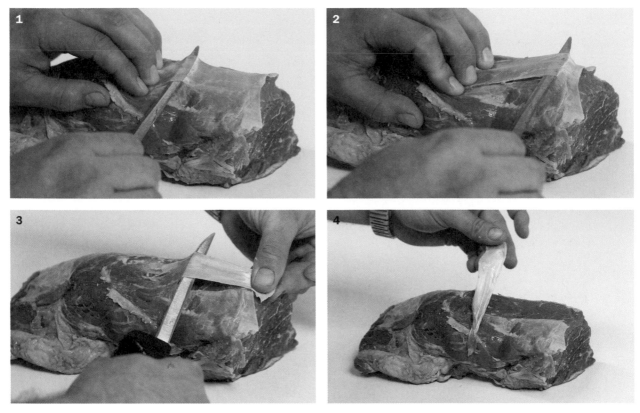

Steps for removing sinew.

More Tips for Processing Game

CONNECTIVE TISSUE AND SINEW

Connective tissue and sinew can easily be removed from each muscle before freezing or after thawing. There simply isn't enough fat or moisture in wild game to overcome the dry, rubbery texture of any sinew or connective tissue. Try to remove as much of this silvery skin as possible before cooking your game.

Using a sharp boning or filet knife, slide the knife just under the white strings of sinew (1) , angle the blade of the knife slightly upwards and push the blade forward (2 and 3). The sinew will cleanly separate from the muscle (4), repeat until all sinew has been removed.

MUSCLE GRAIN

Muscles are comprised of long fibrous grains that run in the direction that the muscle pulls or pushes. These fibers are very similar to those found in a tree. Imagine a 2x4, its strength comes from the long fibers of wood grain that run the length of the board. If we cut a quarter-inch strip lengthwise (with the grain), it cannot easily be broken in half, but if we cut a quarter inch off the end of the board (against the grain), it can be broken with ease. The same holds true for the muscle fibers and grain of meat. When carving roasts, you want to find the grain of the muscle and slice across them. The smaller the length of grain in your slice of meat, the more tender it will feel in the mouth.

Sliced kebab meat versus cubed meat.

The same perfectly cooked piece of meat can be rendered unimaginably tough by cutting it with the grain, because your teeth and jaw muscles will have to do the work that should have been done by the carving knife.

I use this same concept when cutting raw meat for quick-cooking methods. Using slightly frozen, uniform-grained, whole-muscle sections, you can thinly slice raw game meat across the grain to produce very tender petite filets perfect for hot-searing recipes like stir fry. I even cut the meat for grilling and kabobs in a similarly thin manner; two or three of these delicate slices are much easier to chew than one three-quarter-inch cube.

HOME PROCESSING

Once you have successfully brought your game out of the woods, you should begin work on butchering and storing this unique gift of nature as quickly as possible. If you again follow the recipe for success by controlling microorganisms, exposure, fat, and temperature, you will be able to produce delicious wild game capable of being substituted for domestic meat in many of your favorite recipes with great success.

The first step to home processing is to have an area dedicated to processing your game. This area should have:

– A large, hard-surfaced table at a height that is comfortable to use while standing. I prefer stainless steel because, with good care, it will provide a safe and durable work surface for as long as you want to keep it.
– Another area with a table that is comfortable for working while sitting down as some processing jobs require a lot of repetitive motion.
– Access to clean, running water and a large sink.
– Access to a chemical sanitizer such as bleach.
– Access to all the same equipment listed in the field processing section on page 141.
– A well-lit work area.
– All smooth surfaces that are easy to clean.
– Access to a large refrigerator and deep freezer.
– Both an outdoor and an indoor processing area so you can capitalize or avoid the advantages and disadvantages of the weather. Some jobs like skinning game, scaling fish or plucking ducks are just too messy to do inside.
– Ample plastic wrap, butcher paper and labeling tape.

Processing, Preparation and Cuts

MICROORGANISMS

The last vestige for dirt, debris, pests, and contaminants is the hide, skin or feathers of your game. Take care to remove it/them in an area far away from your final processing table, as hair, scales, and feathers are incredibly difficult to remove from the flesh of an animal. The necessary care for skin removal is covered in the individual game processing sections that follow.

Now that you have access to running water and a large sink, it is acceptable to rinse your game of any debris or contaminants it may have picked up in transport or while skinning. You should take particular care in cleaning the wound channel from your kill shot. Large-caliber and even small shot will drive hair, bone fragments and bacteria into the flesh of your game. Thoroughly inspect the wound for any contaminants and rinse well. Always rinse your game from top to bottom under running water, that way any bacteria will wash down and off the meat. Never use a tub of water to rinse game in, as the standing water will only serve to increase the risk of cross-contamination. Once the flesh of your game is completely rinsed clean, you will want to pat it dry with clean disposable towels and place it under refrigeration until you are ready to process it.

EXPOSURE

Always keep the flesh covered tightly with plastic film when processing. Exposure to air is a surefire way to degrade the quality of your game meat. Air will draw moisture out of your game meat and can often dry out the exposed surfaces so much so that they need to be trimmed and discarded. Contact with air will also start the oxidation process, which heightens the unwanted metallic taste of wild meats, discolors the meat to an unappetizing shade of reddish-brown, and can increase the development of rancidity in fat.

It is also extremely important to minimize exposure in the freezer. Using a high-quality vacuum-sealing machine is the most effective way to seal out air and freezer burn. However, plastic wrap and butcher's paper do a better job than a cheap vacuum sealer. Always wrap your finished cuts tightly in plastic wrap, then wrap again in butcher's paper. The plastic wrap protects the meat from exposure to air and freezer burn and the butcher's wrap will protect the integrity of the plastic wrap. To further reduce the possibility of freezer burn ruining more delicate meats like fish and fowl, I will often add 2 to 3 cups of lightly salted water to a heavy freezer bag along with the meat (see photos on the opposite page). When you remove the air from the bag and seal it, the brine will form an even better barrier between the flesh and the freezer.

Processing, Preparation and Cuts

FAT

Fat, regardless if it is high or low temperature, is extremely useful in the kitchen and should never be discarded. I am always amazed by the number of duck hunters who simply remove the breasts and discard the rest of their hard-fought harvest. Not only is there a tremendous abundance of delicious meat being wasted, it is also a great deal of the best cooking fat you can find. Fat can be rendered very easily and can be stored in the freezer for up to 6 months. Small amounts can be broken off the frozen block of rendered fat for use in recipes.

To render fat—collect all fat from the carcass, especially that near the backbone and ribs of the animal. It is okay if the fat has small amounts of meat still attached. (1) Place the fat in a large sauté pan and add just enough water to cover the bottom of the fat. This will protect the fat from sticking and burning to the bottom. (2) Over medium-low heat, warm the fat and liquefy its delicious contents. Be careful not to use too much heat as this will scald and potentially burn the fat. (3) The large pieces of fat will shrink as they liquefy. (4) Stop once the pieces have turned crisp and golden brown. To finish, filter the hot fat through a cheesecloth (opposite).

TEMPERATURE

It is crucial to keep your freshly harvested meat as cold as you can. If your game meat constantly stays around 40°F, you will significantly reduce the growth of any harmful bacteria and slow the transfer of poor tasting fat into the flesh.

Steps for rendering fat.

Filter the hot fat through a cheesecloth and store in an airtight container and freeze until needed.

Whenever possible, try to minimize the amount of time any particular cut of meat is being processed, and keep cuts of meat that are not being worked on stored in the refrigerator or in an ice chest.

It is very important to keep any meat which you plan on grinding extremely cold, even partially frozen. If you run warm meat through a grinder, the mixing and cutting of the soft tissue will make for a very pasty, bright pink and not-so-appetizing final product. Meat is best ground when it is partially frozen. Commercial grinders often add dry ice to their meat to keep the temperature from rising from the heat of the machine and the friction of the grinding process.

The following sections will specifically address the processing techniques used to butcher the four main groups of wild game: large game, small game, fish, and fowl. It is important to have the given types of cuts you want to produce from the game you hunt. If you can process and freeze your game according to the way you want to serve it and in the amount you want to serve, you will find that you are much better at incorporating game meat into your everyday meal plans.

Processing Rabbit

Working with small game is an excellent way to become familiar with gutting and processing. All gutting involves the same steps: sealing off the anus, cutting the diaphragm and esophagus, and pulling down and out to remove.

I recall my first foray with the hands-on realities of skinning and gutting. I was 14 or 15 and had been working the line at a deli in the mall that had sprung up and devoured the cornfields of our small town. One of my coworkers, Jeff, had a love of rabbit that was only outmatched by his love for the constant drone of beagles. After learning that much of the property surrounding the mall was in my family, it wasn't long before he and I had set up an evening hunt. This was my first experience hunting with dogs, and I was enthralled by the strategic circling and the suspense of the approaching pack. Just as impressive was the old .22 rifle Jeff carried in the field. I was hoping that I didn't make a fool of myself with the .410 shotgun I was sporting; if I had a .22, the rabbits' only worry would be the dogs. But with a sudden flash of white and one crisp pop from Jeff's .22, we had our first rabbit of the day. Jeff casually took the rabbit from the mouth of his best hound, and with a quick twist and jerk, removed the rabbit's head. He slid his fingers under the skin of the neck and near effortlessly cleared the hide with one steady pull. A swift clip from his pocket knife and he was three fingers deep in the chest cavity and promptly had the gut pile on the ground. I stood with awe as he dropped the fresh harvest into a plastic grocery bag and tied it to a belt loop. "Your turn next," he quipped, as we trudged off towards the next brush pile. By day's end I had it down, and I have since left several cousins and friends standing equally astonished with dinner in hand.

Rabbit processing tools—cleaver, boning knife, and game shears.

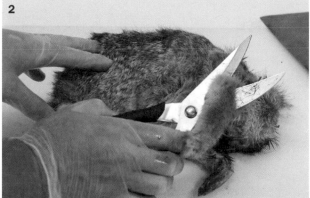

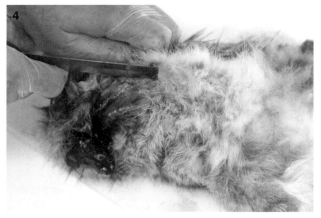

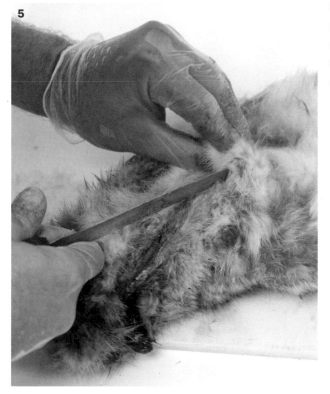

1. Begin by removing the head with the cleaver and discard. **2.** Next remove each front leg at the elbow with the game shears. **3.** Remove each back leg at the knee. Discard all the legs. **4.** Slice the hide, with the boning knife starting at the exposed neck. **5.** Continue slicing over the stomach, being careful to not cut into the paunch.

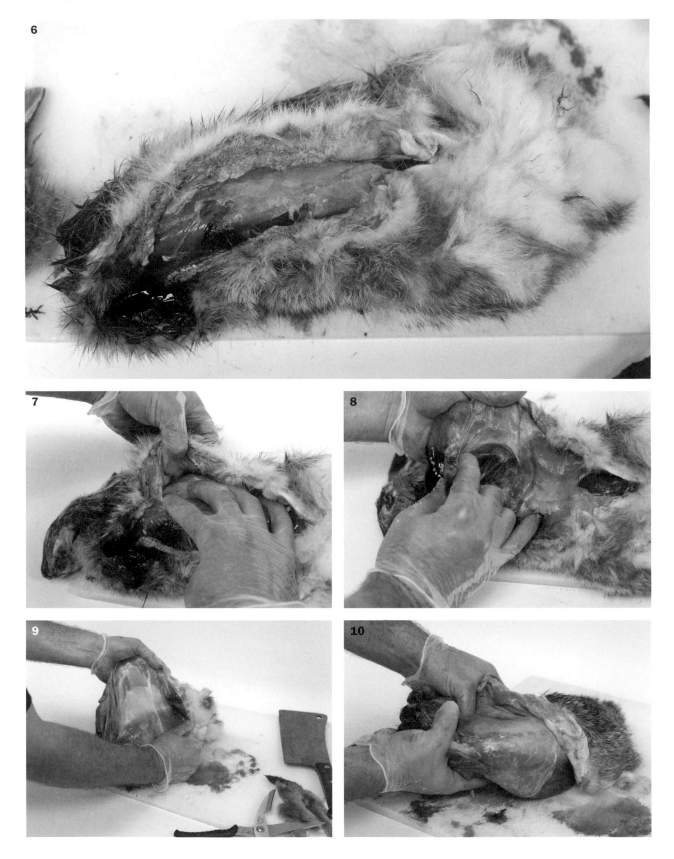

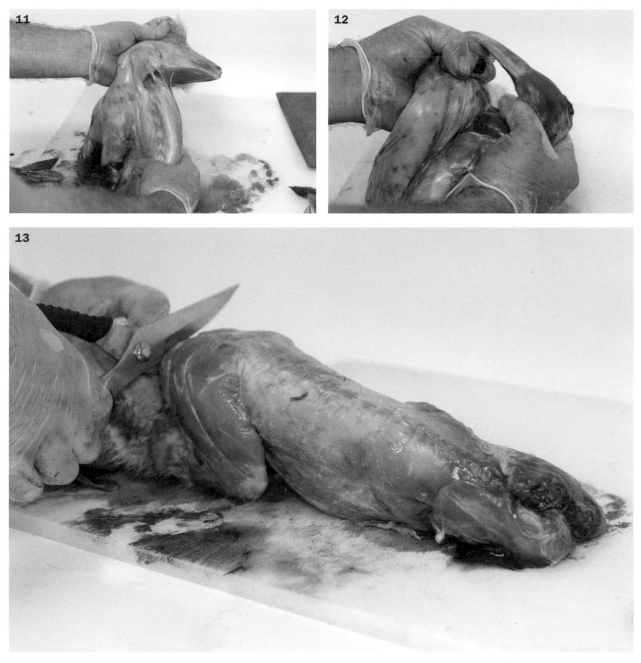

6. Cut through the hide all the way to the tailbone. **7.** Separate the carcass from the hide, pulling back the hide along the cut you just made. **8.** Back the neck out through the hide. **9.** Pull hide over and away from the back. **10.** Pull through each rear leg. **11.** Continue pulling hide back towards tailbone. **12.** Pulling through each rear leg. **13.** Remove hide at tailbone using the game shears.

Processing Rabbit

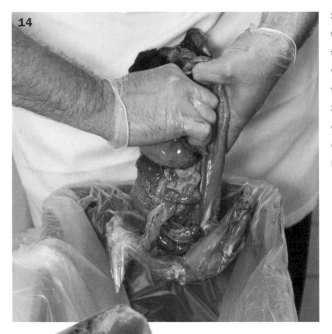

14. Discard all of the unwanted offal into the garbage. Be sure to save the heart and liver. **15.** Clean your work area of any stray hair and return the rabbit to a clean cutting board. **16.** Next cut through the sternum with the game shears. **17.** Slice through the flank skin, starting between the third and fourth rib bone from the end. **18.** Repeat on the other side. **19.** Cutting all the way up and through the flank skin. **20.** Cleave the rib cage and front legs by cutting down through the backbone. **21.** Cleave each rear leg from the loin near the hip bone. **22.** Separate the rear legs by cutting through the tailbone with the cleaver.

Heart

Liver

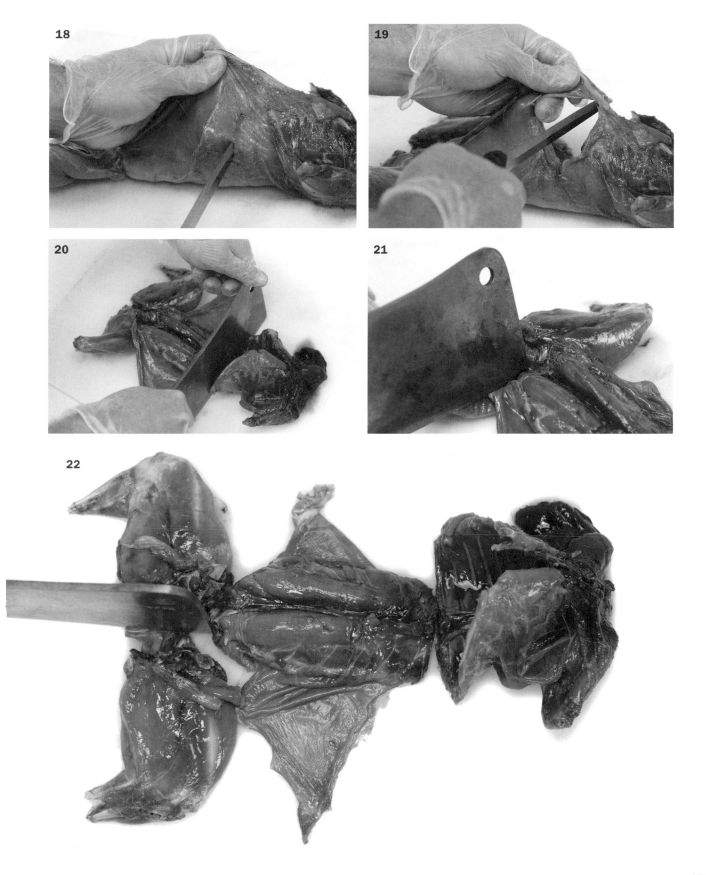

Processing Rabbit

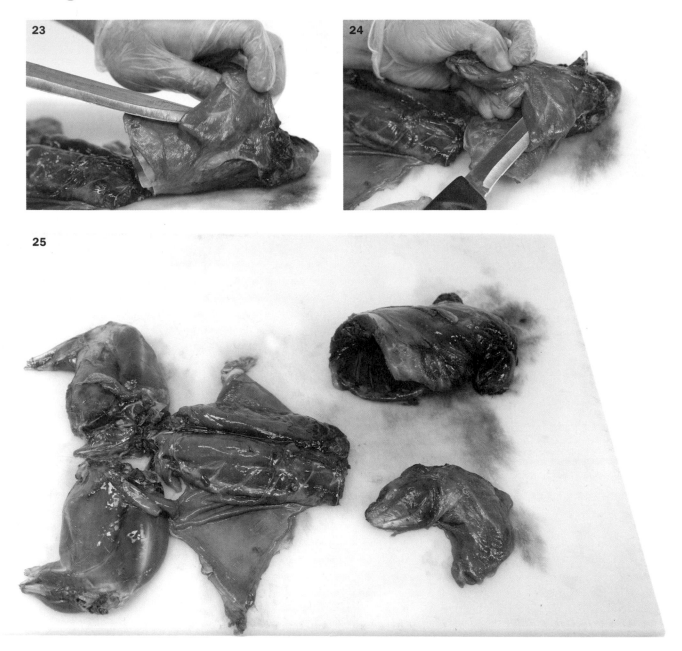

23. If you would like to remove the front legs, start cutting from under the leg with a boning knife. **24.** Hold the leg firmly and cut through the connective tissue holding the shoulder plate to the body. **25.** One rabbit yields two rear legs and thighs, one loin rack, one chest cavity, and two front legs.

Try Chef Jorge Morales' Chicken Fried Rabbit recipe on page 14.

Processing Squirrel

Contrary to rabbits, squirrels have one of the toughest hides to remove. It is easiest when your harvest is fresh, so try to skin it as quickly as possible. Squirrel hair also sticks incredibly well to flesh, so soaking the fur before processing can help keep stray hairs at bay.

Squirrel hunting is a one of my favorite things to do with young or new hunters. It provides many great learning opportunities, and one of my favorites is to show these beginners that squirrels are the only game we hunt that has a collar bone. All our other game species' front quarters can be removed without cutting through bone or socket, but not the squirrel. They have a collarbone much like ours, which connects the upper shoulder to the chest.

You'll need the following tools to process a squirrel—cleaver, boning knife, and game shears.

Processing Squirrel

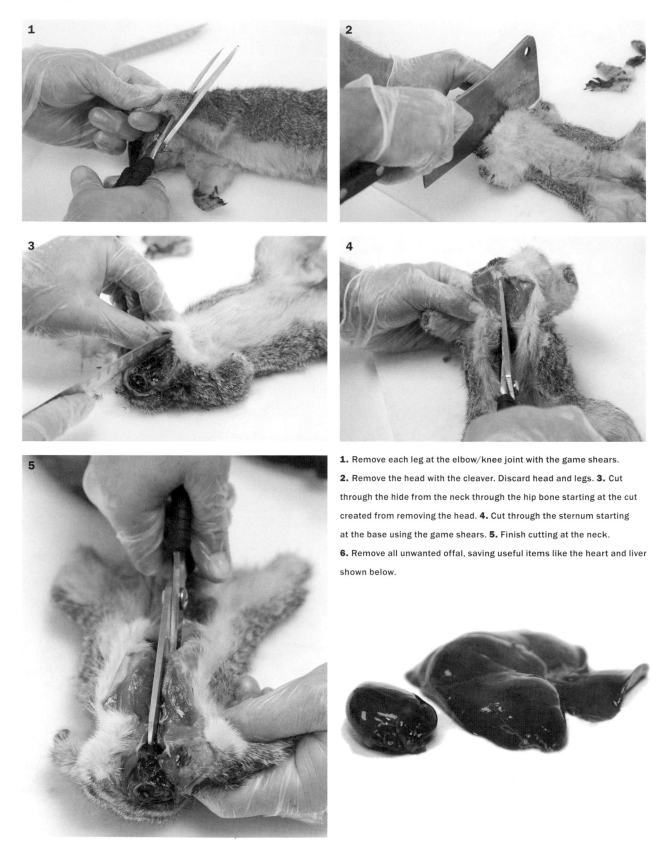

1. Remove each leg at the elbow/knee joint with the game shears.
2. Remove the head with the cleaver. Discard head and legs. 3. Cut through the hide from the neck through the hip bone starting at the cut created from removing the head. 4. Cut through the sternum starting at the base using the game shears. 5. Finish cutting at the neck.
6. Remove all unwanted offal, saving useful items like the heart and liver shown below.

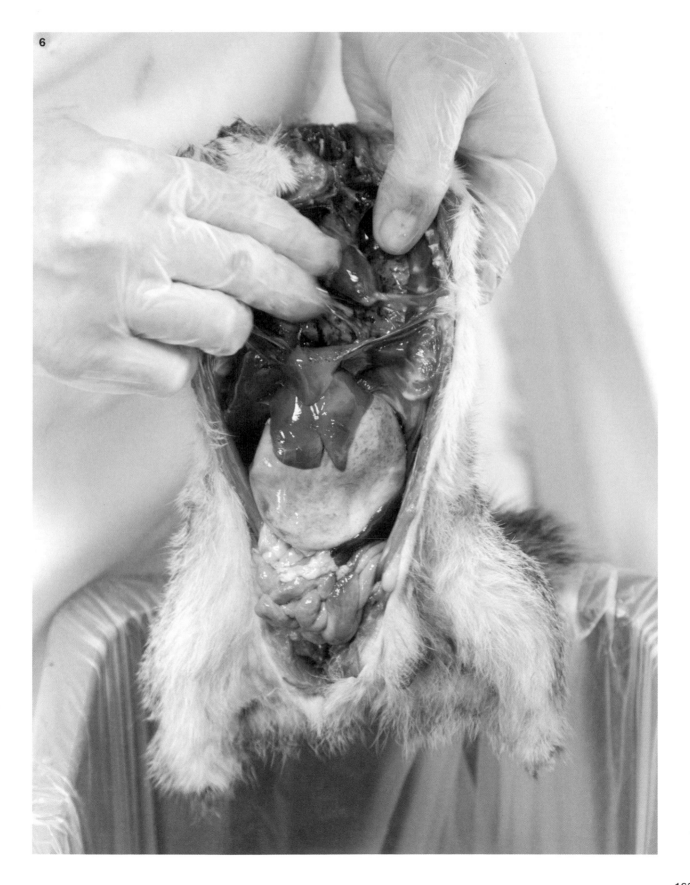

Processing Squirrel

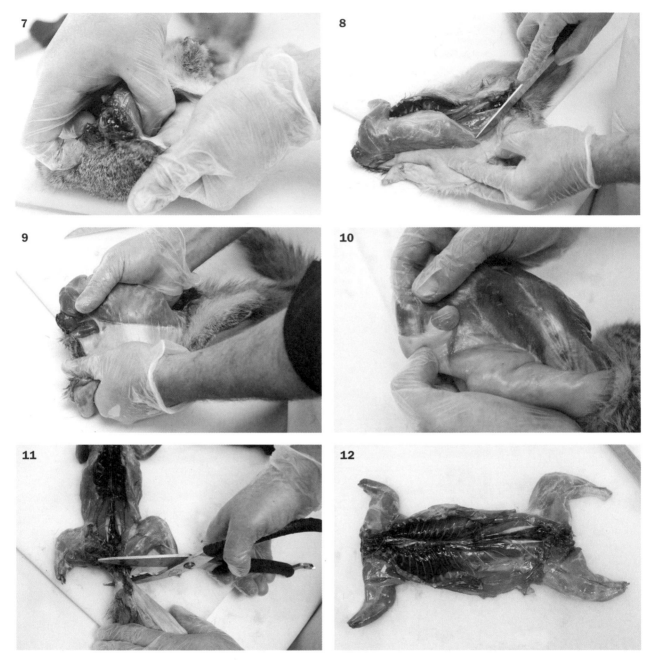

7. Begin peeling the hide back from the flesh starting at the neck. **8.** Use the boning knife to help separate well-attached hide. 9. Peel hide over the back. **10.** Pulling through each leg one at a time. **11.** Detach hide by cutting through at the tailbone. **12.** Clean any hair from your work area and return squirrel to a clean cutting board. **13.** Cut the flank meat between the third and fourth from the last rib bone. **14.** Using the cleaver separate the squirrel into four sections. **15.** One squirrel yields one sternum with front legs, one loin rack and two rear legs with thighs.

Wild Gourmet includes several squirrel recipes. Check out Hank Shaw's Braised Squirrel Aurora on page 7.

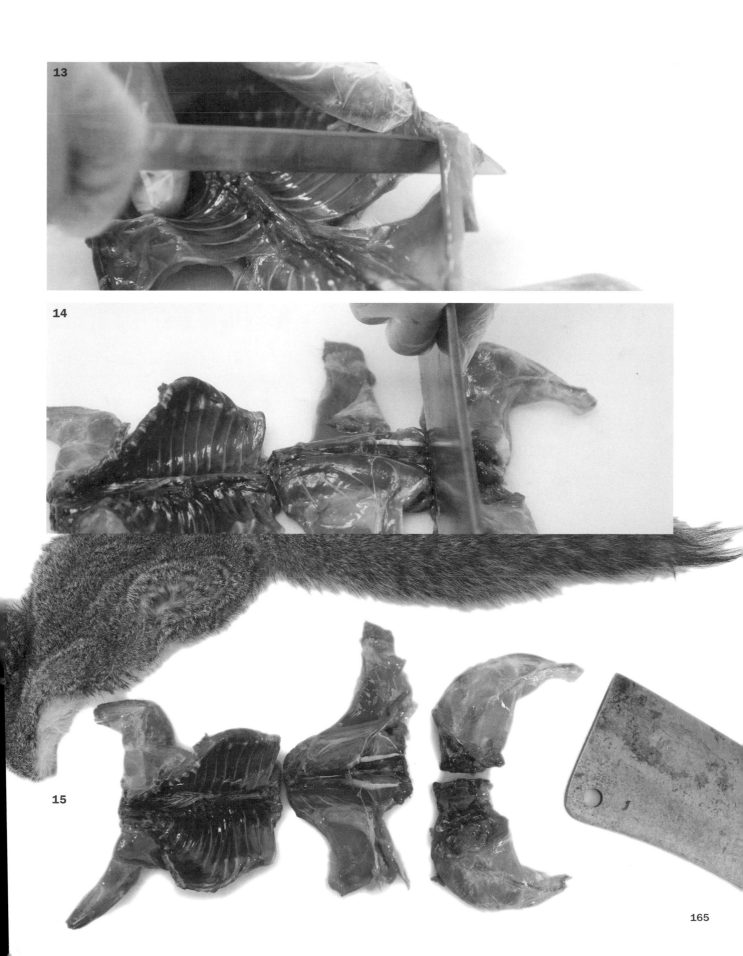

13

14

15

Processing Large Game

A) Traditional round steak

B) Large individual muscles

There are three major components to cooking and serving succulent and tender venison: removing all sinew, cooking to a desired doneness of rare or medium-rare, and crosscutting the grain of muscle fiber into as short of pieces as possible. All of these are done most effectively by separating each whole muscle from the surrounding muscles.

Instead of several large round steaks each comprising the individual muscles in a group (A); you will cleave each muscle from the others and be left with large individual muscles (B).

The sinew of the cross-cut round roast cannot easily be trimmed before cooking, which leaves the work of removing it to the knife of your guest—or worse, their teeth will have the arduous task of masticating it until they can swallow. Alternatively, the whole, individual muscles can be cleaned of excess sinew.

Butchering large animals this way is quite easy as each individual muscle will often separate from its neighbors without too much knife work. Simply follow each muscle to where it attaches to tendon, ligament, or bone, and cut that attachment. Working away from this attachment point, pull or cut the loose connective membrane that divides individual muscles. I cut each muscle into manageable dinner pieces—8 to 10 ounces per guest at your typical dinner table—before freezing. I do love the flavor that the bone and marrow impart on my venison roasts, so I always save the larger bones and incorporate them back into my recipes.

Working in this manner, you can segregate your venison cuts into major categories:
– Grinding venison
– Whole complete muscles, uniform in grain pattern and free of connective tissue
– Prime muscles, tenderloin, backstrap (strip loin and rib eye)
– Bones, offal, neck roast and shank

Outside of the prime muscles, intramuscular fat does not vary widely from cut to cut, so you shouldn't focus on defining each muscle. Rather, aim to create processed pieces that are uniform in grain pattern, free of connective tissue and sized according to your family's needs.

The hide is an exceptionally effective insulator and can hold in the heat of an animal much past an acceptable time frame. Also any sunlight or heat energy will be quickly transferred back into the flesh of your game. This warming of the fat layer just beneath the dermal layers of the hide can greatly affect the taste of your harvest as cervid fat holds much of the "gamey" qualities found in wild meat. I always skin my large game animals as quickly as possible to help cool the animal and to avoid the transfer of fatty tastes. Once the hide is removed you must take extra care to keep exposure to air and other contaminates at a minimum. Large, thick, black plastic bags are perfect for keeping your wild meat from drying out.

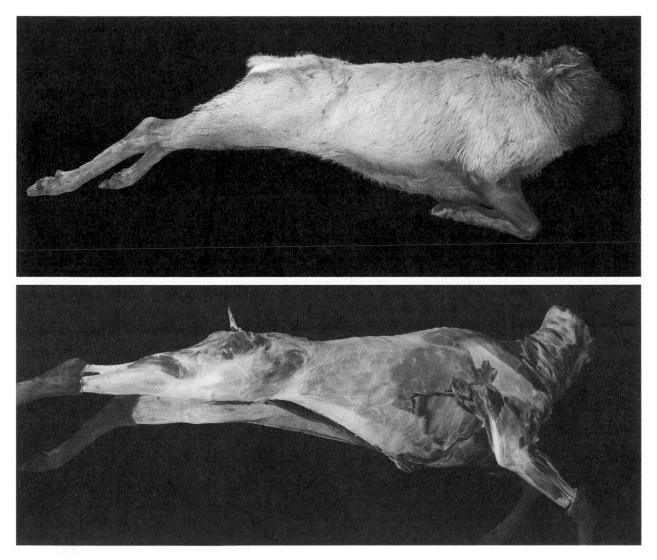

Processing Elk / Skinning

1. Hang your large game using a gambrel, inserted between the end of the femur bone and the heavy tendon located just behind it.
2. Begin by making a cut through the hide all the way around each leg, just below the gambrel.
3. Start pulling and slicing the connective tissue between the hide and the flesh. **4.** Work from your initial cut toward the hip.
5. Repeat for each leg.

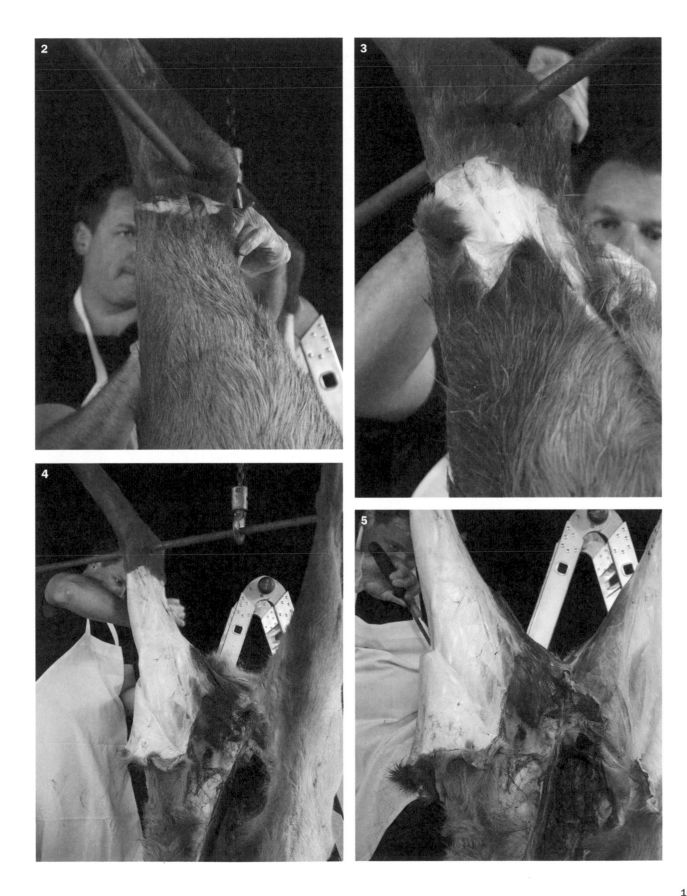

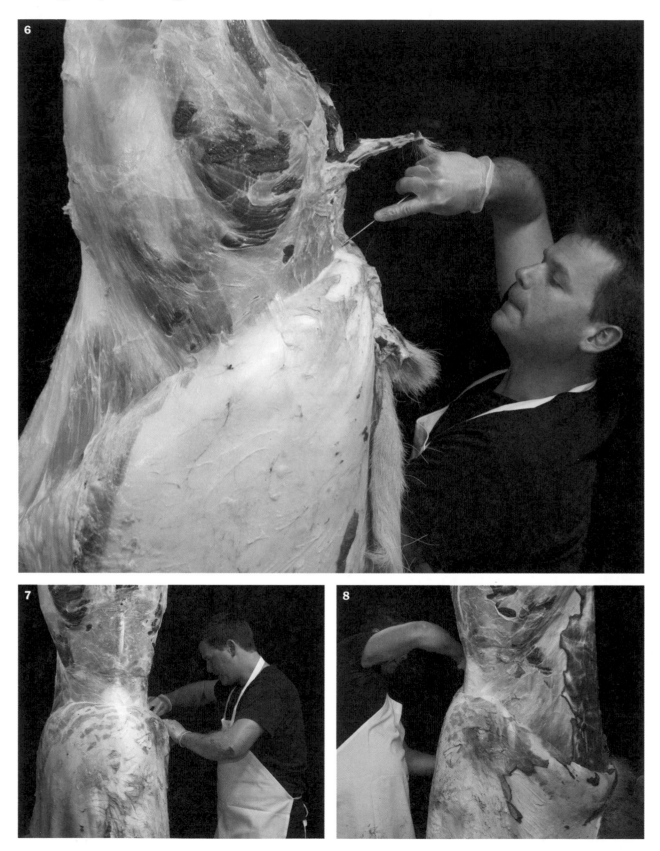

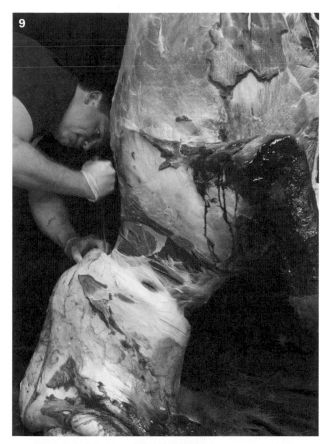

6. Keep pulling the hide down, using your body weight to help separate the hide. **7.** Use a boning knife to cut through toughly connected areas. **8.** As you work into the flank and rib area of the game, you may begin to pick up thin plates of flesh that will not separate easily from the hide. Try to keep the flesh remaining on the hide to a minimum. **9.** Work the hide all the way down the neck as close to the base of the skull as possible. Using a bone saw cut the head and hide off at the base of the skull. **10.** Make a circular cut through the hide of the front legs just above the last joint or use a bone saw to cut off the front legs at the same point. The legs can then be pulled through the hide to separate.

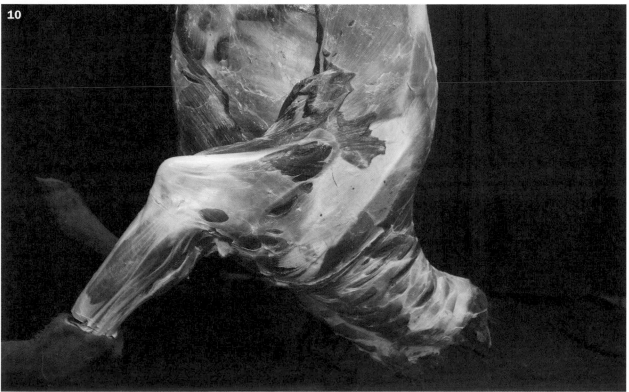

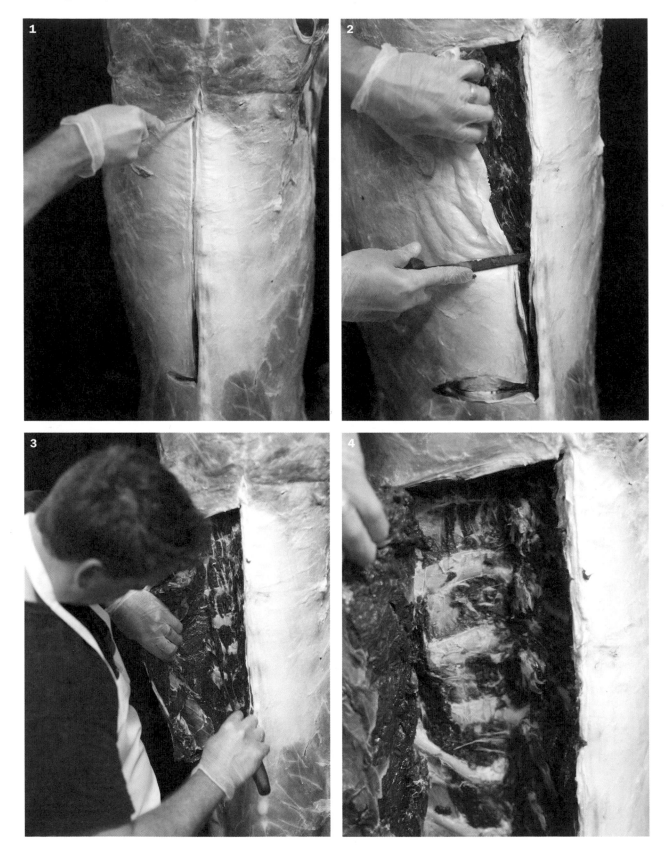

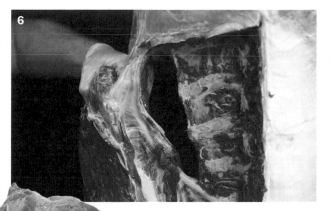

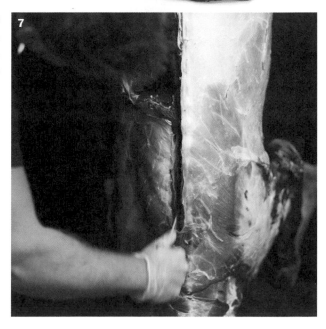

Two cuts are removed here: the rib loin **(A)** and strip loin **(B)**. These can be kept together as a whole back strap or divided between the 12th and 13th rib bone.

A. Rib loin

B. Strip loin

Cervidae is the Latin name for the family of animals that includes all antlered ruminants, like elk, whitetail deer, as well as mule and blacktail deer. Venison is the name given to the flesh of all cervid animals, much like pork is the name given to the flesh of all *Suidae* (pigs) animals.

1. Begin processing by removing the prime muscles of the loin. Make a cut just to the side of the backbone, running from the hips to the shoulders. **2.** Continue cutting down into the meat, following closely to the backbone. You will begin to hit the edges of the vertebrae and will need to cut around these nubs of bone. **3.** After clearing the vertebrae nubs, you will need to turn your knife and begin peeling the loin out, away from the back bone. **4.** Continue separating the loin from the flat bones running perpendicular to the backbone. **5.** The loin is free from bone once you reach the end of these flat bones. **6.** Cut the loin free by slicing the thin connective tissue behind the loin. **7.** Similarly remove the upper loin or rib that runs up to the shoulder.

8. The tenderloin is located on the inside of the chest cavity, beginning near the hips and ending between the third and fourth-to-last rib bone. Clear the fat and connective tissue near the top of the tenderloin and you will see the silverskin of the tenderloin. Clip this silverskin where it attaches to bone. **9.** Slice along the backbone on the inside of the tenderloin for the whole length of the muscle. **10.** The tenderloin is loosely attached and can be pulled out with relative ease, making only a few cuts at well-connected points. **11.** Pull and cut the tenderloin away from the backbone until it is free.

C. Tenderloin with chain and connective tissue still attached

D. Trimmed tenderloin

E. Pismo chain, which is great for grinding into tenderloin burgers

Processing Elk / Shoulder

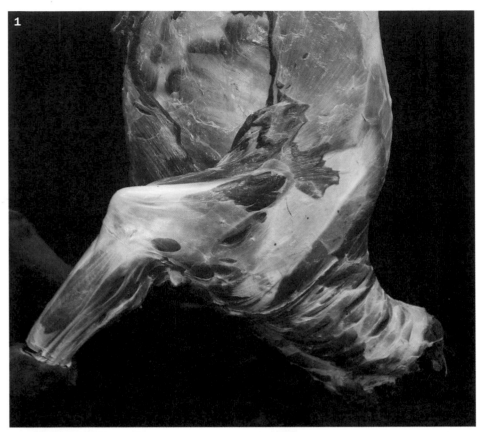

1. The shoulder cuts include the front legs and the chuck, as well as the neck. **2.** Begin by pulling back a front leg and slicing the connective tissue in the "armpit". **3.** Keep pulling each leg away from ribs and slicing connective tissue until it is free. **4.** The front legs have two good whole muscle cuts coming from the blade. Slice all the way around these two muscles as shown. There is a large bone separating them. Cut them free by scraping the meat off the blade of the shoulder.

Use your shanks in Chef Chris Hughes' recipe for Venison Osso Buco on page 31.

G. Two trimmed blade cuts

H. Shoulder clod

I. Bone-in shank (top) and boneless shank (bottom)

177

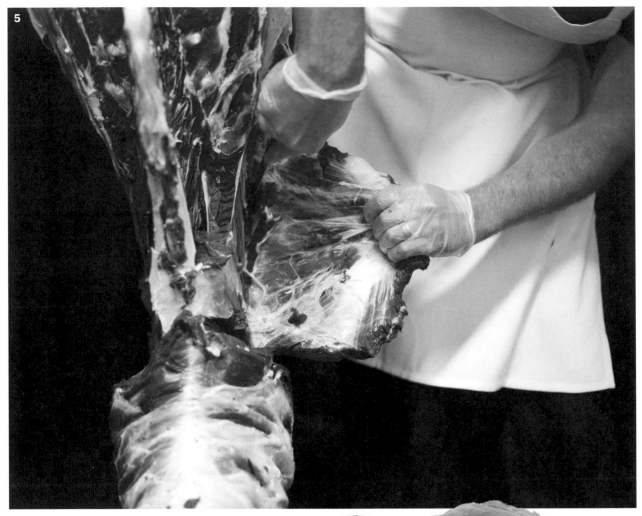

5

5. Cut free the chuck meat (**J**), which rests behind the shoulder along the neck.

See Chef Josh Drage's recipe for Braised Chuck Roast with Puttanesca Sauce on page 58.

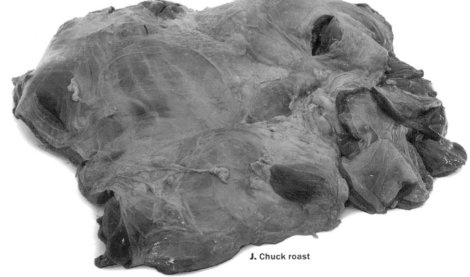

J. Chuck roast

6. Cut the neck off with a bone saw just above the flesh that remains. Neck roasts **(K)** are incredibly flavorful, but can be too gamey for novice consumers. Roast the neck whole and serve very hot to avoid fat coagulation.

Turn to page 21 for Chef Josh Drage's recipe, Braised Venison with Tomatillo and Poblano Peppers featuring a neck roast.

K. Neck roast

6

Processing Elk / Flank and Ribs

1. Remove all skirt **(K)** and flank meat **(L)**, which rests on top of the rib cage. **2.** Remove flank steak and costal rib meat. **3.** Remove the brisket meat **(M)** from the front of the chest. **4.** Remove all belly meat.

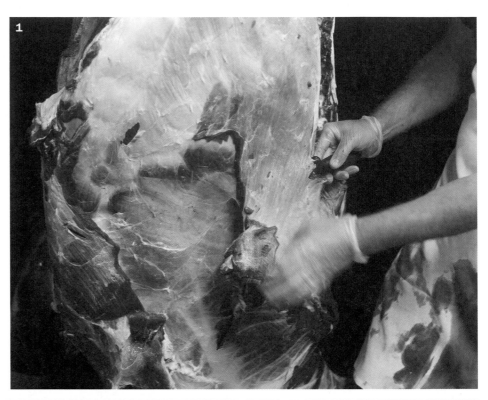

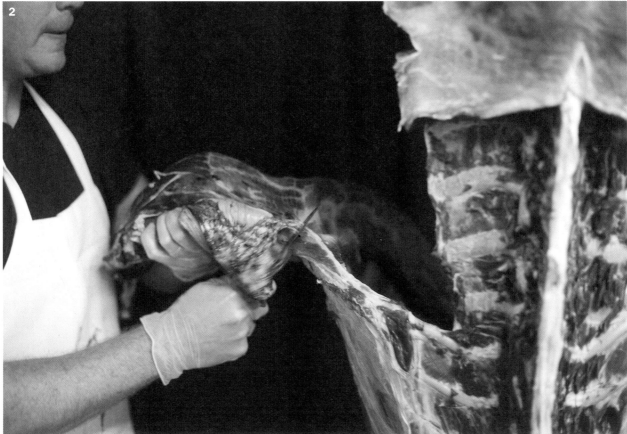

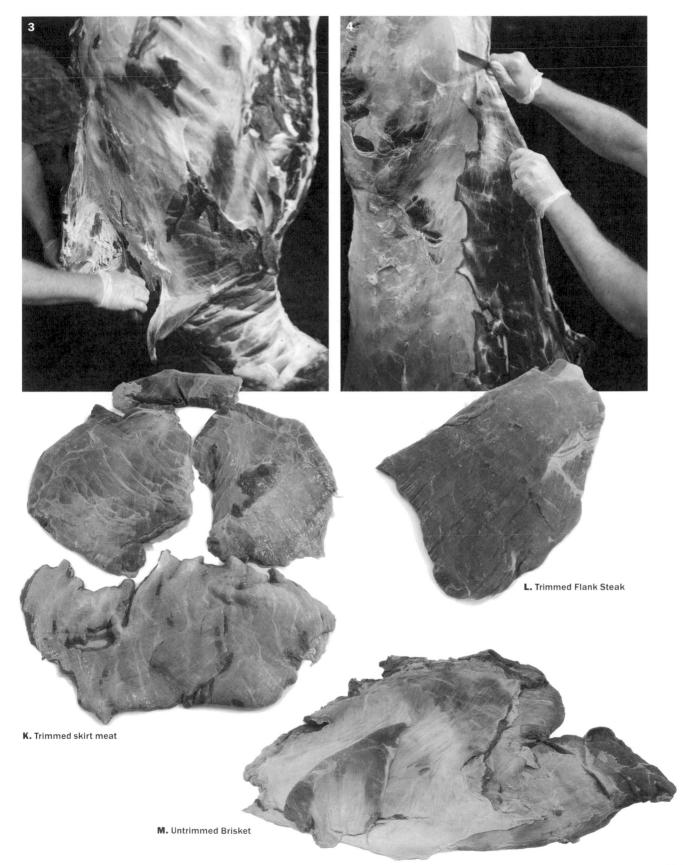

3

4

K. Trimmed skirt meat

L. Trimmed Flank Steak

M. Untrimmed Brisket

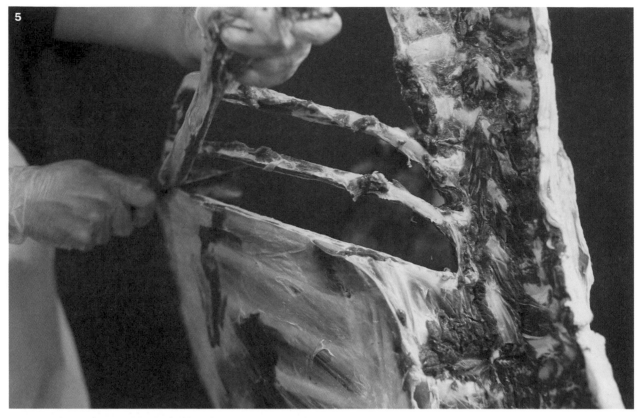

5. Rib meat is incredibly delicious and has its own unique flavor. Do not waste this meat! Cut each intra-rib meat strip **(N)** by cutting the bottom edge clean at the rib. **6.** Be sure when cutting the top of the rib strip to angle your knife upwards so the meat attached to the flat surface of the rib is not wasted.

See Chef Dan Nelson's recipe for Venison Rib Roulettes on page 55.

N. Boneless rib strip

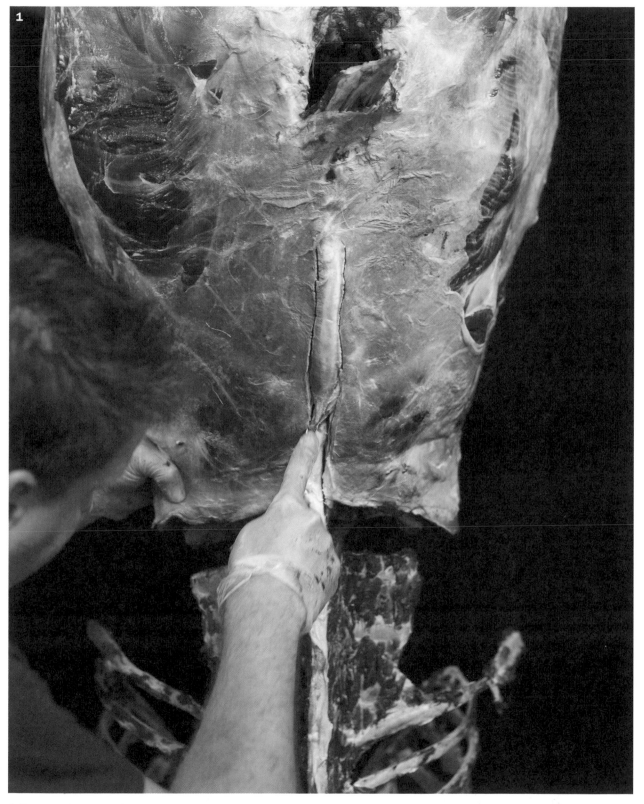

1. To remove the rear legs for processing, cut along the end of the backbone on each side from the upper hip to the tailbone.

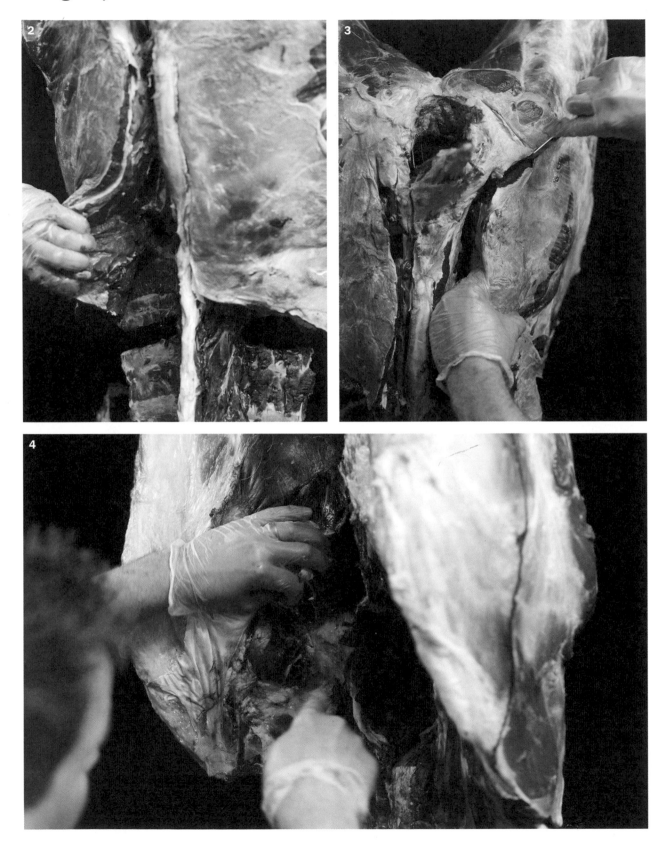

5

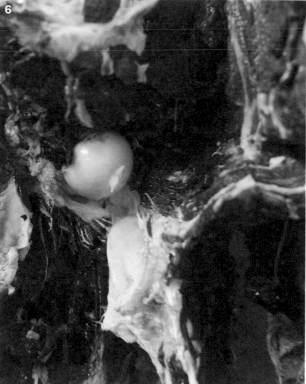

6

2. Pull back a side of the upper hip muscle and cut along the pelvic bone. **3.** Follow the pelvic bone all the way around to the anal hole. **4.** Find the ball of the femur by following pelvic bone to the hip joint with the femur and slice the connective tissue until you can see the femur ball. **5.** Cut along the inside of the pelvic bone. **6.** The connective tissue around the femur ball should be the only thing holding the rear leg on. Cut this tissue and remove the rear leg. **7.** Start tracing and cleaving the individual muscles of the leg.

7

8. The many muscles of the round should be separated individually to make clean, fat and connective-tissue-free cuts of meat. The classic names of each muscle are not as important as the composition of the muscle. Try to create whole sections of muscle that have a uniform grain pattern and very little inter-muscular connective tissue. Cutting just above the stifle join (knee) and removing all the attached muscle will give you the bottom sirloin ball-tip **(O)** and the bottom sirloin tri-tip **(P)**.

8

O. Bottom sirloin ball-tip

P. Bottom sirloin tri-tip

9. Behind the bottom sirloin cuts are the three primary muscles of the inside round (top round). **10.** First remove the outside round flat. **11.** Leaving you with the remaining outside round **(Q)** and the eye of round **(R)**. **12.** Remove the femur by slicing through the stifle joint—this marrow-filled behemoth should always be saved for stocks and soups!

See Chef Dan Nelson's recipe for Wild Game Stock on page 5.

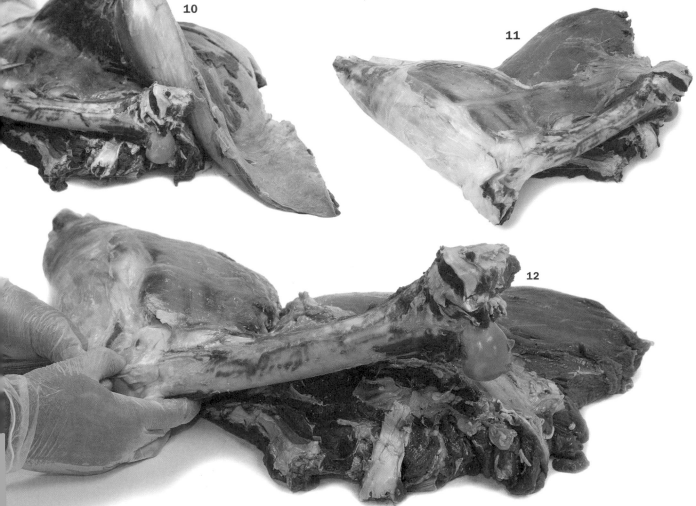

Processing Elk / Round

Q. Outside round flat

R. Eye of found

S. Sirloin

The primary muscles of the outside round.

Make sure to keep all of your trimmings and scrap meat for grinding.

Two trimmed primary muscles of the inside round and the sirloin knuckle.

Processing Duck

Plucking birds is one of the most arduous and messy processing jobs one can have and it rarely produces anything near what we are used to seeing in our supermarkets. Tiny pin feathers and broken feather tips were constantly ruining the appearance of my duck breasts, until I read Hank Shaw's (*honest-food.net*) article on waxing birds. In it he explains how to dip your birds in wax melted and suspended in warm water, after a quick ice bath you crack and peel the wax to reveal near supermarket clean skin—genius! My beautiful wife is the director of a cosmetology college, how had she never suggested that I wax my ducks?

I am still not patient enough to rough pluck and wax all of my ducks. The thick fat on the breasts of ducks and geese is the most crucial to leave on the bird. I begin by rough plucking the small feathers of the breast.

Tool kit for processing duck—game shears, boning knife, and wax.

1

2

See Chef Dan Nelson's recipe for smoking duck tongues on page 67.

3

4

5

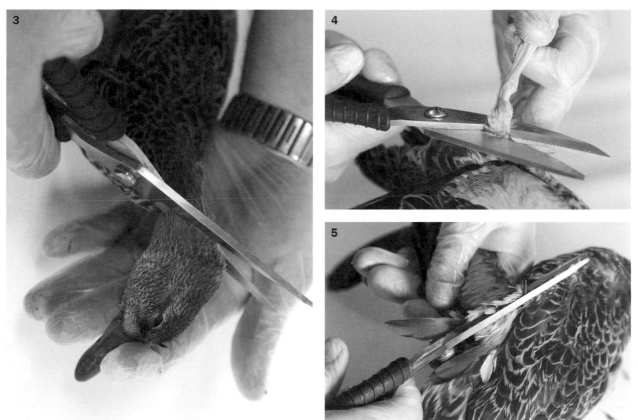

1. Remove tongue at base with game shears. Save your duck tongues and use when you have sufficient number for a recipe. **2.** Remove the tongue bone. It is easiest to peel bone out with your fingers, starting at base of tongue and pulling to remove two filaments which run to tip of tongue.

3. Remove head with game shears where the skull meets the neck. **4.** Remove each foot where the feathers end above the stifle joint. **5.** Remove each wing at the first joint for large ducks and near the body for small ducks.

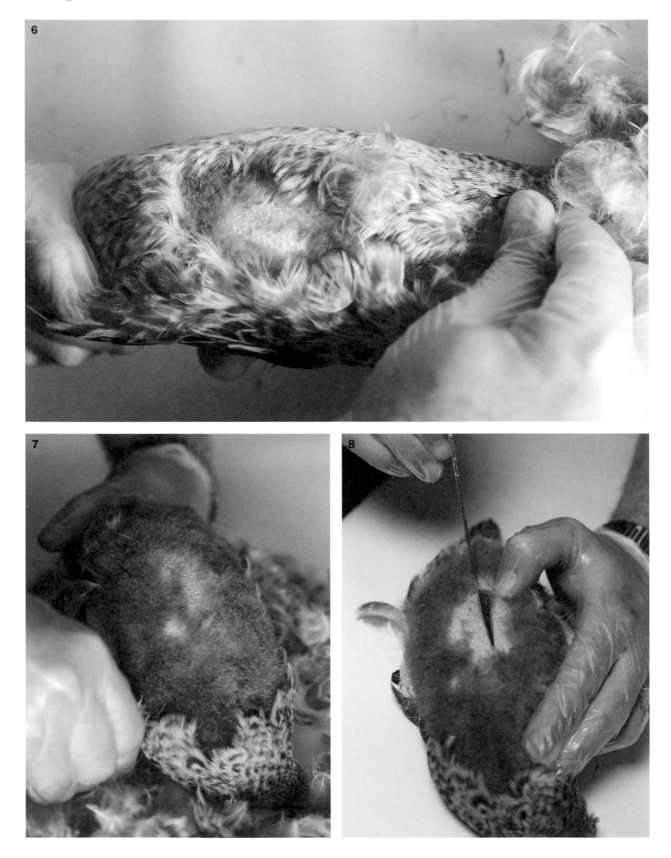

6. Pluck large feathers from breast plate by pulling them up toward the head. **7.** Leave the smaller down feathers to be pulled out by the waxing process. **8.** Slice through the skin on one side of the sternum. Cut tightly along the sternum and down through to the hard breast plate beneath the flesh. **9.** Cut along the base of the breast near the tail.

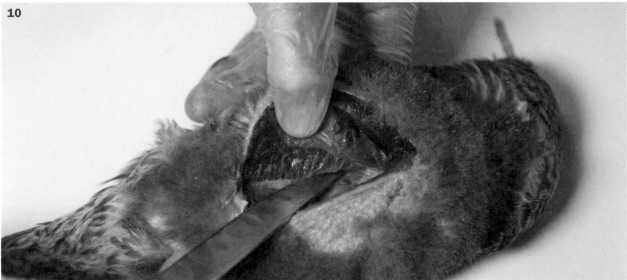

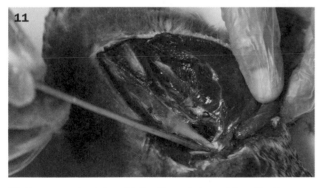

10. Now turn and cut along this hard breast plate, while pulling the breast away. **11.** Find and sever the tendons that connect the breast to the base of the wing and wishbone. **12.** Cut through the skin on the outer edge of the breast to remove. **13.** Repeat these steps on the opposite breast, starting tight at the sternum.

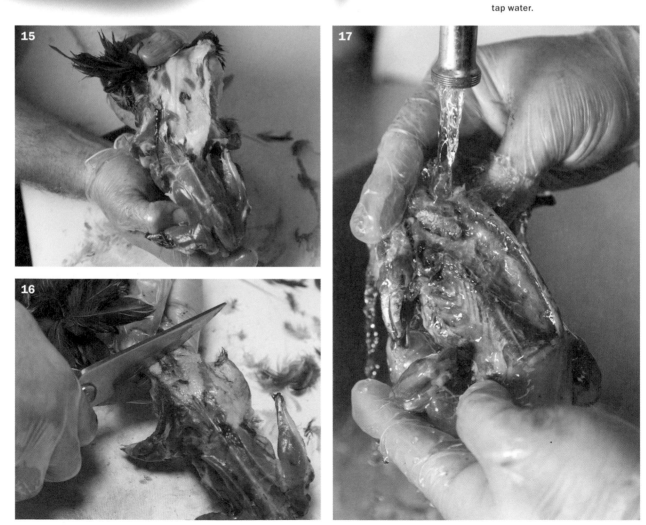

14. Start removing the carcass from the hide by pulling the neck through. **15.** Pull the skin back, while holding the carcass tightly. Each wing will pull through. **16.** Cut the skin from the carcass as far back on the base of the tail as possible. **17.** Rinse carcass thoroughly under cold running tap water.

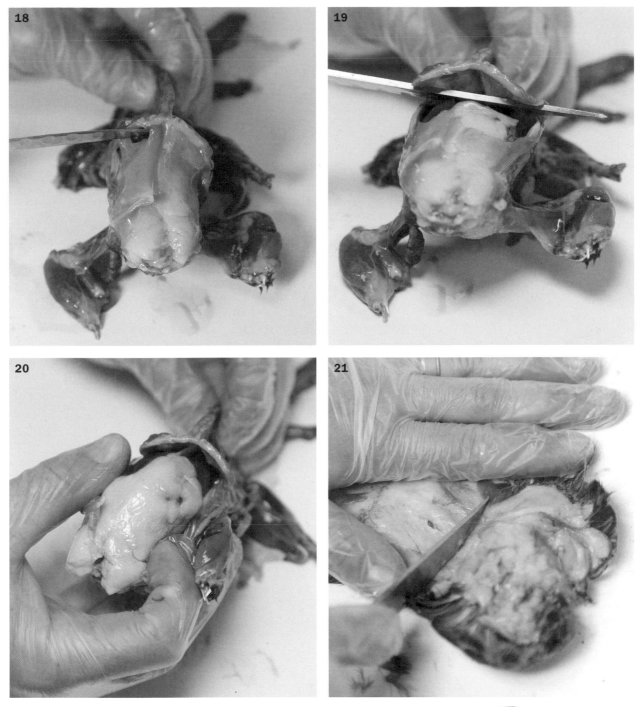

18. Slice through the skin below the chest cavity. **19.** Cut this skin all the way through to give you full access to the guttural cavity. **20.** Pull the offal out through this opening. Be sure to save the delicious liver, gizzard, and heart (shown at right). **21.** Scrape any excess fat from the skin. Start from the center and work to the edges of the skin. Clean off any small feathers and save fat for rendering. See rendering instructions on page 152.

Processing Duck

196

22. Melt 2 to 4 ounces of paraffin wax per breast in hot water, prepare an ice water bath. **23.** Hold the breast and dip only the feather-coated skin into the melted wax, which is floating on the water. Let the feathers soak up as much wax as possible. Then quickly immerse the whole breast into the ice water for 5 to 10 minutes until wax is very hard. **24.** This is what the chilled breast with feathers full of wax will look like. **25.** Crack the wax into pieces. **26.** Peel the wax from the skin to remove all downy feathers. **27.** Keep peeling away the wax, be sure to remove ALL traces of wax. Chill the breast in the ice bath again if necessary to help find small pieces of wax. To dispose of used wax, let the water cool in the refrigerator and then pick the hardened wax from the water and discard.

Nose-to-tail teal duck

Processing Turkey

When processing birds, even those that I pluck and plan on serving whole, I always separate the chest from the back and legs of the bird. These are two very different types of meat and they require different cooking temperatures and durations to be done well. The light protein of the breasts should only be cooked to an internal temperature of 155°F for 15 seconds and no more. The rest of the dark protein should be roasted long enough to reach the crucial 170°F for one to two hours, which breaks down the tougher connective tissues found in the meat. When roasting whole birds, I will fill the cavity with stuffing as normal and set the breast plate on top. That way I can take the breasts out to rest and avoid overcooking, while the rest of the bird finishes. To avoid drying out birds that have no skin, I recommend that you soak cheesecloth in rendered fat and lay this over the bird while roasting.

Wild Turkey Processing Tool Kit—bone saw, game shears, and boning knife. Wild turkey is generally harvested when temperatures are warm, ice packs will help cool your meat without the liquid mess from melting ice.

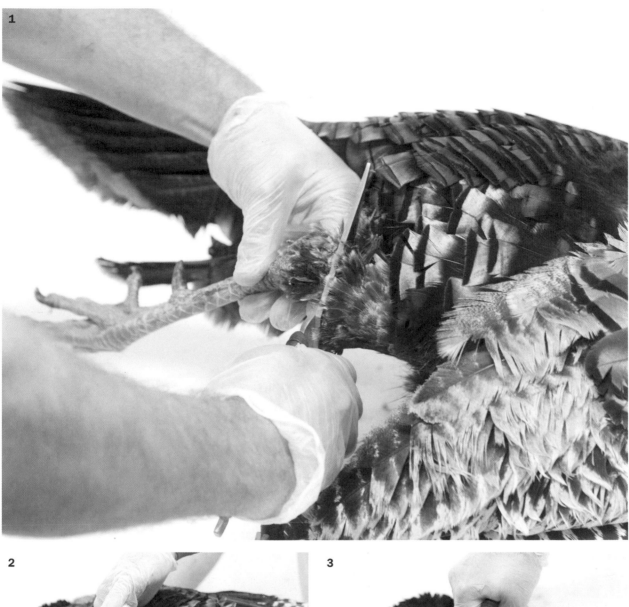

1. Remove legs with game shears or bone saw, just above the knee joint. **2.** Holding the wing out, grab all of the larger flight feathers, pulling them close to the end of the wing. This will reveal the joint where we will remove the wing. **3.** Remove each wing at this joint by cutting through with the game shears.

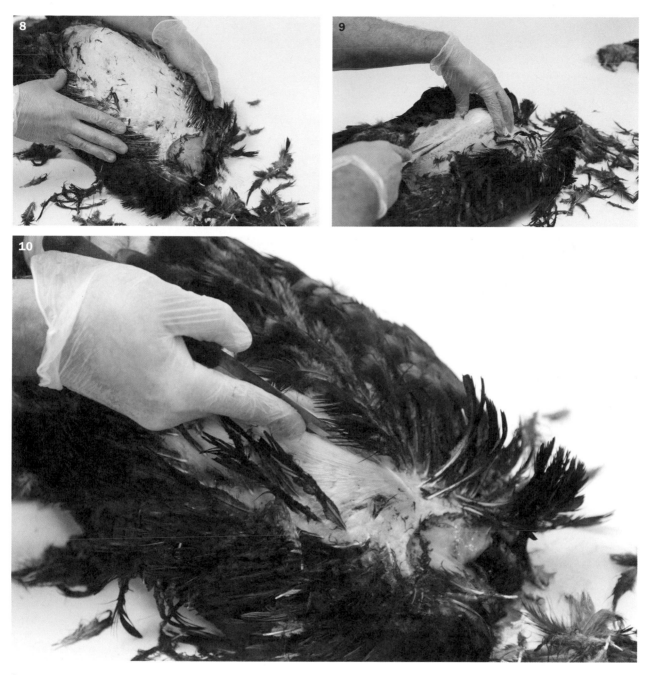

4. Remove the beard by plucking nearby feathers, pinching the beard and a half inch of extra skin on all sides, pull away from chest and cut under the skin and beard with the boning knife. **5.** Using the cut from the beard removal, pull the neck down and out the hole. **6.** Cut through the neck, just below area most affected by the kill shot. Cut off skin and head once neck has been severed. **7.** Pluck feather from breasts and sternum. Pulling feathers towards the head of the turkey. **8.** Remove feathers from 2 to 3 inches surrounding the sternum. **9.** Slice through skin, starting at the base of the sternum. **10.** Cutting through all the way to the neck.

Processing Turkey

11. Above the top of the sternum in gobblers is a red and yellow viscous fatty substance known as the breast sponge. Remove all the sponge tissue. It is easier if the turkey has been thoroughly chilled. Also remove the crop, an extension of the esophagus used to store large quantities of food for future digestion. **12.** Use the boning knife to remove the breast sponge from the breasts. **13.** Continue to remove the skin by pulling away from sternum. **14.** Pull skin over the breast plate and neck. **15.** Pull through each wing. **16.** Pull through each leg. **17.** Keep peeling skin away from flesh, working towards the backbone.

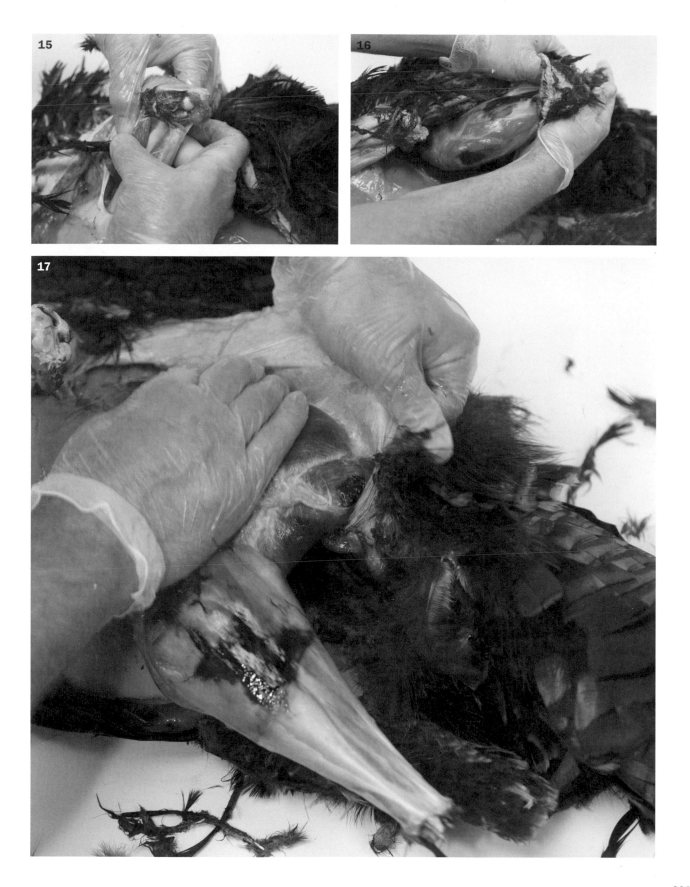

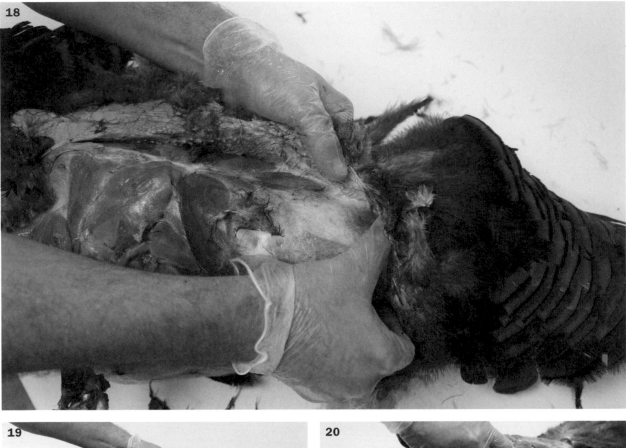

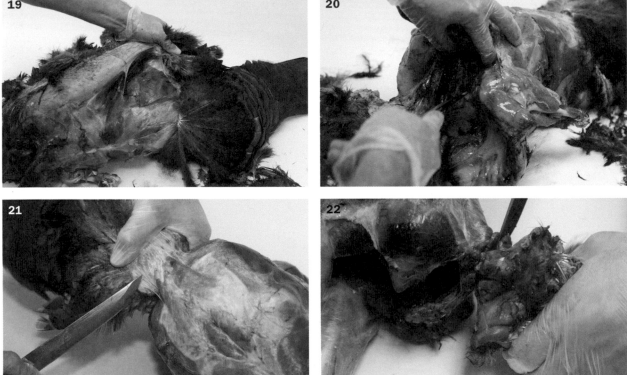

23

18. Push back the skin of the tail. 19. Cut the skin at the base of the tail, leaving plenty of feathers for a tail mount if desired. 20. Remove any breast sponge still remaining. 21. Pull back skin and feather of the tail. 22. Cut through tail bone with boning knife or game shears. 23. Cut through breast meat right where it attaches to the sternum. 24. Follow this cut right up to the end of the wishbone. 25. The breast is now free of the sternum, leaving the tender still attached.

24

25

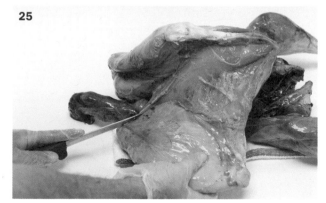

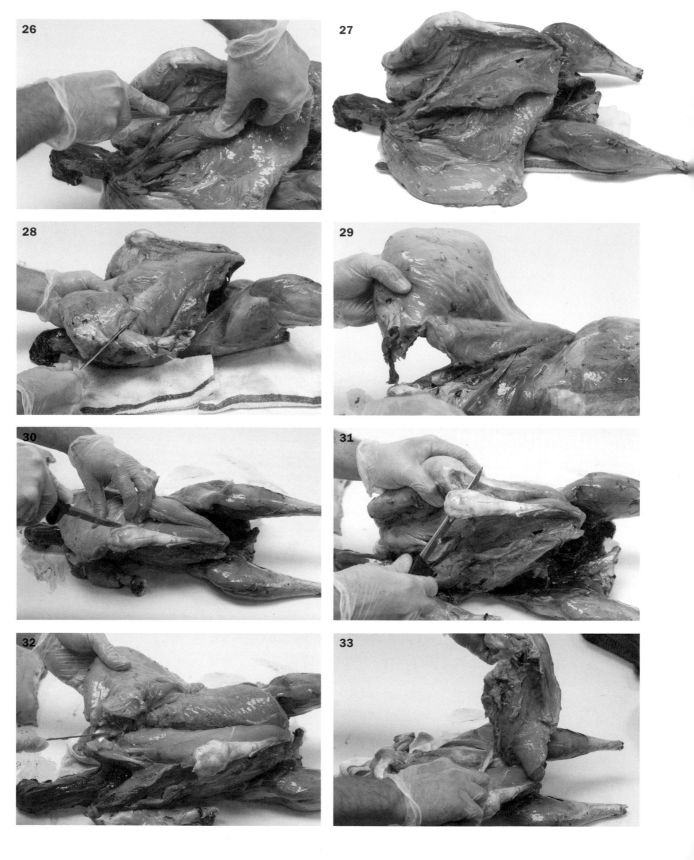

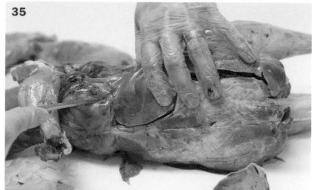

See Chef Dan Nelson's Hickory Cider Glazed Wild Turkey recipe on page 109.

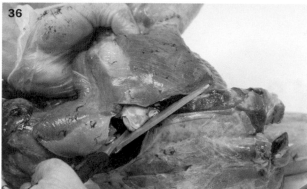

26. Cut close to the sternum and behind the tender. **27.** Clip the tendon that connects the tender to the bone and remove. **28.** Cut the tendons that attach the breast to the shoulder joint. **29.** Cut free the breast by cutting the attached flesh at the backbone. **30-33.** Repeat steps 26 through 29 to remove the other breast. **34.** Cut through the flesh and connective tissue of the rear leg, following the tailbone and backbone. **35.** Be sure to cut around the upper thigh—the most delicious dark meat on a game bird. **36.** Use game shears to cut through hip bone and remove the leg. **37.** The triangular piece of the upper thigh can be removed if desired. **38.** One turkey yields one carcass for stock, two breasts, two tenders and two legs.

Processing Turkey / Gizzard

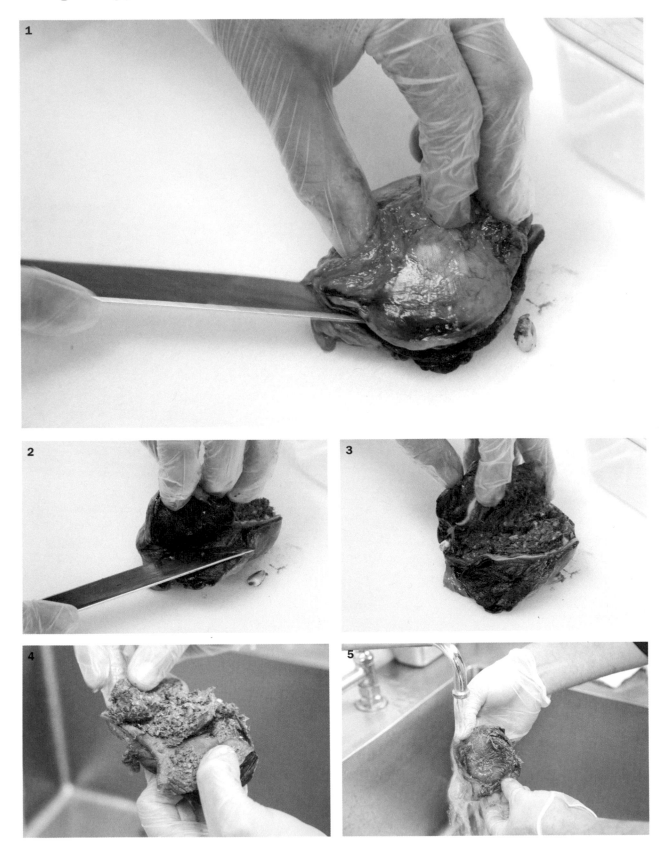

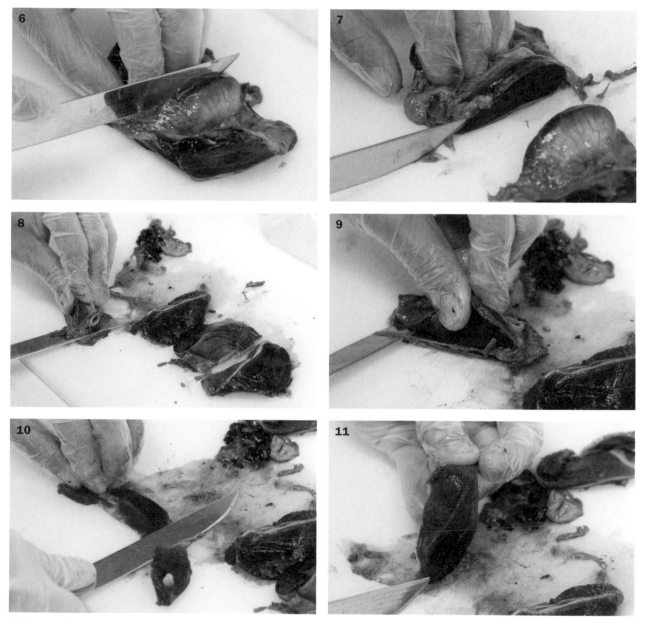

1. Make a half circle cut around the outer edge of the gizzard. **2.** Cutting through all flesh and the tough inner skin of the gizzard called the koilin lining. **3.** Revealing the partially ground food and stones on the inside of the gizzard. **4.** Fold open the gizzard and discard the food paste in a trash can. **5.** Rinse thoroughly under running water. **6.** Place gizzard on a clean cutting board. Cut through the other half circle of the gizzard. **7.** Cut through the thin silverskin connecting the remaining quarters of the gizzard. **8.** Remove any extra fatty and vascular tissue. **9.** Place the koilin layer on the cutting board and slip the boning knife between that layer and the flesh. **10.** Make a small cut separating the koilin layer from the flesh, filleting the koilin layer from the flesh. **11.** Yields four clean pyramids of gizzard.

At right, turkey liver **(A)** and heart **(B)**.

Processing Salmon

Filleting a fish is one skill every outdoor enthusiast should master. The process is the same for virtually every fish. It is a little difficult to get the hang of, but I guarantee at the end of one successful blue-gill fishing trip, you will have it down! The following steps are for a king salmon, but can be applied to any fish.

Tools for processing fish—filet knife, needle nose pliers and game shears.

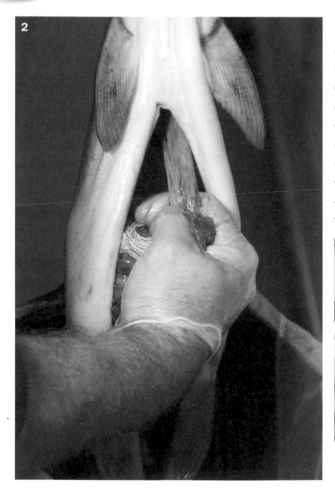

1. Start your gutting cut just below the rib cage of the fish and continue along the belly line to the anus. 2. Reach up into the cavity of the fish grabbing the stomach and upper alimentary canal, remove by hardily pulling out and down the offal. 3. Clear the cavity and pat dry with disposable paper towel.

Processing Salmon

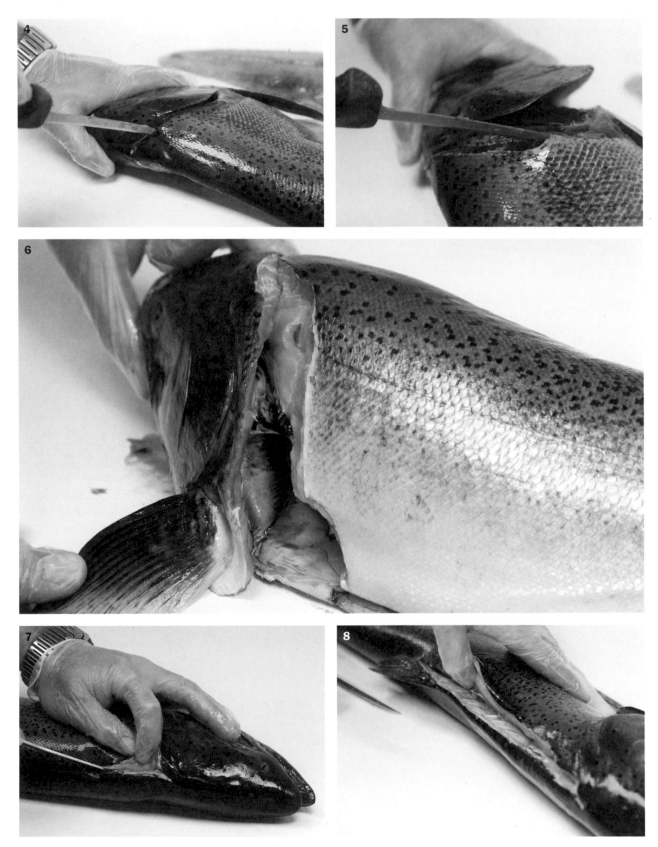

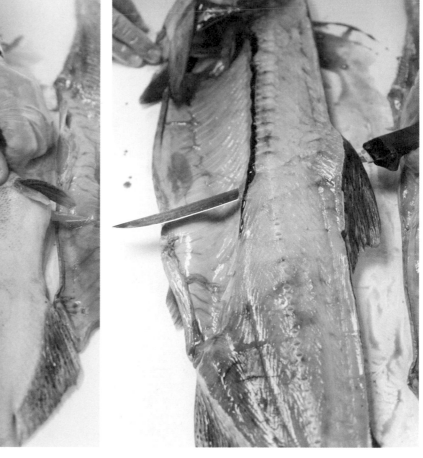

9

10

4. Start your gill cut where the gill plate meets the base of the skull. **5.** Continue cutting along the edge of the gill plate. **6.** Continue your cut behind the pectoral fin and through the belly meat. **7.** Start your dorsal cut at the same point you began your gill cut. **8.** Cut along the dorsal line, deep enough that the tip of your filet knife touches the top of the backbone. **9.** Once your cut reaches the middle of the dorsal fin, insert your filet knife through the fish so that the tip comes through just behind the anus. **10.** This view shows you how the filet knife should be positioned below the spine. **11.** Angle your filet knife down toward the spine of the fish.

11

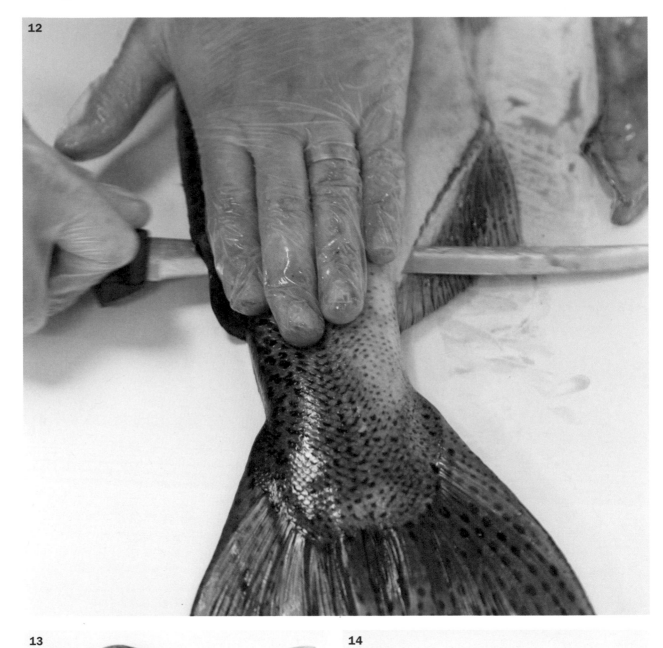

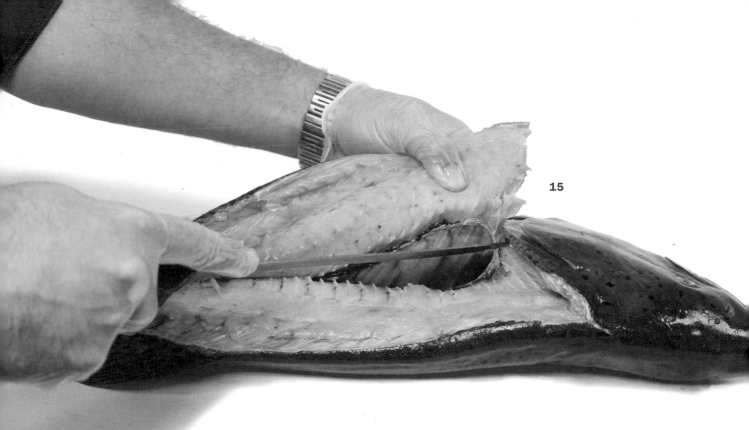

15

12. Press firmly on the flesh of the fish just below your blade, push the blade forward toward the tail. **13.** Your knife will follow above the spin until it cuts through at the base of the tail. **14.** Placing your knife at the same entry point, from mid-dorsal to anus, and cut forward through the rib cage toward the head. **15.** Trim any pieces still connected to the gill plate to remove the filet. Repeat the previous steps for the opposite filet.

Two filets removed from king salmon

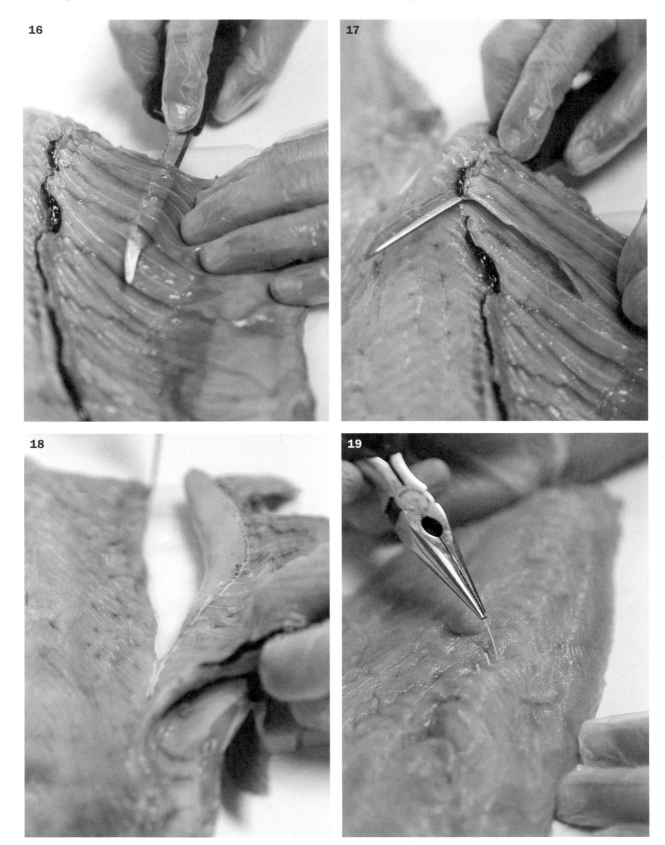

16. Remove the rib cage by sliding your filet knife just behind the ribs. **17.** Angle your blade up toward the ribs and slide the blade through the end of the ribs. **18.** Once the flesh of the belly becomes to thin, cut down and through the skin to remove the ribs and fatty belly meat. Reserve this flap for fish stock or smoking. **19.** Remove the pin bones using needle nose pliers. Pinching firmly on the pin bone, pull up and remove the pin bones, repeat until all bones are removed. **20.** For skin-on filets, cut down into the flesh and through the skin. **21.** To skin fish, begin by cutting down into the flesh at the base of the tail for 2 to 3 inches. **22.** Make a 1-inch slice through the skin you just filleted.

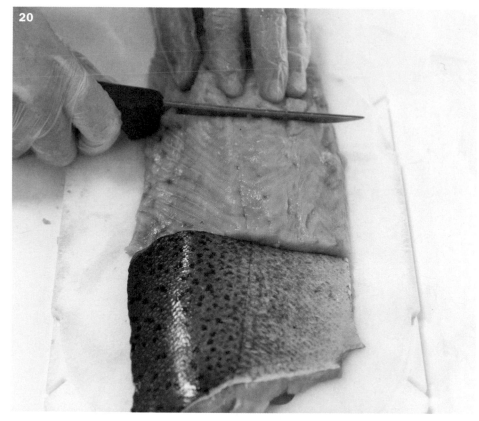

Processing Salmon

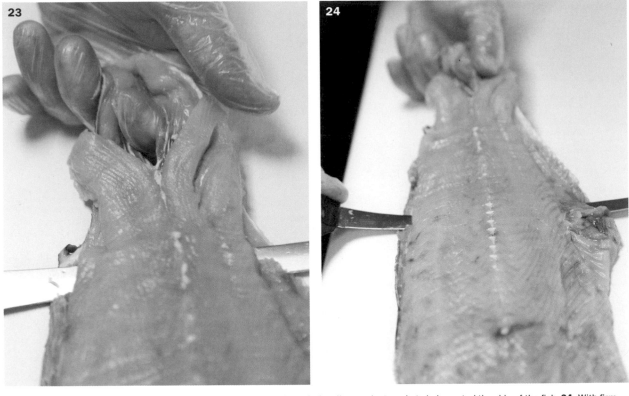

23. Place a finger or thumb through the slice you just made to help control the skin of the fish. **24.** With firm downward pressure on the blade of your knife, push forward with the knife while holding the skin still with the opposite hand. **25.** Your blade should be angled down towards the skin for a clean, waste-free cut.

Skin removed from king salmon filet

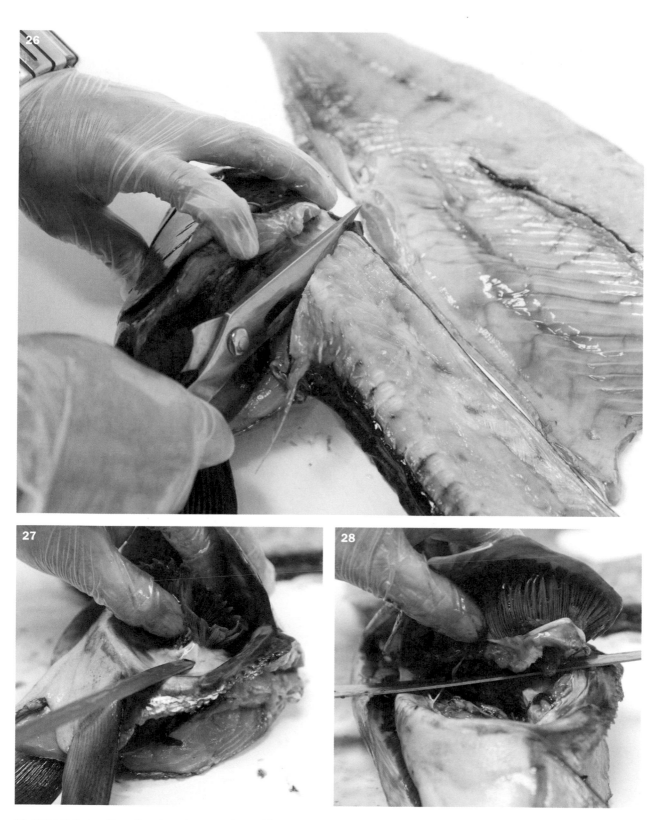

26. Separate the head from the spine using game shears. **27.** Lift up the gills and the top of the gill plate and sever the skin connecting the gills to the flesh. **28.** Place a boning knife into the crease of the cut.

29

29. Firmly push the blade of the boning knife forward and out the nose. Repeat on the opposite gill. **30.** These cuts will remove the collar of the salmon—perfect for smoking. I also push the eyes out, wrap individually and freeze for bait.

Try Chef Susan Prescott-Havers' Vermouth Baked Arctic Char in a Lettuce Shirt on page 95.

30

Conclusion

Growing up in a small town, the grandson of two grain farmers, in the middle of the Great Lakes region gave me ample opportunity to explore the wonders and flow of four distinct seasons and develop a respect for the architecture of nature. Hunting and harvesting wild flora and fauna have always been an integral part of my life story, but a lifetime of experiences is not necessary to find success at hunting. The conservation community and hunter-funded departments of natural resources have quite tirelessly committed much of their time and funding towards fostering new hunter growth. These resources, together with the power of the internet, have significantly eased the ability to locate and take advantage of hunting opportunities.

If you are serious about procuring your protein through hunting and harvesting, you will need to devote some time exploring what you find most enjoyable. Begin by perusing your state's department of natural resources website and look at all of the game seasons and accessible lands. Try to pair a skill set, which you may enjoy and will want to invest time in improving, with the fish, fowl, flora or fauna available in your area. One of the best ways to discover where you derive the most pleasure, is by investing in guided trips. Connecting with professionals on guided hunts gives you immediate access to the knowledge, skills, and equipment necessary to be successful. Guide fees can be substantial, but with rising protein costs, a successful hunt can provide enough meat to offset much of the price tag. Once you begin to narrow in on a favorable skill set and game species, you can expand your familiarity by engaging with conservation organizations. Many organizations have mentorship programs and all are full of people dedicated to the species and the sport, who will truly enjoy sharing their passions with you.

The culinary scene today revolves around forming a deeper more meaningful connection to the nature of the foods we eat. Urban landscapes and backyards everywhere are being colored by gardens, chicken coops, and beehives. Farmers' markets are overflowing with new growers supplying an ever-expanding list of produce niches. For me, there is no stronger connection than that formed hunting for my food—this great meal lived free and wild, until it didn't, and I can't wait to celebrate that by consuming it. Whether you are just starting to discover your desire to consume nature's bounty or are looking to increase the desirability of the game meats you harvest regularly, investing time and energy in successfully caring for your protein will make for a dinner table full of your most memorable meals.

Appendix

Wine Glossary

WHITE WINES

Chardonnay
Complex fruit flavors and often a rich, creamy texture, tastes of green apple, pear, melon, creamy lemon, and sometimes pineapple, rounded out with butterscotch and vanilla.

Chenin Blanc
This white wine can range from dry to very sweet depending on the time of harvest, producing flavors that vary from apple, melon, lime and pear with hints of vanilla and honey.

Marsanne
Marsanne wines are typically colored with straw-like hues, and even fleeting golden-green glints. On the nose, the best examples have a slightly earthy minerality, lifted by notes of honeysuckle and melon.

Pinot Blanc
Pinot Blanc is a lighter flavored white wine with citrus, melon, pear, apricot and perhaps smokey or mineral undertones combined with characteristic high acidity.

Pinot Grigio / Pinot Gris
Pinot Grigio also called Pinot Gris. Generally they qualify as a dry white wine, however some are more fruity, and they tend to be clean and light. They have a citrus or acidic finish, and other flavors include mineral, grapefruit and melon.

Riesling
Riesling wines can be highly aromatic with apple, peach and pear at the forefront mixed with delicate floral undertones and often honey and spice on the nose. On the palate, Rieslings echo the apple, pear and peach along with citrus and tropical nuances.

Rosé
Technically, a Rosé is an "unfinished" red wine with all the refreshing qualities of a white wine mixed with some characteristics of a red. Strawberry and raspberry flavors.

Sauvignon Blanc
Mineral notes with honeysuckle and passion fruit aromas along with fresh melon, lime and grapefruit flavors.

Viognier
Typical notes of Viognier are white floral such as honey-suckle or jasmine, orange blossom and stone fruit flavors, peach, apricot, nectarine, as well as a nice spice component that can be described as baking spices.

RED WINES

Barbera
A medium-bodied red wine whose relatively high acid content gives it an almost tart, but refreshing black cherry flavor. Pairs well with simple, lean or acidic dishes.

Cabernet Franc
This grape has some similarities to Cabernet Sauvignon. It can tend to have a vegetal or herbal aroma and flavor. Generally full bodied.

Cabernet Sauvignon
Considered one of the "noble" wine varietals. Cabernet Sauvignon tends to be a full-bodied wine varietal that can age for decades and are characterized by their high tannin content while supporting the rich fruit characteristics. Common flavors include black currant, chocolate, plum, cherry, blackberry, tobacco and leather aromas.

Charbono
An Italian-style red grape, most wines are very dark purple in color and hold a distinct aroma of plums and other sharp flavors. Full-bodied wine, very tannic and acidic.

Grenache
Medium- to full-bodied, fruit-forward wine. Cherries, black berries, and a plums front for vanilla tannins, and spice.

Malbec
Rich, medium-to-full bodied, plummy, semi-tannic wine often with an earthy or woody secondary taste that goes well with grilled, roasted, or braised red meats.

Merlot
Medium-bodied wine with red fruits, easy tannins and a soft smooth finish. Merlot is a wine of black cherry and plum flavors as well as a light vanilla oak, cedar, clove and mocha.

Petite Sirah
Full-bodied, dark wine with rich meaty flavor. Tends to be very peppery and spicy.

Pinot Noir
Medium-bodied, elegant red wine. Common flavors include strawberry or black cherry.

Rhone Blends
Wonderful combination of rustic and ripe. Gamey, jammy blackberry, pepper, and leather. Blends from all regions are good with juicy, gamey meats and food with common French spices, like rosemary or herbs de Provence.

Syrah
Combines a meaty core of ripe berry fruit with tones that range from herbal to peppery, in a package that tends to be medium-bodied with good acidity and softer tannins. With age, the wines can gain lovely leathery and black olive notes that make them a great match for savory and gamey dishes.

Zinfandel
Robust , full flavored wine with brambly blackberry flavors backed up by some black pepper spice and perhaps a hint of chocolate or violets.

Recommended Cooking Techniques and Internal Temperatures

CHEF DANIEL NELSON

CORE INTERNAL TEMPERATURE

Always take the temperature in the center of the mass in the thickest section of your meat—aim for the "middle of the middle." Digital thermometers are the most preferred; they provide instant readings measured at the tip of the insertion needle. Most dial thermometers take the temperature from a point one-third of the way up the shaft of the needle, making it more difficult to bring that point into the "middle of the middle."

DESIRED DONENESS

Wild game meats are best savored at rare to medium-rare doneness. Eating fine meat is a lot like drinking fine wine. Consumers are usually introduced to the wine spectrum with sweet white wines, as the palate grows it begins to crave the different nuances in wine like dryness, bitterness, earthy-ness, found in deeper red wines. If you are currently only comfortable eating meat at well done, try working backwards bit by bit and your palate will follow. You will soon find yourself comfortable in the medium doneness section and craving the savory juices loaded with umami, found only in rare meats. Be sure to allow for a 3° to 6° rise in the internal temperature, which occurs while resting your cooked meats.

TARGET INTERNAL TEMPERATURES

RARE: 105°F to 115°F
MEDIUM-RARE: 115°F to 130°F
MEDIUM: 130°F to 145°F
MEDIUM WELL: 145°F to 150°F
WELL DONE: 150°F to 165°F

GRILLING — 2 TO 4 MINUTES EACH SIDE

I limit direct-heat grilling to cuts of meat that can be cooked through by four or less minutes each side. Much more than four minutes at high heat will make the surface of game meats extremely dry.

Grill over very hot heat (above 400°F). The rule of four is a good way to measure grill temperatures. If you hold your hand FOUR inches above the grill and at FOUR seconds it becomes unbearable; you have a 400°F grill. Grilling can be used to cook larger cuts of meat by searing for 4 minutes each side and then moving the meat to an indirect heat source at 200°F and cook until your desired doneness.

PAN FRYING — ALWAYS START WITH A SEARING HOT PAN

Wild game for pan frying should be cut thin enough to cook to desired doneness in 4-10 minutes. Pan frying can be used for thin roasts or small whole fish, by searing the sides of the meat and moving the pan to the slow warming heat of an oven.

ROASTING — 250°F TO 350°F OVEN, 8 TO 10 MINUTES OF ROASTING PER INCH OF ROAST

Because wild game roasts should be measured in inches for roasting instead of pounds. The distance the heat has to travel to warm the core is the most crucial factor. Over cooking is easy to do while roasting game meats. I highly recommend using a remote thermometer, which will continually give you accurate temperature readings without having to keep opening the oven and stabbing the roast. Many of these thermometers have alarm features that sound when the meat has reached your set temperature.

POT ROASTING/BRAISING/STEWING — 250°F TO 425°F, 3 TO 8 HOURS

These cooking methods are great for the cuts of meat that contain too much connective tissue for roasting. The goal in these slow, moist, roasting techniques is to get the internal temperature high enough to break down the connective tissues of the meat. This requires that the meat hold temperatures in excess of 170°F. I cook commercial cuts of meat to an internal temperature of 190°F and hold that for 30 to 60 minutes. Wild game suffers too much from that high of a temperature and I have found that the melting of fat and silverskin occurs in meats that I have held at 170°F for 2 hours.

SMOKING — SMOKING FOR 2 TO 8 HOURS AT TEMPERATURES OF 120°F — 200°F

Almost all game can benefit from a little smoking. But, unless you are making jerky, smoking is only used to enhance flavor before the final method of cooking. If you plan to finish cooking your meat after smoking it, keep your temperatures lower than 150°F. If you plan to smoke the meat all the way to your desired doneness, I recommend that you take the low and slow technique to avoid drying out wild game; avoid temperatures above 200°F because they will strip too much moisture from the flesh.

Recommended Cooking Techniques

	TYPE OF GAME	GRILLING	PAN FRY	ROAST	BRAISE	SMOKE
GAME BIRDS	Small Bird 1 to 3 Pounds	•	•	•		•
	Large Bird 4 to 10 Pounds			•	•	•
	Breast	•	•	•		•
	Thighs/Wings			•	•	•
LARGE GAME	Thick Roast Over 4 inches thick			•	•	•
	Thin Roast Under 4 inches thick	•	•			
	Tenderloin	•	•	•		
	Thin Steaks	•	•			
	Ground	•	•			•
	Chuck Roast			•	•	•
	Cross-Cut Roast			•	•	•
	Ribs			•	•	•
	Shank			•	•	•
SMALL GAME	Loin Rack	•	•	•		
	Rear Legs			•	•	•
	Chest & Shoulders			•	•	•
FISH	Whole Under 2 Pounds	•	•	•		•
	Whole Over 2 Pounds	•	•	•		•
	Filet	•	•	•		•

WARNING: Consuming raw or undercooked meats, poultry, seafood, shellfish, or eggs may increase your risk of foodborne illness.

Table 1.
Nutritional Comparison of Wild vs. Domestically Raised Meat Species.

Based on 3 ounce portions:	Wild Rabbit	Farmed Rabbit	Wild Rainbow Trout	Farmed Rainbow Trout	Ground Wild Deer Meat	Ground Grass-fed Beef	Ground Beef 85% lean
NUTRIENTS							
Energy (kcal)	97	116	101	120	134	163	183
Protein (g)	18.53	17.05	17.41	16.95	18.52	16.52	15.8
Total fat(g)	1.97	4.72	2.94	5.25	6.06	10.83	12.75
Total saturated fat (g)	0.587	1.412	0.614	1.176	2.859	4.537	4.986
Total mono-unsaturated fat (g)	0.536	1.276	0.960	1.682	1.143	4.082	5.572
Total poly-unsaturated fat (g)	0.383	0.919	1.051	1.281	0.335	0.452	0.367
Cholesterol (mg)	69	48	50	50	68	53	58
MINERALS							
Ca (mg)	10	11	57	21	9	10	13
Fe (mg)	2.72	1.34	0.60	0.26	2.48	1.69	1.78
Mg (mg)	25	16	26	21	18	16	15
P (mg)	192	181	230	192	171	149	145
K (mg)	321	281	409	320	281	246	251
Na(mg)	43	35	26	43	64	58	56
Zn (mg)	n/a	1.34	0.92	0.38	3.57	3.87	3.81

Data source: U.S. Department of Agriculture, Agricultural Research Service. 2011. USDA National Nutrient Database for Standard Reference, Release 24. Nutrient Data Laboratory Home Page,http://www.ars.usda.gov/ba/bhnrc/ndl. Compiled by Moira Tidball, Cornell Cooperative Extension.

Nutritional Benefits of Wild Game and Fish

MOIRA M. TIDBALL

You are what you eat, whether you're a whitetail deer, rainbow trout, or a human being. Wild game meat tends to be low in fat and high in mineral and protein content due to the diverse diet of wild game animals. Have you ever wondered why a wild salmon and some trout have that beautiful, orange-colored flesh and why other trout don't? It comes from carotenoids that are highly concentrated in their natural diets of invertebrate insects, seafood, and crustaceans[1]. Ruminant animals, such as cows and deer that eat grass have higher concentrations of linoleic acid, a nutrient which helps fight cancer2. The nutrients in their diets are passed up the food chain. In addition, wild game has more lean muscle mass due to a free-range lifestyle and diet. Less fat in the meat equals fewer calories as well. For wild game and fish species that are listed in the United States Department of Agriculture's National Nutrient Database for Standard Reference, there is a notable difference in nutritional content between wild and farm-raised animals[3]. Table 1 (opposite) depicts the nutritional differences between comparable wild and farm-raised species listed in the National Nutrient Database. Table 2 (following pages) depicts nutrition content of wild game and fish species that have known nutritional data in the USDA database.

Researchers at Cornell University have discovered that many species that are hunted and fished are not represented in the National Nutrient Database because of a lack of available nutritional data. They have started to fill this information gap by collecting some of these missing species—starting with brook trout, Canada goose, and ruffed grouse—for nutrient analysis and addition to the National Nutrient Database. Brook trout nutritional information was added in the summer of 2013 and Canada goose and ruffed grouse should be included by the end of 2014. Table 3 (page 232) depicts fish species and wild game that are legal to hunt in the state of New York but are missing from the USDA National Nutrient Database. More work has to be done to compile the nutritional content of all edible wild game and fish species from across the country, so consumers can be informed about what they are eating. Current nutrition information and updated information from this research can be found at *wildharvesttable.com*.

Health Advisories and References for Eating Wild Game and Fish

As healthy a meat source as wild game and fish may be, certain precautions need to be taken to ensure the quality and safety of the meat.

In 1991, a nationwide ban was placed on using lead shot for waterfowl hunting. Mostly this was done for environmental reasons and to protect birds

1   Britton, George, and Frederick Khachik. "Carotenoids in Food." Chap. 3 In *Carotenoids*, edited by George Britton, Hanspeter Pfander and Synnøve Liaaen-Jensen. Carotenoids, p54: Birkhäuser Basel, 2009.

2   French, P., C. Stanton, F. Lawless, O'Riordan E.G., and et al. 2000. "Fatty Acid Composition, Including Conjugated Linoleic Acid, of Intramuscular Fat from Steers Offered Grazed Grass, Grass Silage, Or Concentrate-Based Diets." *Journal of Animal Science* 78 (11): 2849-55.

3   Tidball, M., KG Tidball, and P. Curtis. 2014. "The Absence of Wild Game and Fish Species from the USDA National Nutrient Database for Standard Reference: Addressing Information Gaps in Wild Caught Foods." *Ecology of Food and Nutrition*, 53:1-7, p. 142-148.

Table 2.
Nutrition content of wild game and fish species that have known nutritional data in the USDA database.

Nutrition Information Per 3 oz. portion		Energy (kcal)	Protein (g)	Fat (g)	Total saturated fat (g)	Total Mono-unsaturated fat (g)	Total Poly-unsaturated fat (g)	Cholesterol (mg)	Calcium (mg)	Iron (mg)
LARGE GAME	Antelope	97	19	1.7	0.63	0.48	0.37	81	3	2.71
	Black bear	132	17.8	7	NA	NA	NA	NA	NA	6.1
	Boar, wild	104	18.3	2.8	0.84	1.11	0.41	NA	10	NA
	Caribou	108	19.2	2.8	1.1	0.86	0.4	71	14	4
	Deer*	120	23	2.4	0.95	0.67	0.47	85	5	3.4
	Elk	94	19.5	1.2	0.45	0.31	0.25	47	3	2.35
	Moose	87	18.9	0.6	0.19	0.13	0.2	50	4	2.73
SMALL GAME	Beaver	124	20.5	4.1	NA	NA	NA	NA	13	5.9
	Muskrat	138	17.7	6.9	NA	NA	NA	NA	21	NA
	Opossum*	188	25.7	8.7	1	3.2	2.5	110	14	3.9
	Rabbit	97	18.5	2	0.6	0.5	0.38	69	10	2.7
	Raccoon*	217	24.8	12.3	3.5	4.4	1.78	82	12	6
	Squirrel	102	18.1	2.7	0.3	1	0.79	71	2	4
FISH	Black bass	97	16	3.1	0.66	1.2	0.9	58	68	1.2
	Brook trout	94	18	2.3	0.51	0.69	0.66	51	21	0.32
	Catfish, channel	81	13.9	2.4	0.61	0.77	0.74	49	12	0.26
	Lake whitefish	114	16.2	5	0.77	1.7	1.83	51	22	0.31
	Northern pike	75	16.4	0.6	0.1	0.13	0.17	33	48	0.47
	Shad	167	14.4	11.7	2.66	4.87	2.78	64	40	0.82
	Sunfish	76	16.5	0.6	0.12	0.1	0.21	57	68	1.02
	Walleye	79	16.3	1	0.21	0.25	0.38	73	94	1.1
FOWL	Duck Wild breast meat only	105	16.9	3.6	1.1	1	0.5	65	3	3.8
	Pheasant Wild meat only	113	20	3	1.1	0.99	0.5	66	11	0.98
	Quail Wild meat only	114	18.5	3.9	1.1	1.1	0.99	60	11	3.83
OTHER	Crayfish	65	13.6	0.8	0.13	0.15	0.25	97	23	0.71
	Frog Legs only	62	13.9	0.26	0.07	0.045	0.087	42	15	1.3

Nutrients based on raw meat except where indicated with *

Source: USDA National Nutrient Database for Standard Reference, updated March 2014, compiled by Moira Tidball, Cornell Cooperative Extension

Magnesium (mg)	Phosphorus (mg)	Potassium (mg)	Sodium (mg)	Zinc (mg)	Selenium (mcg)	Vitamin C (mg)	Thiamin (mg)	Riboflavin (mg)	Niacin (mg)	Vitamin A (IU)	Total Folate (mcg)
23	160	300	43	1.09	NA	0	0.27	0.49	NA	0	NA
NA	138	NA	NA	NA		NA	0.13	0.58	2.7	221	NA
NA	102	NA	NA	NA	NA	0	0.33	0.09	3.4	0	NA
22	177	251	48	3.4	NA	0	0.27	0.61	4.7	0	3
23	202	318	51	2.1	9.7	0	0.22	0.48	6.37	0	3
20	137	265	49	2.04	NA	0	NA	NA	NA	0	NA
20	134	270	55	2.38	NA	3.4	0.05	0.23	4.25	0	NA
21	202	296	43	NA	23	1.7	0.05	0.19	1.6	0	NA
19	187	235	70	NA	NA	4.3	0.08	0.44	5.3	0	NA
29	236	372	1.9	1.9	15.5	0	0.09	0.31	7.2	0	8
25	192	321	43	NA	8	0	0.03	0.05	5.5	0	NA
26	222	338	67	1.9	15.3	0	0.5	0.44	4	0	9
20	146	259	88	NA	7.9	0	0.06	0.18	3.4	0	NA
26	170	303	60	0.55	10.7	1.7	0.06	0.06	1.06	85	13
24	209	354	38	0.47	NA	NA	0.12	0.09	2.5	NA	NA
20	178	304	37	0.43	NA	0.6	0.18	0.06	1.16	42	8
28	230	269	43	0.84	10.7	0	0.12	0.1	2.6	102	13
26	187	220	33	0.57	10.7	3.2	0.05	0.05	1.96	60	13
26	231	326	43	0.31	31	0	0.128	0.204	7.14	90	13
26	153	298	68	1.32	10.7	0.8	0.068	0.06	1.02	24	13
26	178	331	43	0.53	10.7	0	0.23	0.14	1.95	60	13
19	158	228	48	0.63	11.8	5.3	0.35	0.26	2.9	45	21
17	196	223	31	0.82	NA	0.07	0.13	5.75	140	140	5 (DFE)
21	261	201	43	2.3	14.8	6.1	0.24	0.24	6.97	48	6
23	218	257	49	1.1	NA	1	0.06	0.27	1.88	45	31
17	125	242	4	0.85	12	0	0.12	0.21	1	42	13

Table 3.
Wild game and fish species that are legal to hunt in New York, but are missing from the USDA Nutrient Database.

Species Listed in NYS DEC Hunting & Fishing Regulations, but no nutritional facts listed in the USDA National Nutrient Database for Standard Reference	Analysis in USDA National Nutrient Database?	Closest Species Listed in Database
Brant (Branta bernicla)	Needs analysis	domesticated goose
Brook trout (Salvelinus fontinalis)	Being analyzed	trout, mixed species
Bullhead (Ameiurus nebulosus)	Needs analysis	catfish, channel, wild, raw
Coot (Fulica Americana)	Needs analysis	duck, wild
Crappie (Pomoxis nigromaculatus)	Needs analysis	N/A
Crow (Corvus brachyrhynchos)	Needs analysis	N/A
Duck, multiple species	Needs analysis	duck, wild
Gallinule (Gallinula chloropus)	Needs analysis	N/A
Canada goose (Branta canadensis)	Being analyzed	domesticated goose
Lake trout (Salvelinus namaycush)	Needs analysis	trout, mixed species
Landlocked salmon (Salmo salar)	Needs analysis	Atlantic salmon
Merganser (Mergus merganser)	Needs analysis	duck, wild
Muskellunge (Esox masquinongy)	Needs analysis	N/A
Pickerel (Esox niger)	Needs analysis	N/A
Porcupine (Erethizon dorsatum)	Needs analysis	N/A
Rail (Rallus)	Needs analysis	N/A
Ruffed grouse (Bonasa umbellus)	Being analyzed	N/A
Snapping turtle (Chelydra serpentine)	Needs analysis	green turtle (illegal to harvest in NY)
Snipe (Gallinago gallinago)	Needs analysis	N/A
Snow goose (Chen aerulescens)	Needs analysis	domesticated goose
White-tailed deer (Odocoileus virginianus)	Needs analysis	game meat, deer
Wild turkey (Meleagris gallopavo)	Needs analysis	domesticated turkey, all classes
Woodchuck (Marmota monax)	Needs analysis	N/A
Woodcock (Scolopax minor)	Needs analysis	N/A
Yellow perch (Perca flavescens)	Needs analysis	perch, mixed species

and animals from ingesting lead fragments. More recent studies[4] have shown that animals and upland birds harvested with lead ammunition have residual lead throughout the carcass that raises blood lead levels in humans who ingest it! Even if the meat around the entry wound is removed, lead fragments can still be found in meat from the animal. Lead is a neurotoxin that is particularly harmful to pregnant women and young children as it impacts developing brains. The good news is that lead ingestion and poisoning can be prevented by hunting with ammunition that doesn't contain lead! Look for steel, copper, or tungsten to use when hunting for meat.

Health advisories and pollutants may also be of concern when consuming wild fish. Mercury, PCBs (polychlorinated biphenyls) and other insecticides have been found in certain fish species, especially older fish and fish that consume other fish. Some waterways are more polluted with these chemicals, and fish should not be consumed from these water sources, especially by pregnant women and small children because exposure to these chemicals can harm the developing nervous system. Waterfowl, especially diving ducks, feeding in these same waters can also contain PCBs and chemicals. In most states, the Department of Public Health publishes fish and game advisories every year. These advisories outline how much and what kinds of fish and game can be consumed, how often and by whom for the various waterways in the state. Contact your department of health or your state's department of environmental conservation to learn more. The New York State Department of Environmental Conservation has loads of good information about hunting and fishing regulations, along with health advice and how-to advice. Ultimately hunting and fishing and consuming our quarry helps us to be good stewards of the land. Thoughtful consumption of wild game and fish can positively impact the health of our bodies, the species we hunt, and the land and waters where we all live.

MOIRA M. TIDBALL

Moira Tidball is the Human Ecology Nutrition Resource Educator for Cornell Cooperative Extension in Seneca County, New York. She holds a Master's degree in Community Nutrition and received classic culinary training while obtaining an undergraduate degree from Boston University's School of Hospitality Administration. She created the Wild Harvest Table website, *wildharvesttable.com*, as a resource for game and fish recipes, nutrition information, and preparation techniques. She is working with colleagues in the Department of Natural Resources at Cornell University on research regarding extension of the locavore movement to wild game and fish consumption and how that pertains to nutrition, food security, and increased participation in outdoor recreation and restoration activities.

4   Iqbal, S., W. Blumenthal, C. Kennedy, F.Y. Yip, S. Pickard, W.D. Flanders, K. Loringer, K. Kruger, K.L. Caldwell, and M. Jean Brown. 2009. "Hunting with lead: Association between blood lead levels and wild game consumption". Environmental Research. 109 (8): 952-959.

Gourmet Gone Wild

Find healthy food hiding in the woods, fields, and streams near you!

Go Wild! Many Americans are going wild for healthy, local, sustainable food options. Are you one of these newcomers?

Harvesting one's own meat through legally fishing, hunting, or trapping is the pinnacle of local and sustainable procurement of protein. Not only is the meat harvested locally, it also puts the hunter/angler in charge of every step of the treatment of that protein. Hunters and anglers can ensure their animals are treated humanely, their meat is handled safely, and the environment has not been degraded in the process; in fact, it has most likely been enhanced! Also, wild fish and game are some of the leanest, healthiest, and most sustainable proteins available today. Venison, for instance, can provide you with most of your recommended daily intake of iron, zinc, phosphorus, B6 and copper—and don't forget, lots of lean protein. Also, wild fish and game are free of industrial feedlots, growth hormones, antibiotics, and other additives many contemporary foodies find disagreeable.

Plus, you may not realize that when you choose to legally hunt and fish, your license fees and equipment taxes directly fund conservation. How great is that? So, get out there, enjoy the adventure of harvesting your own meal, and then enjoy cooking and sharing that tasty adventure with friends.

Gourmet Gone Wild®

THE PERFECT PROGRAM FOR HEALTHY LIVING

Never thought about wild fish and game as a solution to your local, sustainable food needs? In Michigan—and now spreading across the nation—a new program called Gourmet Gone Wild® (GGW), is taking the food scene by storm. Gourmet Gone Wild® introduces new, non-hunting and angling audiences to wild fish and game as a local, unique, sustainable food source and connects with those people interested in gaining a greater connection to their food. The program showcases wild fish and game as a healthy and delicious cuisine that can be prepared easily at home. The GGW program seeks to challenge the popular myths that wild game is tough, hard to cook or "gamey" as well as quashing other stereotypes associated with hunting.

During each GGW event, participants sample professionally prepared wild fish and game entrées paired with local wine and beer, while learning about the health benefits of eating local and the role hunters and anglers play in conserving natural resources. Participants receive a cooking demonstration by our GGW professional chef, who showcases how wild proteins can easily rival non-game options when properly prepared.

JORDAN PUSATERI BURROUGHS

ERIN McDONOUGH

HUNTING AND FISHING DOES MORE THAN FEED US

- Boosts the economy by bringing in 90 billion dollars to the U.S. economy
- Contributes to fish and wildlife conservation (via license sales and excise tax)
- Controls fish and wildlife populations
- Connects individuals with nature

235

wild
turkey
etzel roll

net gone, wild
ate in healthy, local eating™

After GGW, participants are invited to attend a Gourmet Gone Wild-er event which provides hands-on opportunities to connect them with hunting, fishing and conservation in their own communities. This hands-on local event is designed to introduce individuals to hunting, fishing, and conservation activities, while continuing to highlight the culinary and health benefits of eating wild fish and game. Some GGW-er events take individuals directly into the field or stream to harvest game or fish. Others may consist of processing fish and game, or shooting sports workshops that give individuals the basic tools and confidence they need to get started in harvesting nature's bounty. Participants get to try an aspect of hunting or fishing in a risk-free and minimal commitment format. At the conclusion of these hands-on events, participants sample a delicious wild game or fish snack prepared by the GGW chef. By first introducing participants to the health and culinary side of wild game and then getting them outdoors, we hope to light the spark that can lead individuals to take control of their food in a way they may never have thought possible.

We understand that many GGW or GGW-er participants may never become hunters and anglers, but we believe the vast majority will accept hunting and angling as a positive, acceptable way to obtain a healthy, local food source. We also believe participants will become members of the new generation who buy hunting or fishing licenses to promote healthy habitats, join conservation organizations, and lobby state or local governments to conserve wildlife and habitat.

How you can become involved

You may be thinking GGW sounds like a great program but wonder how you can become involved. Check out the GGW website at *gourmetgonewild.org* and share with others in your area or ask your state's fish and wildlife agency to start a Gourmet Gone Wild program. Purchase a hunting or fishing license to do your part to help manage your state's fish and wildlife. Contact local conservation organizations or your fish and wildlife agency and volunteer for one of their programs; you may be able to assist with on-the-ground conservation projects. Lastly, become a certified hunter safety instructor and pass on the tradition. Yes, you, alone can make a difference!

Gourmet Gone Wild was created in partnership with Michigan State University, Michigan United Conservation Clubs, Michigan Department of Natural Resources, and the Boone and Crockett Club. Gourmet Gone Wild is trademarked by Michigan United Conservation Clubs. Use is prohibited without prior written consent. To learn more about GGW, visit gourmetgonewild.org or email gourmetgonewild@mucc.org.

GOALS OF THE GOURMET GONE WILD PROGRAM

- **Awareness**—Attract a new generation of lifelong conservationists by articulating the vital role that hunting and angling play in managing our natural resources, namely through providing wild meat sources.
- **Image**—Increase the number of people who support hunting and fishing and improve the public perception and image of hunters and anglers.
- **Opportunity**—Ignite the curiosity and desire to want to harvest and prepare wild fish and game at home.
- **Action**—Instill the desire to preserve and protect natural resources, our outdoor heritage, and the unique character of the state and region.

JON BONNELL \ TEXAS

 DANIEL BOULUD \ NEW YORK

 TRAVIS BRUST \ VIRGINIA

 MICHAEL CHIARELLO \ CALIFORNIA

 JOSH DRAGE \ MONTANA

 CHRIS HUGHES \ TEXAS

 BOB HURLEY \ CALIFORNIA

 EMERIL LAGASSE | LOUISIANA

 SCOTT LEYSATH \ CALIFORNIA

 JORGE MORALES \ MONTANA

 DANIEL NELSON \ MICHIGAN

 HOLLY PETERSON \ CALIFORNIA

 SUSAN PRESCOTT-HAVERS \ WYOMING

 ANTHONY SCANIO \ LOUISIANA

 HANK SHAW \ CALIFORNIA

Meet the Chefs

CHEF JON BONNELL

Chef Jon Bonnell pairs his native Texas heritage with classic culinary training to create inventive and delicious dishes featuring decidedly Texan ingredients to inspire the palette. Distinguished as one of the foremost experts on fine wild game and Texas cuisine, his innate understanding of flavor combinations and perfected techniques entices diners to experience new culinary creations. With a passion for sharing knowledge with others, there is never a technique or recipe he won't share.

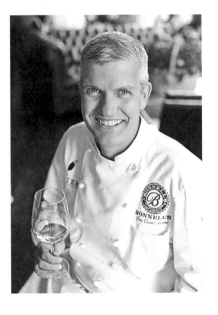

Chef Bonnell is a graduate of Vanderbilt University and the prestigious New England Culinary Institute. He has authored two cookbooks *Jon Bonnell's Fine Texas Cuisine* and *Jon Bonnell's Texas Favorites.* Chef Bonnell has cooked at the famed James Beard House in New York City in 2004, 2005 and 2008. He has been featured on NBC's "The Today Show", CBS's "The Early Show" and "This Morning", ABC's "Nightline" and "GMA Now, Better TV", as well as The Food Network's "BBQ with Bobby Flay" and "Meat & Potatoes". His namesake restaurant, Bonnell's Fine Texas Cuisine in Fort Worth, has won the "Award of Excellence" from Wine Spectator each year since 2004 and has been consistently rated among the top restaurants in the state by Zagat. His newest restaurant concept, WATERS | Bonnell's Coastal Cuisine, opened to rave reviews in March 2013.

RESTAURANTS
Bonnell's Fine Texas Cuisine
Fort Worth, TX

WATERS | Bonnell's Coastal Cuisine
Fort Worth, TX

BOOKS
Jon Bonnell's Fine Texas Cuisine

Jon Bonnell's Texas Favorites

CHEF DANIEL BOULUD

Daniel Boulud is Chef-Owner of several award-winning restaurants and the Feast & Fêtes catering company. While he hails from Lyon, France, it is in New York that he has truly mastered the dining scene and is today considered one of America's leading culinary authorities. Raised on his family's farm in the village of St. Pierre de Chandieu, the chef remains inspired by the rhythm of the seasons and menus driven by fine ingredients. Since arriving in the U.S. in 1982, Boulud has become renowned for the contemporary appeal he adds to soulful cooking rooted in French tradition.

Daniel Boulud's New York City restaurants include DANIEL, a three Michelin star Relais & Châteaux member; the elegant one Michelin star Café Boulud with its adjacent Bar Pleiades; the more casual db Bistro Moderne; Bar Boulud and DBGB Kitchen and Bar. His Manhattan destinations on the Upper West Side include, Boulud Sud and Épicerie Boulud. Beyond Manhattan the chef has created Café Boulud in Palm Beach and db Bistro Moderne in downtown Miami, Florida. The Chef has extended his culinary reach internationally with Maison Boulud in Beijing's Legation Quarter and a new db Bistro Moderne at Singapore's Marina Bay Sands. Bar Boulud, his first restaurant in the United Kingdom opened in London's Mandarin Oriental in May 2010. In 2012, two new partnerships were forged with legendary names in hospitality, when Daniel Boulud and his restaurant management team opened a Café Boulud in Toronto's Four Seasons hotel and a Maison Boulud in Montréal's Ritz-Carlton. Daniel will return to Vegas in partnership with the The Venetian® Las Vegas in early 2014 as well as open a DBGB Kitchen & Bar in Washington D.C.'s City Center in mid-2014.

RESTAURANTS

DANIEL, Café Boulud, db Bistro Moderne, Bar Boulud, DBGB Kitchen and Bar all of New York

And numerous other across the U.S. and internationally

TOP BOOKS

DANIEL: My French Cuisine

Braise: A Journey Through International Cuisine

TV

After Hours with Daniel

Boulud's culinary accolades include James Beard Foundation awards for "Outstanding Restaurant," "Outstanding Restaurateur," "Best Chef, New York City" and "Outstanding Chef of the Year." In addition, he has been named "Chef of the Year" by the Culinary Institute of America and Chevalier de la Légion d'Honneur by the French government. Restaurant DANIEL has been cited as "one of the ten best restaurants in the world" by the International Herald Tribune, has earned three Michelin stars and Wine Spectator's "Grand Award", and is ranked eighth among Restaurant Magazine's "World's 50 Best Restaurants." The Chef's culinary style is reflected in his eight cookbooks, including the most recent *DANIEL: My French Cuisine* (Grand Central Publishing, 2013) and his "After Hours with Daniel" television series.

TRAVIS BRUST

Travis Brust was named executive chef for the Williamsburg Inn in March 2011. Chef Brust has been instrumental in the creation of Regency Room and Terrace Room menus and worked with the culinary staff in creating meals for visiting dignitaries and royalty during his career at the Inn. He joined the Williamsburg Inn culinary staff in 2002 during an apprenticeship working as a cook in night production and returned to the Inn in 2004 as a lead line cook until he was named sous chef in 2005. He was promoted to executive sous chef in 2008, chef du cuisine in 2009 and executive chef at the age of 29.

Under Chef Brust's leadership, the Inn has introduced special dining events such as Virginia Wine and Moonlight, a four-course dinner served on the terrace under the full moon; Smoke and Spirits, offering fine cigars, smoked meats and cheeses accompanied by scotches, bourbons and cognacs; and Art of Fine Food and Spirits, a cooking demonstration and tasting of the perfect culinary accompaniment to cocktails made with vodka, gin, bourbon or scotch. He excels in the preparation of such classics as rack of lamb and chateaubriand as well as innovative pairings of regional foods from local purveyors. In October of 2012, he led a Williamsburg Inn culinary team in the preparation and presentation of a six-course Regency Room-inspired reception and dinner at the James Beard House in New York City.

RESTAURANT
Williamsburg Inn
Williamsburg, VA

His culinary career began when he was a teenager washing pots in a small fine dining restaurant in Mongaup Valley, N.Y., when the appetizer cook broke his leg. He was asked to step in, thereby discovering his passion for cooking – and he has been in the kitchen ever since.

His career has taken him from apprenticeships and internships in nearly every position in the kitchens of the Balsams Grand Resort Hotel in Dixville Notch, NH, Russini's Restaurant in Forestburg, NY, the American Club in Kohler, Wis., the Gasparilla Inn in Gasparilla, FL., Jupiter Island Club in Jupiter Island, FL., Wigwam Resort in Phoenix, AZ, and the Williamsburg Inn.

In April 2003, Travis was one of the first four chefs to complete and pass the Pro Chef Level One exam given at the Culinary Institute of America in Hyde Park, NY. He received the Johnson and Wales Grand Award for Professionalism in 2003 and in 2004 was named Chapter Chef of the Year of the ACF Chapter of Northern New Hampshire. He has received multiple gold and silver medals in state and regional culinary competitions. He is the chairman of the Culinary Apprenticeship Board of the Virginia Chefs Association.

Chef's most recent accomplishment was receiving the grand award of first place at the inaugural World Food Championship's, World Chefs Challenge in November of 2012. Chef competed again in 2013 with a second place finish in Las Vegas. He was greatly honored in February 2014 with receiving the 2013 Chef of the Year award from the Virginia Chefs Association which he holds the Vice-Presidency position.

MICHAEL CHIARELLO

Michael Chiarello is an award-winning chef and owner of critically acclaimed Bottega restaurant in the Napa Valley. He made his mark by combining his Southern Italian roots with the distinctive hallmarks of Napa Valley living. From his earliest childhood experiences – created around his mother's California kitchen with his extended Italian family of butchers, cheesemakers and ranchers -Michael Chiarello dreamed of becoming a chef one day. Decades later, he has realized his dream, and much more.

Upon graduating from the Culinary Institute of America (CIA), Michael

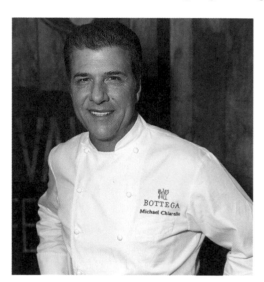

began to shape his career into what he would become: an acclaimed chef, highly-rated vintner, culinary & lifestyle trends pioneer, noted author, and Emmy®-winning television host on Food Network and Cooking Channel. Throughout his achievements, he incorporates his passion for seasonal, sustainable living – and the artisan purveyors who make it possible – into his endeavors. His unique perspective on good food & healthy living, spiced with a dose of old-world charm, inspires friends and family to create meaningful memories around their table. His passion for a food-centric life is shared with his fans, restaurant guests, television viewers and Napa Valley visitors alike.

Michael was named Chef of the Year by Food & Wine Magazine in 1985, just three years after graduating from the CIA. He received the CIA's Chef of the Year Award in 1995, and was just named CIA's 2011 Alumni of the Year. Michael's books have received awards and nominations from both IACP and James Beard Foundation. In the mid-90's, his specialty food innovations earned his olive oil business, Consorzio Flavored Oils, the Best Product Line Award at the International Fancy Food Show. After turning his enthusiasm for sustainability to his own vineyards in 1999, he created Chiarello Family Vineyards, and his small-production wines are consistently high-scoring. And since 2000, Michael has been the tastemaker behind the NapaStyle retail line of artisanal foods, kitchenware and home decor.

Michael has been a national television host of his own shows for over a decade on PBS, Food Network and Cooking Channel, and has appeared on the highest rated food competition shows on television as well. His Emmy Award®-winning show "Easy Entertaining with Michael Chiarello", began in 2003 and still airs daily. In 2009, he took second place as finalist on Bravo's inaugural "Top Chef Masters", and has appeared as a judge on "Top Chef" and "Top Chef Masters". In Fall 2011, he joined another highly-rated cooking show, "The Next Iron Chef", also on Food Network. A popular celebrity guest chef, Michael has been a regular contributor to NBC's "The Today Show", CBS's "The Early Show", "Martha Stewart Living Radio", "Regis & Kelly", and the San Francisco Chronicle's "Inside Scoop Voices" column. Michael lives among his Napa Valley vineyards.

RESTAURANT
Bottega
Napa Valley, CA

TOP BOOKS
Michael Chiarello's Live Fire: 125 Recipes for Cooking Outdoors

Bottega: Bold Italian Flavors from the Heart of California's Wine Country

JOSHUA DRAGE

Executive Chef Josh Drage began his culinary career at just 12 years old in his mother's kitchen in a small cabin outside of Anchorage, Alaska. With a preference of cooking rather than doing the dishes, Drage proved himself to be a quick learner, with a careful attentiveness of what to learn and who to learn it from.

Drage earned his Bachelor's Degree in Environment Studies from the University of Montana, and after a two-year service in the Alaskan Forestry Industry, realized his culinary calling. He then enrolled at the Scottsdale Culinary Institute in Arizona in 2002, where he studied classic techniques and began his culinary career.

Upon graduation from the Culinary Institute, Drage served as the grill cook at Tarbell's neighborhood restaurant and was quickly promoted to Sous Chef in 2004. This was a fantastic opportunity to work with a great team, building, directing, and implementing the seasonal, local and organic menu at Tarbell's. His career then led him back to Montana to Higgin's Alley restaurant in Missoula. It was here that he excelled as the chef de cuisine, constantly tinkering, improving and refining the menu.

Drage's culinary program will be in keeping with the Ranch's philosophy, one of simplicity, authenticity and comfort. The ingredient-driven cuisine is a gourmet adaptation of traditional ranch fare, enhanced by the integrity of local Montana producers. The natural and organic meat and produce will be sourced from the neighboring valleys to ensure the cuisine remains honest, bold and healthy; which truly defines life in Montana and on the Ranch at Rock Creek.

RESTAURANT
Ranch at Rock Creek
Philipsburg, Montana

CHRIS HUGHES

Chris and Maeve Hughes own Broken Arrow Ranch, which produces wild game meats, and Diamond H Ranch, which produces quail.

Broken Arrow Ranch has provided wild game meats of the highest quality to discriminating chefs and individual consumers nationwide since 1983.

The Hughes harvest only truly wild animals—not farm-raised or pen-raised animals—roaming free on ranches that are typically 2,000 to 250,000 acres (that's about 400 square miles). The free-ranging animals subsist on a wide variety of natural vegetation available to them, which gives the meat a more complex flavor—not bland like farmed game meat, but also not "gamey."

Broken Arrow Ranch worked closely with government inspection agencies to develop a unique field harvesting technique that was sanitary, fully inspected and humane. This technique results in meat harvested from truly wild, stress-free animals and provides an efficient population management program for area ranchers. Animals are harvested from distances of 50 to 200 yards away using a sound-suppressed rifle. The harvested animals are then processed under government inspection in our mobile processing unit.

The Hughes work with about 100 Texas ranches as an integral part of their animal population management programs. Our field harvesting methods helps ranchers maintain naturally sustainable deer and antelope populations to prevent overgrazing, which preserves the herd and land as a future resource. It also provides ranchers with a supplemental income source.

Diamond H Ranch is a small batch quail farm in Bandera, TX. It is quickly earning a reputation for producing the highest quality quail in the country. They know details matter and every decision is made with a focus on producing the best quail possible.

The Hughes think happy quail make better quail. Their quail are raised on an all-natural diet with plenty of space to roam and ample sunlight. Antibiotics or medication are never used. The quail are bred, hatched, raised, harvested and processed all on their farm, eliminating stress caused by transporting the quail to multiple sites throughout their life, which is the more common practice.

BUSINESS
Broken Arrow Ranch and Diamond H Ranch, Texas

BOB HURLEY

In the summer of 1988 Chef Bob Hurley planted his roots firmly in the California Wine Country, first as a chef at Domaine Chandon, then later as Executive Chef at the Napa Valley Grille.

In November 2002 he opened his own restaurant, Hurley's Restaurant, in Yountville, California. Chef Hurley describes his menu as local California cuisine high in flavor and influenced by the Mediterranean so that it fits very well with wine. The regular menu offers a wide array of options. The "Wine Country" theme allows diversity so that it is not tied down to a particular style or ethnicity. It is creative food done simply and he always has two or three wild game selections as well. The menus are revised about three times each year to take advantage of seasonal changes, particularly with produce and seafood. Fall brings on wonderful risottos with wild mushrooms and squashes, and in the chilly winter it's time for the deep rich braises with root vegetables and hearty potato based soups. His summer menu lightens up again with fresh vine ripened heirloom tomatoes, sweet corn, and wonderful summer stone fruit.

RESTAURANT
Hurley's Restaurant
Yountville, CA

Chef Bob Hurley is a world traveler and a devotee of the culture, cuisine and lifestyle of many other countries. His years of trekking and working around the world provide the basis for his theory that Napa Valley is no longer a melting pot of cuisines from the rest of the world; but they have come together to create a Napa Valley regional cuisine.

Always the first to respond to the needs of the non-profit sector, Chef Hurley has been a regular participant in charitable events including Guide Dogs for the Blind, the Veterans Home of Yountville Luncheon and Pathway Home Programs, Napa Valley Wine Auction, Copia: American Center for Wine, Food and the Arts, the Napa Valley Academy Awards AIDS benefit, the Napa Valley Mustard Festival, VIP chef for Hands Across the Valley food bank, the Staglin Family Vineyard Music Festival for Mental Health and many others. Other Napa Valley community events he actively participates in are the Napa Valley Film Festival, Sense Yountville, Flavor! Napa Valley, Yountville Festival of Lights and is an active board member of the Lincoln Theater Center For the Arts located at the historic Yountville Veterans Home. He also finds time to do a large number of food and wine demonstrations.

Chef Hurley has brought his Napa Valley cuisine to the famous James Beard House in New York City several times and was also named a Shining Star Chef by Cooking Light Magazine. He has been a regular on San Francisco's Bay TV and has appeared several times on the award-winning California food show, "Bringing it Home with Laura McIntosh". Chef Hurley is a featured chef on the nationally syndicated PBS special "The Great Chefs of Napa Valley".

EMERIL LAGASSE

Chef Emeril Lagasse is the chef/proprietor of 13 restaurants, including three in New Orleans (Emeril's, NOLA and Emeril's Delmonico); four in Las Vegas (Emeril's New Orleans Fish House, Delmonico Steakhouse, Table 10 and Lagasse's Stadium); two in Orlando (Emeril's Orlando and Emeril's Tchoup Chop); three at the Sands Casino Resort Bethlehem in Pennsylvania (Emeril's Italian Table, Emeril's Chop House and Burgers And More by Emeril) and one in Charlotte, N.C. (e2 emeril's eatery).

As a national TV personality, he has hosted more than 2,000 shows on the Food Network and is the food correspondent for ABC's "Good Morning America." He is also the host of "Fresh Food Fast" and "The Originals with Emeril" appearing on the Cooking Channel. His latest TV show, "Emeril's Florida", began its second season in January 2014 on the Cooking Channel. Lagasse also joined the judges' table on "Top Chef New Orleans"—season 11 of Bravo's hit food series "Top Chef".

Lagasse is the best-selling author of 18 cookbooks, including *Emeril's New New Orleans Cooking* which introduced his creative take on Creole cuisine. His latest cookbook, *Cooking with Power,* was released in October 2013.

In 2002, Lagasse established the Emeril Lagasse Foundation to support children's educational programs that inspire and mentor young people through the culinary arts, nutrition, healthy eating, and important life skills. To date, the Foundation has donated more than $5.5 million to children's causes in New Orleans, Las Vegas and on the Gulf Coast. In 2013, Lagasse was named the Humanitarian of the Year by the James Beard Foundation for his dedicated efforts to further the culinary arts in America, as well as his philanthropic work supporting children's educational programs through his Foundation.

Lagasse's restaurant company, Emeril's Homebase, is located in New Orleans and houses culinary operations, a test kitchen for recipe development, and a boutique store for his signature products.

Emeril Lagasse joined the Martha Stewart family of brands in 2008; Martha Stewart Living Omnimedia (NYSE: MSO) acquired the assets related to Emeril's media and merchandising business, including television programming, cookbooks, the Emerils.com website and his licensed kitchen and food products.

RESTAURANTS
Emeril's, NOLA, and Emeril's Delmonico
New Orleans, LA

And numerous other across the U.S. and internationally

TOP BOOKS
Cooking with Power

Emeril's New New Orleans Cooking

From Emeril's Kitchens: Favorite Recipes from Emeril's Restaurants

TV
Fresh Food Fast

The Originals with Emeril

Emeril's Florida

SCOTT LEYSATH

Since the late 1980s Scott Leysath has been recognized as a leading authority on proper preparation of fish and game. Building on a corporate restaurant management background, Leysath opened his own Sacramento, California restaurant in 1987. Along with innovative fish and game items on the daily menu, he invited sportsmen to bring in their bagged fish and game so he could show them how it is supposed to taste. His reputation for extraordinary fish and game cooking led to his catering enterprise, Silver Sage Caterers, which provided exceptional meals for Northern California sporting groups such as Ducks Unlimited, California Waterfowl Association, National Wild Turkey Federation, Mule Deer Federation, Rocky Mountain Elk Foundation, California Deer Association and Safari Club International for over a decade.

Scott is a regular contributor for a handful of outdoor publications, plus he has authored two popular cookbooks. He spent four years on HGTV's "Home Grown Cooking with Paul James". When not in front of the camera giving useful cooking tips or preparing dishes, Scott scripted, coordinated and directed the show's cooking segments. He makes weekly personal appearances on outdoor-related television and radio programs nationwide. His "Sporting Chef" TV show earned popular acclaim, including back-to-back Excellence in Craft Awards from the Southeastern Outdoor Press Association.

In 2005, Scott joined forces with Donny McElvoy, host of "The Outdoor Advantage" TV show. Their new show, "HuntFishCook", does just that. They hunt, fish, cook and explore all things outdoors. The show combines two very different hosts from two different coasts. It's fun, entertaining and, along the way, the viewer will learn a great deal about how to get their fish and game to the table and what to do with it once you drag it home. Every week, Scott also prepares a new waterfowl recipe on "Ducks Unlimited TV" on OLN.

Scott began working for corporate entities, conducting wild game cooking demonstrations prior to a five-course wild game dinner. Word of mouth demand soon exceeded Scott's available time, but he managed to execute over 125 dinners each year. He also appears at numerous hunting and fishing lodges, private residences, country clubs and banquet facilities. He has established relationships with chefs, caterers and restaurant operators throughout the U.S., especially in the southeast, Texas and the Rocky Mountain states.

Chef Leysath appears at numerous outdoors/sportsman and food expositions where he entertains attendees with his subtle wit and culinary mastery. He practices what he calls "short attention span cooking", knowing that learning is an active process and that guests not entertained will move on to other venues. In a period of less than one-hour, Scott will prepare up to ten fabulous fish and game dishes while watching guests devour each one as it is prepared.

TV
HuntFishCook

The Sporting Chef TV Show

BOOKS
The Sporting Chef's Better Venison Cookbook

The Sporting Chef's Favorite Wild Game Recipes

JORGE MORALES

Originally from Miami, Florida, I was lured into the culinary world during my early years in college. I worked my way up through the industry to achieve status of current Executive Chef of Plonk Missoula. Over the years, I have worked under influential leaders of the American culinary profession like Chef Douglas Rodriquez of Patria N.Y.C, Chef Matthew Kenny of Matthew's N.Y.C and Chef Abe Risho of Silk Road Montana who have helped shape my style and depth of knowledge. They have also inspired me to study culture, cuisines, and cooking techniques that shaped my cross culture style. My culinary philosophy and passion reflects the growing movement towards a healthier and down-to-earth lifestyle. Working with neighboring farmers to seek out the finest regional and local produce, is the essence of my cuisine.

RESTAURANT
Plonk Missoula
      Missoula, MT

DANIEL NELSON

Chef Dan is an avid sportsman who has always had a passion for cooking and was often in charge of the family meals from a very young age. The first professional kitchen he worked in was at the Old Dixie Inn, a wild game restaurant ran by Master Chef Dave Minor. This early experience, followed by many years of professional experience while attaining his degree from Michigan State University, paved a path connecting his inner sportsman and culinary inquisitor. Chef Dan has spent the last decade perfecting wild game cuisine and working to bring great wild game to the plates of both hunters and non-hunters interested in healthy, sustainable, and delicious table fare. Turn to page 136 for the chapter, "Wild Game Processing, Preparation, and Cuts" written by Chef Dan to learn more about his work.

RESTAURANT
Eagle Eye Golf and Banquet Center
East Lansing, MI

HOLLY PETERSON

After working as a chef, wine expert and educator for years in France and Germany, Chef Peterson returned home to Napa Valley where she runs her multi-faceted business, FLOURISH.

Chef Holly Peterson's FLOURISH – Events, Edibles and Expressions is built on Chef Peterson's rich and varied background. Her multi-dimensional approach to the culinary arts has allowed Chef Peterson to work throughout the world in every aspect of the food and wine industry.

Her philosophy of nourishment, health, enjoyment and luxury can be distilled to one descriptive word – Flourish.

From Breathtaking "once-in-a-lifetime" events to intimate and stunning winery celebrations, Chef Peterson has the culinary expertise, discerning eye, creative touch and experience to insure the most successful events.

Chef Peterson's client list includes numerous American and French wineries, renowned cooking schools, Fortune 500 companies, resorts, Olympic athletic teams, and restaurants around the world. Her work has taken her from Air Museums to our Embassy in Paris to Mount Everest.

Chef's traditional training at La Varenne in Paris, combined with a creative spirit and philosophy of using only the freshest produce and humanely raised meats allow her to create delicious, impressive menus, and very special event-tailored products.

To benefit cancer research, one of her newest creations are "Robin's Eggs" event chocolates. These hand-painted precious jewels have a luscious shell of rich, dark chocolate and a delicate center of lovely turmeric white chocolate cream blended with other favored ingredients like ginger, saffron, coffee and raspberry. Each flavor is a combination of ingredients that are deliciously delectable and also treasured ingredients known to fight cancer.

Chef Peterson's Sea Star Sea Salt is one of the worlds most pristine sea salts available, harvested from the nature preserve of France's Sea of Brittany – considered by nature experts to be "the cleanest ocean in the world."

Flourish Perfume is another creation of Chef Peterson's. It is a deep sensual fragrance reflecting the fresh ocean breeze, fig leaves and a garden of antique roses – some of Chef Holly Peterson's favorite aromas. An oil base rather than an alcohol based fragrance, it is much closer to the body, and those around you only smell this heavenly scent when next to you, rather than from across the room. It whispers, rather than shouts.

Chef Peterson is an accomplished photographer and her food photography gives the viewer a chef's perspective of the beauty of simple fruits, vegetables and flowers. Her photographs express her belief that the presentation of the food we eat is as important as its flavors and health benefits.

BUSINESS
Flourish
Napa Valley, CA

252

SUSAN PRESCOTT-HAVERS

Susan was born under a wandering star; British by birth but growing up in Kenya, Africa before attending Durham University in England for an Arabic and Economics degree,

After a period as a research analyst at the British Foreign Office she entered the commercial world in administrative, marketing and account management roles in England, Bahrain, Jordan, Belgium, France and the USA. Her life time passion for food and wine led her to attend l'Ecole de Cordon Bleu in Paris where she obtained the prestigious Grande Diplôme in cuisine and patisserie in 1988.

She also has post-grad qualifications in marketing and naturopathic nutrition and has completed programs at Cornell School of Hotel Management and Steven Spurrier's L'Academie du Vin wine school in Paris. She owned her own restaurant and catering business in Brussels, Belgium for 4 years including external catering for large corporations and embassies.

Susan loves preparing country style food with more than a hint of Europe plus a few delightful surprises whilst occasionally catering extravagant gourmet dinners to more discerning food cognoscenti.

She has taught cooking skills to young people in France and at the Peninsula Boys and Girls Club of America in California. Susan has also counseled adults who wish to improve their culinary skills in short but intensive culinary retreats.

RESTAURANT
The Historic Elk Mountain Hotel
Between Laramie and Rawlins, WY

ANTHONY SCANIO

Anthony Scanio has a "love affair," as he calls it, with New Orleans. A New Orleans native, Scanio has been immersed in the city's culture and cuisine since birth. In fact, his earliest childhood memory is uniquely from the Crescent City: Riding down Canal Street—in a high chair—during the Elks Orleans parade on Mardi Gras day in 1973. Scanio infuses these New Orleans experiences, coupled with his world travels and love of history, into the Creole-inspired food he creates for Emeril's Delmonico restaurant on St. Charles Avenue.

Scanio didn't begin his culinary career until he was in his late '20s, when

he decided to shift his career path from English teacher to chef, enrolling in Delgado Community College's culinary arts program in New Orleans. He cut his chops in the industry at New Orleans restaurants Café Indo followed by Herbsaint, where he studied under James Beard award-winning chefs Donald Link and Stephen Stryjewski. He and his wife then moved to Italy, where he spent about a year studying the country's cuisine and staging in Rome.

Scanio joined the Emeril's family at Delmonico in 2005 as a line cook. Following Hurricane Katrina, he moved to Emeril's Orlando before returning to Delmonico as sous chef in 2006. He was promoted to executive sous chef in 2009. Today, Scanio leads the kitchen at Delmonico and oversees all facets of its culinary operations, from sourcing products, to managing the restaurant's in-house dry-aging program for beef, duck and charcuterie, to working with local farmers, and crafting ambitious nightly tasting menus for guests at his kitchen table.

Scanio's vision and flavor for Delmonico is expressed through his Creole heritage and fresh, clean, ingredient-based approach to cooking. He's returning to the roots of Creole cooking—homey, approachable, fresh and diverse—and including ingredients and techniques that have been long forgotten to reinterpret the dishes for today's tastes, keeping in tradition with Chef Emeril's signature "New New Orleans" cuisine.

RESTAURANT
Emeril's Delmonico
New Orleans, LA

HANK SHAW

I write. I fish. I dig earth, forage, raise plants, live for food and kill wild animals. I drink Balvenie, Barolo or Budweiser with equal relish and wish I owned a large swath of land I could play on. I spend my days thinking about new ways to cook and eat anything that walks, flies, swims, crawls, skitters, jumps—or grows. I am the omnivore who has solved his dilemma. This is my story.

Honest food is what I'm seeking. Nothing packaged, nothing in a box, nothing wrapped in plastic. I eat meat, and I'm not keen on factory farms, so I either hunt it myself or buy it from real people who raise animals humanely. Other than pork fat for charcuterie and the occasional octopus, I have not bought meat or fish for our home more than a handful of times since 2005. I am a constant forager, angler, hunter, gardener and fan of farmer's markets, and eating locally and making good food from scratch is what I do. Seasonality rules my diet: In winter, I would rather eat a well-cooked turnip than asparagus from Chile.

I am a former line cook, I've caught fish and dug clams for a living and, after 19 years as a political reporter for newspapers ranging from New York to Virginia to Wisconsin, Minnesota and California, I now pay the bills writing about food, fishing, foraging and hunting. On occasion, I also cater events around Northern California and beyond.

As a food writer, my work has been published in *Food & Wine*, *Organic Gardening*, *The Art of Eating*, *Field and Stream*, *Gastronomica*, *Edible Sacramento*, *Pheasants Forever* magazine, *Delta Waterfowl Magazine* and several other publications. I was written up in the March 2009 issue of *Field & Stream* magazine for my wild game cookery, which was an honor. I've been featured on a few TV shows, too. I've been on Andrew Zimmern's "Bizarre Foods America" twice, and have been on Steve Rinella's "Meateater" and am a contributor to Scott Leysath's "The Sporting Chef."

My first book, *Hunt, Gather, Cook: Finding the Forgotten Feast*, was released in 2011 by Rodale Books. My hope is that the book will help open the world of foraging, hunting and fishing to those interested in food, but who may have never hunted mushrooms or picked up a gun or cast a rod and reel before. It is also my hope that hunters who want to expand their skills to foraging, or anglers who want to hunt, or foragers who want to fish, will find value in this book.

My second book, *Duck, Duck, Goose: Recipes and Techniques for Ducks and Geese, both Wild and Domesticated*, was released by Ten Speed Press in October 2013. This book I hope will be useful both to waterfowl hunters and home cooks alike. I tried to include everything you'd want to know about cooking ducks and geese, and the recipes work just as well for store-bought birds as wild ones.

Hunter Angler Gardener Cook won Best Food Blog by the James Beard Foundation in 2013, and was nominated in 2009 and 2010. I was honored to win a Bert Greene Award from the International Association of Culinary Professionals for Best Food Blog in both 2010 and 2011.

BLOG
Hunter Angler Garden Cook

BOOKS
Hunt, Gather, Cook: Finding the Forgotten Feast

Duck, Duck, Goose: Recipes and Techniques for Ducks and Geese, both Wild and Domesticated

Recipe Index

About the Boone and Crockett Club

The Boone and Crockett Club was founded in 1887 by Theodore Roosevelt. Daniel Boone and Davy Crockett were the famous, heroic archetypes of the 1800s, known for their hunting adventures and exploration of the wilderness they opened for western expansion of the United States, hence the symbolic name chosen for the Club. Key members of the Club have included Theodore Roosevelt, George Bird Grinnell, Madison Grant, Charles Sheldon, Gifford Pinchot, Frederick Burnham, Charles Deering, John Lacey, J. N. "Ding" Darling and Aldo Leopold.

The Club, through Roosevelt and these early leaders of the American conservation movement, saw a crisis in humanity's impact on wildlife and their habitat and called people to action to change America's direction. They initially focused on protecting wild places and impeding the killing of game and fish for markets. The result of the Club's efforts to establish a foundation and framework for conservation in America includes what has lately become known as the North American Model for Wildlife Conservation.

The Club's efforts were aimed at the development and passage of the Timberland Reserve Act, which reserved approximately 36 million acres for national forests. The Club worked to develop the Yellowstone Park Protection Act, which expanded the size of the Park, established laws for its protection, and became the model piece of legislation for all future national parks. The Club played a major role in establishing many other areas for use by the public, including the Glacier National Park, Mount McKinley National Park, Pelican Island National Wildlife Refuge, National Key Deer Refuge, Holt Collier National Wildlife Refuge and Theodore Roosevelt National Wildlife Refuge, to name a few.

The Club played a major role in impeding the massive killing of wild animals for meat, hide and plume markets, which resulted in the Club developing and working for passage of the Lacey Act and other modern day game laws. Other significant pieces of legislation the Club was involved in included the Reclamation Act, National Wildlife Refuge System Act, Migratory Bird Conservation Act, Federal Aid in Wildlife Restoration Act, Healthy Forests Restoration Act and what is commonly called the "Farm Bill."

The Club and its members were also active in establishing other conservation organizations such as the New York Zoological Society, Camp Fire Club of America, National Audubon Society, American Wildlife Institute, Save the Redwoods League, Ducks Unlimited, North American Wildlife Foundation, National Wildlife Federation, and more recently, the highly-effective American Wildlife Conservation Partners.

In 1906, the Club established the National Collection of Heads and Horns as a repository for the vanishing big game of the World and to enlist public support for their protection. In 1932, the Club published the first Records of North American Big Game. It has consistently published records books and has held big

MISSION

It is the mission of the Boone and Crockett Club to promote the conservation and management of wildlife, especially big game, and its habitat, to preserve and encourage hunting and to maintain the highest ethical standards of fair chase and sportsmanship in North America.

game trophy awards programs since the 1940s. The highly-popular Boone and Crockett scoring system was adopted in 1950 and is still the most popular scoring system in the world and one of the few based on science and fair-chase principles.

The Club has long advocated for the need for science to be the backbone of professional wildlife research and management, including the establishment of Cooperative Wildlife Research Units at the nation's land grant universities.

Historically, the Club has been involved in education through the publication of its many books, starting with *American Big Game Hunting* (1893). Others include *Hunting and Conservation* (1925), *American Game Mammals and Birds* (1930), *Crusade for Wildlife* (1961), *An American Crusade for Wildlife* (1975), *The Black Bear in Modern North America* (1979) and many others.

Beginning in the 1990s, the Club began focusing on private lands and conceptualized and worked for passage of several programs to protect, restore and enhance wildlife habitat on those lands. These include the Wetlands Reserve Program (1991), Wildlife Habitat Incentives Program (1996), Grassland Reserve Program (2002), Healthy Forests Reserve Program (2003), Emergency Forest Restoration Program (2007) and Endangered Species Recovery Program (2007).

The Club has established a legacy of historic achievements in shaping the conservation policies of the United States and its role in big game records keeping throughout North America. The legacy of the Club was built upon the following cornerstones of the conservation movement: creation and establishment of the National Forest System, National Park System, National Wildlife Refuge System and the federal agencies to oversee those systems; the establishment of modern day game laws; and promoting ethical hunting of wildlife. In the past 20 years, the Club has worked to create a system for the conservation of private lands.

With the political, economic, social, technological and environmental changes, this impressive system of hunting and conservation that the Club established will not sustain itself without solving the many challenges it faces.

If the Club is to continue as an effective and influential organization, we must continue to not only evaluate, adjust and fine tune our program of work, but adapt it to the political, economic, social, technological and environmental changes facing North America.

Hunting and conservation are at a "crossroads" in North America. The challenges to them are great, but the historic achievements and the financial, political, communication and scientific assets of the Club's members place the Boone and Crockett Club in a unique position, unlike any other conservation organization, to successfully address them.

We continue to challenge ourselves to not only protect our investment in hunting and conservation, but advance it for future generations.

To learn more about the Boone and Crockett Club, our history, as well as our current programs, visit *boone-crockett.org*. If you're interested in supporting our mission and vision for the future, considering becoming a Boone and Crockett Club Associate and receiving our quarterly magazine *Fair Chase*. Details can be found on our web site or by calling 406-542-1888.

Acknowledgments

Producing Boone and Crockett Club's first ever cookbook required us to reach out to numerous individuals for their assistance and expertise. We would like to express appreciation to everyone who helped us with this endeavor, especially those who went above and beyond.

Within the B&C office, we had several staff members who don't typically work in our publishing department lend their knowledge to the project.

Mark Mesenko, B&C's digital strategies manager, is a professional photographer who specializes mainly on large-scale outdoor and landscape projects. Mark spent countless hours researching food photography techniques and gaining the knowledge needed to produce the cover image for *Wild Gourmet*, as well as numerous photographs throughout the book.

The original concept for *Wild Gourmet* was developed by B&C's Vice President of Communications Marc C. Mondavi. The trade edition was printed and bound by Friesens in Altona, Manitoba, Canada. Final copyediting for the components other than recipes was provided by Julie Cowan at WordCritter Creative. The book was designed and produced by B&C's Director of Publications Julie L. Tripp with additional design collaboration by Karlie Slayer, B&C's Creative Services Manager.

Amy Hutchison, who handles B&C's customer service department, isn't afraid to have an adventure or two in her kitchen with her husband and two daughters. Her love for preparing new dishes helped tremendously as she reviewed every recipe in the book to ensure the directions were clear and concise. Our goal was to provide recipes that virtually anyone could prepare with relative ease. She also spent a great deal of time proofing the ingredient lists and the instructions for processing the various game animals.

Abra Loran, B&C's assistant controller, and **Justin Spring**, B&C's assistant director of Big Game Records, provided game cuts for our photography sessions. Justin and his wife Rebecca also field-tested several of the recipes and provided additional insight into the instructions for those recipes. Additionally, we are grateful to several other staff members who brought in props, antiques, and cookware for our photography sessions.

B&C's Vice President of Communications **Marc Mondavi** of Charles Krug Winery lent us a very helpful hand with his executive assistant **Debi Stone**. She was on the front line coordinating recipes, photography, and biographies for most of the chefs featured in *Wild Gourmet*, as well as keeping Marc on task with his contributions to the book! She was great to work with, and the book would not have been possible without her efforts.

Food stylist **Kimberlee Carlson** was an amazing resource for the three days that we turned the library at B&C headquarters into our own food photography studio. She worked side-by-side with us as we foraged into the exciting world of food photography. Her experience working with food and food preparation provided the knowledge and instilled confidence in our project. We are deeply thankful for her patience and insight.

We would like to recognize chef **Dan Nelson**—the official chef for the Gourmet Gone Wild® program and executive chef at Eagle Eye Golf and Banquet Center in East Lansing, Michigan—for his dedication to providing the most comprehensive game processing chapter I've ever read. He volunteered more nights and weekends to this project than I'm sure I will ever fully understand. His attention to detail along with his desire to provide as much information as possible will be appreciated by anyone who turns to his chapter and goes through his step-by-step illustrated processing sections. He was assisted by photographer **Matthew Wesener,** who provided all of the processing imagery, a task that is not easy to portray with both great artistic view and compassion for the subject. A special thank you also needs to be extended to B&C professional member **Jordan Burroughs** for bringing Chef Dan into the fold on this project. She also connected us with **Moira Tidball** who provided the chapter on wild game nutrition.

Lastly, we need to thank the chefs who so generously contributed their time, recipes, and photography to this book. Be sure to read the "Meet the Chefs" section beginning on page 241. This is an all-star cast and we know you will enjoy their work.

This project would not have been possible without each of these individuals. Thanks to all of them for their dedication to the Boone and Crockett Club and our mission.

Julie L. Tripp — *B&C Director of Publications*